Mexican
Spanish
PHRASEBOOK & DICTIONARY

Acknowledgments

Editors Jodie Martire, Kristin Odijk, Branislava Vladisavljevic
Series Designer Mark Adams
Layout Designers Carol Jackson, Joseph Spanti
Language Writers Cecilia Carmona, Rafael Carmona

Thanks

Grace Dobell, Chris Love, Tony Wheeler

Published by Lonely Planet Publications Pty Ltd

ABN 36 005 607 983

4th Edition – May 2016
ISBN 978 1 74321 4480
Text © Lonely Planet 2016
Cover Image Juice vendor in Mexico City
Tony Anderson/Getty ©

Printed in China 10 9 8 7 6 5 4 3 2

Contact lonelyplanet.com/contact

MIX
Paper from
responsible sources
FSC™ C021741

Look out for the following icons throughout the book:

'Shortcut' Phrase
Easy to remember alternative to the full phrase

Q&A Pair
'Question-and-answer' pair – we suggest a response to the question asked

Look For
Phrases you may see on signs, menus etc

Listen For
Phrases you may hear from officials, locals etc

Language Tip
An insight into the foreign language

Culture Tip
An insight into the local culture

How to read the phrases:
- Coloured words and phrases throughout the book are phonetic guides to help you pronounce the foreign language.
- Lists of phrases with tinted background are options you can choose to complete the phrase above them.

These abbreviations will help you choose the right words and phrases in this book:

f feminine	**m** masculine	**pol** polite
inf informal	**pl** plural	**sg** singular
lit literal		

Contents

PAGE 6

 About Mexican Spanish
Learn about Mexican Spanish, build your own sentences and pronounce words correctly.

PAGE 29

Travel Phrases
Ready-made phrases for every situation – buy a ticket, book a hotel and much more.

 Basics 29

 Practical 39

 Social — 105

Safe Travel — 153

Food — 167

INTRO **Mexican Spanish**

español mexicano es·pa·*nyol* me·*khee*·ka·no

Who speaks Mexican Spanish?

OFFICIAL LANGUAGE

MEXICO

WIDELY UNDERSTOOD

ARGENTINA · BELIZE
BOLIVIA · CHILE · COLOMBIA
COSTA RICA · CUBA
DOMINICAN REPUBLIC
ECUADOR · EL SALVADOR
EQUATORIAL GUINEA
GUATEMALA · HONDURAS
NICARAGUA · PANAMA
PARAGUAY · PERU · PUERTO
RICO · SPAIN · URUGUAY
USA · VENEZUELA

Why Bother

Even if you can't roll your *r*'s like Speedy González, communicating with locals is crucial, as Mexicans well know. It was La Malinche, the enslaved Mayan mistress of conquistador Hernán Cortés, who ultimately facilitated the Spanish conquest by interpreting for him.

Distinctive Sounds

The strong and rolled r, and kh (as in the Scottish *loch*).

Spanish in the World

Over the last 500 years, Spanish in Mexico has

110 MILLION
speak Mexican Spanish as their first language

evolved differently to the Spanish spoken in Europe. You'll easily recognise Spaniards by the 'lisp' in their speech – ie *cerveza* (beer) is ser·*ve*·sa in Mexico but ther·*ve*·tha in Spain.

Spanish in Mexico

What sets Mexican Spanish apart from other Latin American Spanish varieties is the rich vocabulary. In addition to the influence by indigenous Náhuatl and Mayan languages, there's strong impact from US English, especially in the northern border areas.

False Friends

Warning: many Spanish words look like English words but have a different meaning altogether, eg *éxito ek*·see·to is 'success', not 'exit' (which is *salida* sa·*lee*·da in Spanish).

Language Family

Romance (developed from Vulgar Latin spoken by Romans during the conquest of the Iberian Peninsula from the 3rd to the 1st century BC). Close relatives include Portuguese, Italian, French and Romanian.

Must-Know Grammar

Spanish has a formal and informal word for 'you' (*Usted* oos·*ted* and *tú* too respectively). Also, verbs have a different ending for each person, like the English 'I do' vs 'he/she does'.

ABOUT INTRODUCTION

Donations to English

Numerous. Thanks to Columbus' discovery of the New World in 1492, there's a large corpus of words from indigenous languages that have entered English via Mexican Spanish. You may recognise *avocado, chocolate, coyote, tomato* ...

5 Phrases to Learn Before You Go

 Where can I buy handicrafts?
¿Dónde se puede comprar artesanías?
don·de se pwe·de kom·prar ar·te·sa·nee·as

Star buys in Mexico are the regional handicrafts produced all over the country, mainly by the indigenous people.

 Which *antojitos* do you have?
¿Qué antojitos tiene? *ke an·to·khee·tos tye·ne*

'Little whimsies' (snacks) can encompass anything – have an entire meal of them, eat a few as appetisers, or get one on the street for a quick bite.

 Not too spicy, please.
No muy picoso, por favor. *no mooy pee·ko·so por fa·vor*

Not all food in Mexico is spicy, but beware – many dishes can be fierce indeed, so it may be a good idea to play it safe.

 Where can I find a *cantina* nearby?
¿Dónde hay una cantina cerca de aquí?
don·de ai oo·na kan·tee·na ser·ka de a·kee

Ask locals about the classical Mexican venue for endless snacks, and often dancing as well.

 How do you say ... in your language?
¿Cómo se dice ... en su lengua?
ko·mo se dee·se ... en su len·gwa

Numerous indigenous languages are spoken around Mexico, primarily Mayan languages and Náhuatl. People will appreciate it if you try to use their local language.

10 Phrases to Sound Like a Local

Hey!	¡Oye!/¡Oiga! inf/pol	o·ye/oy·ga
How's things?	¿Qué tal?	ke tal
What's new?	¿Qué onda?	ke on·da
Cool, dude!	¡Chido, güey!	chee·do gway
Awesome!	¡Cámara!	ka·ma·ra
Check this out!	¡Checa ésto!	che·ka es·to
Wow, really?	¡Órale!	o·ra·le
Are you serious?	¿Te cae?	te kai
You must be kidding!	¡No manches!	no man·ches
Whatever.	Me vale.	me va·le

ABOUT MEXICAN SPANISH

Pronunciation

Mexican Spanish pronunciation differs slightly from the Castilian Spanish spoken in Spain. The most obvious difference is the lack of the lisping 'th' sound which is found in Castilian Spanish. With a bit of practice you'll soon get the basics.

Vowel Sounds

SYMBOL	ENGLISH EQUIVALENT	SPANISH EXAMPLE	TRANSLITERATION
a	run	agua	*a*·gwa
e	red	número	*noo*·me·ro
ee	bee	día	*dee*·a
o	dog	ojo	*o*·kho
oo	book	gusto	*goos*·to

Vowels in Mexican Spanish are quite short and fairly closed. The sound remains level, and each vowel is pronounced as an individual unit. There are a few cases where two vowel sounds become very closely combined (so-called 'diphthongs'):

SYMBOL	ENGLISH EQUIVALENT	SPANISH EXAMPLE	TRANSLITERATION
ai	aisle	bailar	bai·*lar*
ay	say	seis	says
ow	house	autobús	ow·to·*boos*
oy	boy	hoy	oy

Consonant Sounds

SYMBOL	ENGLISH EQUIVALENT	SPANISH EXAMPLE	TRANSLITERATION
b	big	barco	*bar*·ko
ch	chili	chica	*chee*·ka
d	din	dinero	dee·*ne*·ro
f	fun	fiesta	*fye*·sta
g	go	gato	*ga*·to
k	kick	cabeza, queso	ka·*be*·sa, *ke*·so
kh	as in the Scottish 'loch'	gente, jardín, México	*khen*·te, khar·*deen*, *me*·khee·ko
l	loud	lago	*la*·go
m	man	mañana	ma·*nya*·na
n	no	nuevo	*nwe*·vo
ny	canyon	señora	se·*nyo*·ra
p	pig	padre	*pa*·dre
r	run (but strongly rolled, especially *rr*)	ritmo, mariposa, burro	*reet*·mo, ma·ree·*po*·sa, *boo*·ro
s	so	semana, zarzuela, Xochimilco	se·*ma*·na, sar·*swe*·la, so·chee·*meel*·ko
t	tin	tienda	*tyen*·da
v	a soft 'b' (between 'v' and 'b')	veinte	*vayn*·te
w	win	guardia, Oaxaca	*gwar*·dya, wa·*ha*·ka
y	yes	llave, viaje, ya	*ya*·ve, *vya*·khe, ya

Word Stress

Words in Spanish have stress, which means you emphasise one syllable over another. Rule of thumb: when a written word ends in *n*, *s* or a vowel, the stress falls on the second-last syllable. Otherwise, the final syllable is stressed. If you see an accent mark over a syllable, it cancels out these rules and you just stress that syllable instead. Don't worry if you can't remember these details – our coloured phonetic guides give you the stressed syllable in italics.

Plunge in!

Don't worry too much about pronunciation. Just take your cue from the locals when it comes to the sounds and intonation of Mexican Spanish. The coloured phonetic guides we've provided for every phrase give you all the correct sounds and the stressed syllables. Even if you pronounce them as if they were English, you should be understood just fine.

ABOUT PRONUNCIATION

~ SPANISH ALPHABET ~

A a	a	**J j**	*kho*·ta	**R r**	*e*·re
B b	be *lar*·ga	**K k**	ka	**S s**	*e*·se
C c	se	**L l**	*e*·le	**T t**	te
D d	de	**M m**	*e*·me	**U u**	oo
E e	e	**N n**	*e*·ne	**V v**	be *kor*·ta
F f	*e*·fe	**Ñ ñ**	*e*·nye	**W w**	*do*·ble ve
G g	khe	**O o**	o	**X x**	*e*·kees
H h	a·che	**P p**	pe	**Y y**	ee *grye*·ga
I i	ee la·*tee*·na	**Q q**	koo	**Z z**	*se*·ta

The letters *ch* and *ll* are no longer officially considered separate letters but they're still sounds in their own right.

~ SPELLBOUND ~

The relationship between Mexican Spanish sounds and their spelling is quite straightforward and consistent. Here are the rules:

c	before *e* or *i* pronounced as the 's' in 'so';	cerveza, cita	ser·*ve*·sa, *see*·ta
	before *a, o* and *u* pronounced as the 'k' in 'kick'	carro, corto, cubo	*ka*·ro, *kor*·to, *koo*·bo
g	before *e* or *i* pronounced as the 'ch' in the Scottish *loch*;	gente, gitano	*khen*·te, khee·*ta*·no
	before *a, o* and *u* pronounced as the 'g' in 'go'	gato, gordo, guante	*ga*·to, *gor*·do, *gwan*·te
gue, gui, güi	as the 'g' in 'go' (*u* is not pronounced unless there are two dots above it)	guerra, Guillermo	*ge*·ra, gee·*yer*·mo
		güiski	*gwees*·kee
h	not pronounced	haber	a·*ber*
j	as the 'ch' in the Scottish *loch*	jardín	khar·*deen*
ll	as the 'y' in 'yes'	llave	*ya*·ve
ñ	as the 'ny' in 'canyon'	niño	*nee*·nyo
qu	as the 'k' in 'kick' (*u* is not pronounced)	quince	*keen*·se
x	usually as the 'ch' in the Scottish *loch*; as 's' in some place names; as 'ks' in other words	México, Xochimilco, próximo	me·*khee*·ko, so·chee·*meel*·ko, *prok*·see·mo
z	as the 's' in 'soup'	zorro	*so*·ro

ABOUT MEXICAN SPANISH

Grammar

This chapter is designed to explain the main grammatical structures you need in order to make your own sentences. Look under each heading – listed in alphabetical order – for information on functions which these grammatical categories express in a sentence. For example, demonstratives are used for giving instructions, so you'll need them to tell the taxi driver where your hotel is, etc. A glossary of grammatical terms is included at the end of the chapter to help you.

Adjectives & Adverbs

Describing People/Things • Doing Things

Adjectives in Spanish have different endings depending on whether the noun is masculine or feminine, and singular or plural (see **gender** and **plurals**).

		~ ADJECTIVES ~	
m sg	**fantastic hotel**	hotel fantástico	o·*tel* fan·*tas*·tee·ko
f sg	**fantastic hammock**	hamaca fantástica	a·*ma*·ka fan·*tas*·tee·ka
m pl	**fantastic books**	libros fantásticos	*lee*·bros fan·*tas*·tee·kos
f pl	**fantastic artworks**	obras fantásticas	*ob*·ras fan·*tas*·tee·kas

Adjectives generally come after the noun in Spanish. However, adjectives of quantity (such as 'much', 'a lot', 'little/few', 'too

much') and possessive adjectives (cg 'my' and 'your') always
precede the noun. See also **demonstratives** and **possessives**.

many tourists	muchos turistas (lit: many-m-pl tourists)	*moo*·chos too·*rees*·tas
my hat	mi sombrero (lit: my hat)	mee som·*bre*·ro

Most adverbs in Spanish are derived from adjectives by adding
the ending *-mente* ·*men*·te to the singular feminine form of
the adjective (ie the form ending in *-a*), just like adding '-ly' to
adjectives in English. In Spanish, adverbs are generally placed
after the verb they refer to.

a slow train	un tren lento (lit: a-m-sg train slow-m-sg)	oon tren *len*·to
to speak slowly	hablar lentamente (lit: to-speak slowly)	ab·*lar* len·ta·*men*·te

Articles

Naming People/Things

Spanish has two words for 'a/an': *un* oon and *una* *oo*·na. The
gender of the noun determines which one you use. *Un* and *una*
also have plural forms – *unos* *oo*·nos and *unas* *oo*·nas (some).

~ INDEFINITE ARTICLES ~

m sg	**a taco**	un taco	oon *ta*·ko
m pl	**some tacos**	unos tacos	*oo*·nos *ta*·kos
f sg	**a house**	una casa	*oo*·na *ka*·sa
f pl	**some houses**	unas casas	*oo*·nas *ka*·sas

The articles *el* el and *la* la both mean 'the'. Whether you use *el*
or *la* also depends on the gender of the noun. For the plural,
use *los* los and *las* las for masculine and feminine. See also
gender and **plurals**.

ABOUT GRAMMAR

	~ DEFINITE ARTICLES ~		
m sg	**the donkey**	el burro	el *boo*·ro
m pl	**the donkeys**	los burros	los *boo*·ros
f sg	**the shop**	la tienda	la *tyen*·da
f pl	**the shops**	las tiendas	las *tyen*·das

Be

Describing People/Things • Making Statements

Spanish has two words for the English verb 'be': *ser* ser and *estar* es·*tar*, which are used depending on the context.

~ USE OF *SER* (TO BE) ~		
permanent characteristics of persons/things	Cecilia is very nice.	Cecilia es muy amable. se·*see*·lya es mooy a·*ma*·ble
occupation or nationality	Marcos is from Mexico.	Marcos es de México. *mar*·kos es de *me*·khee·ko
time or location of events	It's 3 o'clock.	Son las tres. son las tres
possession	Whose backpack is this?	¿De quién es esta mochila? de kyen es es·*ta* mo·*chee*·la

~ USE OF *ESTAR* (TO BE) ~		
temporary characteristics of persons/things	The meal is cold.	La comida está fría. la ko·*mee*·da es·*ta free*·a
time or location of persons/things	We are in Coyoacán.	Estamos en Coyoacán. es·*ta*·mos en ko·yo·a·*kan*
a person's mood	I'm happy.	Estoy contento/a. m/f es·*toy* kon·*ten*·to/a

ABOUT GRAMMAR

~ *SER* – PRESENT TENSE ~

I	am	yo	soy	yo	soy
you sg inf	**are**	tú	eres	too	e·res
you sg pol	**are**	Usted	es	oos·ted	es
he/she	**is**	él/ella	es	el/e·ya	es
we	**are**	nosotros/ nosotras m/f	somos	no·so·tros/ no·so·tras	so·mos
you pl	**are**	Ustedes	son	oos·te·des	son
they	**are**	ellos/ellas m/f	son	e·yos/e·yas	son

~ *ESTAR* – PRESENT TENSE ~

I	am	yo	estoy	yo	es·toy
you sg inf	**are**	tú	estás	too	es·tas
you sg pol	**are**	Usted	está	oos·ted	es·ta
he/she	**is**	él/ella	está	el/e·ya	es·ta
we	**are**	nosotros/ nosotras m/f	estamos	no·so·tros/ no·so·tras	es·ta·mos
you pl	**are**	Ustedes	están	oos·te·des	es·tan
they	**are**	ellos/ellas m/f	están	e·yos/e·yas	es·tan

Demonstratives

Giving Instructions • Indicating Location • Pointing Things Out

To point something out the easiest phrases to use are *es* es (it is), or *eso es* e·so es (that is). To say 'this is' use *este es* es·te es if it's a masculine object and *esta es* es·ta es if it's a feminine.

Esta es mi licencia. es·ta es mee lee·*sen*·sya
This is my drivers license.
(lit: this-**f-sg** is my drivers-license)

There are three 'distance words' in Spanish, depending on
whether something or someone is close (this), away from you
(that), or even further away in time or distance (that over
there). See also **gender** and **plurals**.

~ DEMONSTRATIVES ~

	m sg		m pl	
this (close)	éste	es·te	éstos	es·tos
that (away)	ése	e·se	ésos	e·sos
that (further away)	aquél	a·*kel*	aquéllos	a·*ke*·yos
	f sg		f pl	
this (close)	ésta	es·ta	éstas	es·tas
that (away)	ésa	e·sa	ésas	e·sas
that (further away)	aquélla	a·*ke*·ya	aquéllas	a·*ke*·yas

Diminutives

Naming People/Things

Mexicans frequently use diminutives, which are nouns whose
endings have been altered in order to soften their intensity,
emphasise smallness, express endearment or even show politeness. A person's name can be made diminutive as a way
of expressing affection, especially towards a child or younger
sibling.

Diminutives are created by changing the ending of the noun
to *-ito* ·*ee*·to for a masculine noun, or *-ita* ·*ee*·ta for a feminine
noun. Less commonly, diminutives may be formed with *-illo*
·*ee*·yo, *-illa* ·*ee*·ya, *-ico* ·*ee*·ko and *-ica* ·*ee*·ka endings.

~ NOUN ~	~ DIMINUTIVE NOUN ~	~ USED FOR ~
un momento oon mo·*men*·to one moment	**un momentito** oon mo·men·*tee*·to just a moment (lit: a-**m-sg** moment- little-**m-sg**)	showing politeness
dos semanas dos se·*ma*·nas two weeks	**dos semanitas** dos·se·ma·*nee*·tas just two weeks (lit: two weeks-little-**f-pl**)	softening intensity
perro *pe*·ro dog	**perrito** pe·*ree*·to doggy (lit: dog-little-**m-sg**)	emphasizing smallness
Pablo *pab*·lo Paul	**Pablito** pab·*lee*·to (dear) Paul (lit: Paul-little-**m-sg**)	expressing endearment/ affection

Gender

Naming People/Things

In Spanish, all nouns – words which denote a thing, person or concept – are either masculine or feminine. The dictionary will tell you what gender a noun is, but here are some handy tips to help you determine gender:

» a word is masculine/feminine if referring to a man/woman
» words ending in *-o* or *-or* are often masculine
» words ending in *-a*, *-d*, *-z* or *-ión* are often feminine

In this book, masculine forms appear before the feminine forms. If you see a word ending in *-o/a*, it means the masculine form ends in *-o*, and the feminine form ends in *-a* (ie replace *-o* with *-a* to make it feminine). The same goes for the plural endings *-os/as*. If you see an *(a)* between brackets at the end of a word, eg *escritor(a)* es·*kree*·tor/es·kree·*to*·ra, it means you have to add that ending to make the word feminine. In other cases we spell out the whole word. See also **adjectives**, **articles** and **possessives**.

Have

Possessing

Possession can be indicated in various ways in Spanish (see also **possessives**). The easiest way is by using the verb *tener* te·*ner* (have).

I have two sisters.	Tengo dos hermanas.
	(lit: I-have two sisters)
	ten·go dos er·*ma*·nas

~ TENER – PRESENT TENSE ~

I	have	yo	tengo	yo	*ten*·go
you sg inf	**have**	tú	tienes	too	*tye*·nes
you sg pol	**have**	Usted	tiene	oos·*ted*	*tye*·ne
he/she	**has**	él/ella	tiene	el/e·ya	*tye*·ne
we	**have**	nosotros/ nosotras m/f	tenemos	no·so·tros/ no·so·tras	te·*ne*·mos
you pl	**have**	Ustedes	tienen	oos·*te*·des	*tye*·nen
they	**have**	ellos/ellas m/f	tienen	e·yos/e·yas	*tye*·nen

Negatives

Negating

To make a negative statement, just add the word *no* no before the main verb of the sentence:

I don't like cooking.	No me gusta cocinar.
	(lit: not me it-pleases cooking)
	no me *goo*·sta ko·see·*nar*

Contrary to English, double negatives are not only acceptable but necessary in Spanish:

| **I have nothing to declare.** | No tengo nada que declarar. (lit: not I-have nothing to declare) no *ten*·go *na*·da ke dek·la·*rar* |

Personal Pronouns

Making Statements • Naming People/Things

Personal pronouns ('I', 'you' etc) change form in Spanish depending on whether they're the subject or the object of a sentence. It's the same in English, which has 'I' and 'me' as the subject and object pronouns (eg 'I see her' and 'She sees me'). The subject pronoun is often omitted in Spanish as the subject is understood from the corresponding verb form (see also **verbs**).

| **I'm a student.** | Soy estudiante. (lit: I-am student) soy es·too·*dyan*·te |

~ SUBJECT PRONOUNS ~

I	yo	yo	**we**	nosotros m nosotras f	no·*so*·tros no·*so*·tras
you sg inf	tú	too	**you** pl	Ustedes	oos·*te*·des
you sg pol	Usted	oos·*ted*			
he/she	él/ella	el/e·ya	**they**	ellos m ellas f	*e*·yos *e*·yas

Mexicans use two different words for the singular 'you'. When talking to someone familiar to you or younger than you, it's usual to use the informal form *tú* too, rather than the polite form *Usted* oos·*ted*. The polite form should be used when you're meeting someone for the first time, talking to someone much older than you, or when you're in a formal situation (eg when talking to the police, customs officers etc). In this book we have chosen the appropriate form for the situation. Note that in Mexico you use the word *Ustedes* oos·*te*·des for the plural 'you' – whether or not it's a formal situation.

See also **be** and **have**.

Plurals

Naming People/Things

Forming plurals is easy – in general, if the word ends in a vowel, you add -*s* for plural. If the nouns ends in a consonant (or *y*), you add -*es*:

~ SINGULAR ~			~ PLURAL ~		
bed	cama	*ka*·ma	**beds**	camas	*ka*·mas
woman	mujer	moo·*kher*	**women**	mujeres	moo·*khe*·res

Possessives

Possessing

A common way of indicating possession is by using possessive adjectives before the noun they describe. As with any other adjective, they always agree with the noun in number (singular or plural) and gender (masculine or feminine). See also **gender** and **plurals**.

This is our daughter.	Ésta es nuestra hija.
	(lit: this-f-sg is our-f-sg daughter)
	es·ta es *nwes*·tra ee·kha

In the table opposite, the forms separated by a slash are used with a singular/plural noun.

~ POSSESSIVE ADJECTIVES ~

my	mi/ mis	mee/ mees	**our**	nuestro/ nuestros m nuestra/ nuestras f	*nwes·tro/* *nwes·tros* *nwes·tra/* *nwes·tras*
your sg inf	tu/ tus	too/ toos	**your** pl inf	vuestro/ vuestros m vuestra/ vuestras f	*vwes·tro/* *vwes·tros* *vwes·tra/* *vwes·tras*
your sg pol	su/ sus	soo/ soos	**your** pl pol	su/ sus	*soo/* *soos*
his/ **her**	su/ sus	soo/ soos	**their**	su/ sus	*soo/* *soos*

In Spanish, ownership can also be expressed by using the word
de de (of).

That's my friend's **backpack.**	Esa es la mochila de mi amigo. (lit: that-**f·sg** is the-**f·sg** backpack of my friend-**m**) *e·sa es la mo·chee·la de mee* *a·mee·go*

Alternatively, you can use the verb *tener* (see **have**).

Prepositions

Giving Instructions • Indicating Location • Pointing Things
Out

Like English, Spanish uses prepositions to explain where
things are in time or space. Common prepositions are listed in
the table below. For more prepositions, see the **dictionary**.

~ PREPOSITIONS ~

after	después de	*des·pwes* de	**from**	de	de
at (time)	a	a	**in (place)**	en	en
before	antes de	*an·tes de*	**to**	a	a

ABOUT GRAMMAR

Questions

Asking Questions • Negating

To ask a simple 'yes/no' question, just make a statement but raise your intonation towards the end of the sentence, as you would in English. The inverted question mark in written Spanish prompts you to do this.

Is that the main square? ¿Eso es el zócalo?
(lit: that-**m-sg** is the-**m-sg** main-square)
e·so es el so·ka·lo

It's not impolite to answer questions with a simple *sí* see (yes) or *no* no (no) in Spanish, even when you'd like to say 'Yes it is/ does', or 'No, it isn't/doesn't'.

As in English, there are also question words for more specific questions. These words go at the start of a sentence.

~ QUESTION WORDS ~

How?	¿Cómo?	ko·mo
How many?	¿Cuántos? **m pl** ¿Cuántas? **f pl**	kwan·tos kwan·tas
What?	¿Qué?	ke
When?	¿Cuándo?	kwan·do
Where?	¿Dónde?	don·de
Which?	¿Cuál? **sg** ¿Cuáles? **pl**	kwal kwa·les
Who?	¿Quién? **sg** ¿Quiénes? **pl**	kyen kye·nes
Why?	¿Por qué?	por ke

Verbs

Doing Things • Making Statements

There are three verb categories in Spanish, depending on
whether the infinitive ends in *-ar*, *-er* or *-ir*, eg *hablar* ab·*lar*
(talk), *comer* ko·*mer* (eat), *vivir* vee·*veer* (live). Tenses are
formed by adding various endings for each person to the verb
stem (after removing *-ar*, *-er* or *-ir* from the infinitive) or to the
infinitive, and for most verbs these endings follow regular
patterns. The verb endings for the present, past and future
tenses are presented in the tables on the following pages. For
negative forms of verbs, see **negatives**.

~ PRESENT TENSE ~

		hablar	**comer**	**vivir**
I	yo	hablo	como	vivo
you sg inf	tú	hablas	comes	vives
you sg pol	Usted	habla	come	vive
he	él	habla	come	vive
she	ella	habla	come	vive
we	nosotros m nosotras f	hablamos	comemos	vivimos
you pl	Ustedes	hablan	comen	viven
they	ellos m ellas f	hablan	comen	viven

See also **be** and **have** for present-tense forms of these verbs.

~ PAST TENSE ~

		hablar	comer	vivir
I	yo	hablé	comí	viví
you sg inf	tú	hablaste	comiste	viviste
you sg pol	Usted	habló	comió	vivió
he	él	habló	comió	vivió
she	ella	habló	comió	vivió
we	nosotros m nosotras f	hablamos	comimos	vivimos
you pl	Ustedes	hablaron	comieron	vivieron
they	ellos m ellas f	hablaron	comieron	vivieron

In the future tense, all three verb categories have the same endings added to the infinitive (dictionary form of the verb):

~ FUTURE TENSE ~

		hablar	comer	vivir
I	yo	hablaré	comeré	viviré
you sg inf	tú	hablarás	comerás	vivirás
you sg pol	Usted	hablará	comerá	vivirá
he	él	hablará	comerá	vivirá
she	ella	hablará	comerá	vivirá
we	nosotros m nosotras f	hablaremos	comeremos	viviremos
you pl	Ustedes	hablarán	comerán	vivirán
they	ellos m ellas f	hablarán	comerán	vivirán

CULTURE TIP

The Meaning of 'México'

The mysterious origins of the word *México* *me*·khee·ko have long been the subject of debate. One of the most popular theories is that *México* literally means 'navel of the moon' in the indigenous Náhuatl language, derived from *meztli mes*·tlee (moon) and *xictli* *sheek*·tlee (navel). Another theory associates the name with the Náhuatl word *metl* metl (maguey plant). In the 15th and 16th centuries some clerics tried vainly to establish a link between *México* and the Hebrew word *Mesi* (Messiah). Other theories include words which mean 'place of springs' and 'that which kills by an obsidian arrow'.

In 1998, a 'Round Table on the True Meaning of the Word México' was convened in an attempt to lay the issue to rest once and for all. The panel agreed unanimously that the Aztecs who founded Mexico City called themselves *mexítin* me·shee·teen (Mexicans) in honour of their leader Mexítli, known affectionately as 'Mexi'. Add the Náhuatl suffix *-co* ·ko (place of) and you get *México*: 'Place of the Mexicans'.

ABOUT GRAMMAR

Word Order

Making Statements

Sentences in Spanish have a basic word order of subject–verb–object, just like in English. However, the subject pronoun is generally omitted because the subject is obvious from the corresponding verb form (see **verbs**):

I study business.
Yo estudio comercio.
(lit: I I-study business)
yo es·*too*·dyo ko·*mer*·syo
Estudio comercio.
(lit: I-study business)
es·*too*·dyo ko·*mer*·syo

See also **negatives** and **questions**.

~ GLOSSARY ~

adjective	a word that describes something – 'he was the **greatest** mariachi of his time'
adverb	a word that explains how an action is done – 'he sang **beautifully**'
article	the words 'a', 'an' and 'the'
demonstrative	a word that means 'this' or 'that'
direct object	the thing or person in the sentence that has the action directed to it – 'and the crowd loved **him**'
gender	classification of *nouns* into classes (like masculine and feminine), requiring other words (eg *adjectives*) to belong to the same class
indirect object	the person or thing in the sentence that is the recipient of the action – 'the public yelled to **him**'
infinitive	dictionary form of a *verb* – 'to **play** more'
noun	a thing, person or idea – 'the **ensemble** was excited'
number	whether a word is singular or plural – 'and they performed more **songs**'
personal pronoun	a word that means 'I', 'you' etc
possessive adjective	a word that means 'my', 'your' etc
possessive pronoun	a word that means 'mine', 'yours' etc
preposition	a word like 'for' or 'before' in English
subject	the thing or person in the sentence that does the action – 'the **musicians** played for hours'
tense	form of a *verb* that tells you whether the action is in the present, past or future – eg 'run' (present), 'ran' (past), 'will run' (future)
verb	a word that tells you what action happened – 'and **went** home late'
verb stem	part of a *verb* that doesn't change – eg '**play**' in '**play**ing' and '**play**ed'

Basics

Understanding

KEY PHRASES

Do you speak English?	¿Habla/Hablas inglés? pol/inf	a·bla/a·blas een·gles
I don't understand.	No entiendo.	no en·tyen·do
What does ... mean?	¿Qué significa ...?	ke seeg·nee·fee·ka ...

Q Do you speak English?	¿Habla/Hablas inglés? pol/inf a·bla/a·blas een·gles	
Q Does anyone speak English?	¿Hay alguien que hable inglés? ai al·gyen ke a·ble een·gles	
A I (don't) speak Spanish.	(No) Hablo español. (no) a·blo es·pa·nyol	
A I speak a little.	Hablo un poquito. a·blo oon po·kee·to	
Q Do you understand?	¿Me entiende/entiendes? pol/inf me en·tyen·de/en·tyen·des	
A I (don't) understand.	(No) Entiendo. (no) en·tyen·do	
How do you pronounce this?	¿Cómo se pronuncia ésto? ko·mo se pro·noon·sya es·to	
How do you write ...?	¿Cómo se escribe ...? ko·mo se es·kree·be ...	
What does ... mean?	¿Qué significa ...? ke seeg·nee·fee·ka ...	

| **Could you please repeat that?** | ¿Puede repetirlo, por favor?
 pwe·de re·pe·teer·lo por fa·vor |
| **Could you please speak more slowly?** | ¿Puede hablar más despacio, por favor?
 pwe·de a·blar mas des·pa·syo por fa·vor |

| ✂ | **Slowly, please!** | ¡Despacio, por favor! | des·pa·syo por fa·vor |

| **Could you please write it down?** | ¿Puede escribirlo, por favor?
 pwe·de es·kree·beer·lo por fa·vor |
| **I'd like to learn some of your (indigenous) language.** | Me gustaría aprender un poco de su lengua (indígena).
 me goos·ta·ree·a a·pren·der oon po·ko de soo len·gwa (een·dee·khe·na) |

BASICS UNDERSTANDING

LANGUAGE TIP

False Friends
Beware of words which sound like English words but have a different meaning altogether.

embarazada f   *em·ba·ra·sa·da*   pregnant
not 'embarrassed', which is *apenado/a* m/f *a·pe·na·do/a*

éxito m   *ek·see·to*   success
not 'exit', which is *salida* *sa·lee·da*

injuria f   *een·khoo·ree·a*   insult
not 'injury', which is *herida* *e·ree·da*

parientes m pl   *pa·ryen·tes*   relatives
not 'parents', which is *padres* *pa·dres*

Numbers & Amounts

KEY PHRASES

How much?	¿Cuánto?	kwan·to
a little	un poco	oon po·ko
a lot	mucho	moo·cho

Cardinal Numbers

1	uno	oo·no
2	dos	dos
3	tres	tres
4	cuatro	kwa·tro
5	cinco	seen·ko
6	seis	says
7	siete	sye·te
8	ocho	o·cho
9	nueve	nwe·ve
10	diez	dyes
11	once	on·se
12	doce	do·se
13	trece	tre·se
14	catorce	ka·tor·se
15	quince	keen·se
16	dieciséis	dye·see·says
17	diecisiete	dye·see·sye·te
18	dieciocho	dye·see·o·cho

19	diecinueve	dye·see·*nwe*·ve
20	veinte	*vayn*·te
21	veintiuno	vayn·tee·*oo*·no
30	treinta	*trayn*·ta
40	cuarenta	kwa·*ren*·ta
50	cincuenta	seen·*kwen*·ta
60	sesenta	se·*sen*·ta
70	setenta	se·*ten*·ta
80	ochenta	o·*chen*·ta
90	noventa	no·*ven*·ta
100	cien	*syen*
200	doscientos	do·*syen*·tos
1,000	mil	meel
1,000,000	un millon	oon mee·*yon*

Ordinal Numbers

1st	primero/a m/f	pree·*me*·ro/a
2nd	segundo/a m/f	se·*goon*·do/a
3rd	tercero/a m/f	ter·*se*·ro/a

Useful Amounts

How much?	¿Cuánto/a? m/f	*kwan*·to/a
How many?	¿Cuántos/as? m/f pl	*kwan*·tos/as
a little	un poco	oon *po*·ko
a lot/much	mucho/a m/f	*moo*·cho/a
many	muchos/as m/f pl	*moo*·chos/as
some	algunos/as m/f pl	al·*goo*·nos/as

For other useful amounts, see **self-catering** (p182).

BASICS TIMES & DATES

Times & Dates

KEY PHRASES

What time is it?	¿Qué hora es?	ke *o*·ra es
At what time ...?	¿A qué hora ...?	a ke *o*·ra ...
What date?	¿Qué día?	ke *dee*·a

Telling the Time

When telling the time in Mexico, 'It is ...' is expressed by *Son las ...* son las ... followed by a number. The exceptions are *Es la una* es la *oo*·na (It's one o'clock), *Es mediodía* es me·dyo·*dee*·a (It's midday) and *Es medianoche* es me·dya·*no*·che (It's midnight).

Q What time is it?	¿Qué hora es? ke *o*·ra es
A It's one o'clock.	Es la una. es la *oo*·na
A It's (10) o'clock.	Son las (diez). son las (dyes)
A Quarter past one.	Es la una y cuarto. es la *oo*·na ee *kwar*·to
A Twenty past one.	Es la una y veinte. es la *oo*·na ee *vayn*·te
A Half past (eight).	Son las (ocho) y media. son las (*o*·cho) ee *me*·dya
A Twenty to (eight).	Son veinte para las (ocho). son *vayn*·te *pa*·ra las (*o*·cho)
A Quarter to (eight).	Son cuarto para las (ocho). son *kwar*·to *pa*·ra las (*o*·cho)

Ⓠ At what time ...?	¿A qué hora ...?	a ke o·ra ...
Ⓐ At one o'clock.	A la una.	a la oo·na
Ⓐ At (eight) o'clock.	A las (ocho).	a las (o·cho)
Ⓐ At (4.40pm).	A las (cuatro y cuarenta de la tarde).	a las (kwa·tro ee kwa·ren·ta de la tar·de)

in the morning	de la mañana	de la ma·nya·na
in the afternoon	de la tarde	de la tar·de
in the evening	de la noche	de la no·che
sunrise	amanecer m	a·ma·ne·ser
dawn	madrugada f	ma·droo·ga·da
morning	mañana f	ma·nya·na
day	día m	dee·a
afternoon	tarde f	tar·de
evening	noche f	no·che
night	noche f	no·che
sunset	atardecer m	a·tar·de·ser

The Calendar

Monday	lunes m	loo·nes
Tuesday	martes m	mar·tes
Wednesday	miércoles m	myer·ko·les
Thursday	jueves m	khwe·ves
Friday	viernes m	vyer·nes
Saturday	sábado m	sa·ba·do
Sunday	domingo m	do·meen·go

January	enero m	e·ne·ro
February	febrero m	fe·bre·ro
March	marzo m	mar·so
April	abril m	a·breel
May	mayo m	ma·yo
June	junio m	khoo·nyo
July	julio m	khoo·lyo
August	agosto m	a·gos·to
September	septiembre m	sep·tyem·bre
October	octubre m	ok·too·bre
November	noviembre m	no·vyem·bre
December	diciembre m	dee·syem·bre

Q **What date?**	¿Qué día?	ke dee·a
Q **What's today's date?**	¿Qué día es hoy?	ke dee·a es oy
A **It's (17 November).**	Es el (diecisiete de noviembre).	es el (dye·see·sye·te de no·vyem·bre)

summer	verano m	ve·ra·no
autumn	otoño m	o·to·nyo
winter	invierno m	een·vyer·no
spring	primavera f	pree·ma·ve·ra

Present

now	ahora	a·o·ra
right now	ahora mismo	a·o·ra mees·mo
today	hoy	oy
tonight	esta noche	es·ta no·che

> **LANGUAGE TIP**
>
> **Multiple Meanings**
> It's worth remembering that the word *mañana*
> ma·*nya*·na means 'tomorrow', but *la mañana*
> la ma·*nya*·na means 'morning'. More rarely, *mañana* can
> mean 'later on' (especially in bureaucratic situations). Also,
> *la madrugada* la ma·droo·*ga*·da can mean 'daybreak' or 'the
> small hours of the morning', depending on the context.

this morning	esta mañana	es·ta ma·*nya*·na
this afternoon	esta tarde	es·ta *tar*·de
this week	esta semana	es·ta se·*ma*·na
this month	este mes	es·te mes
this year	este año	es·te *a*·nyo

Past

yesterday	ayer	a·*yer*
yesterday morning	ayer en la mañana	a·*yer* en la ma·*nya*·na
yesterday afternoon	ayer en la tarde	a·*yer* en la *tar*·de
yesterday evening	ayer en la noche	a·*yer* en la *no*·che
day before yesterday	antier	an·*tyer*
(three days) ago	hace (tres días)	*a*·se (tres *dee*·as)
since (May)	desde (mayo)	*des*·de (*ma*·yo)
last night	anoche	a·*no*·che
last week	la semana pasada	la se·*ma*·na pa·*sa*·da
last month	el mes pasado	el mes pa·*sa*·do
last year	el año pasado	el *a*·nyo pa·*sa*·do

BASICS TIMES & DATES

> **CULTURE TIP**
>
> **Meeting Etiquette**
> Being late for an appointment isn't the end of the world in Mexico. In situations where punctuality is important, make sure you add *a la hora europea* a la *o*·ra e·oo·ro·*pe*·a (meaning 'exactly') after arranging a time to meet. Family obligations always take precedence over social or business meetings, and if you're invited to a party it's expected that you'll arrive between 30 minutes to an hour later than the specified time.

Future

tomorrow	mañana	ma·*nya*·na
tomorrow morning	mañana en la mañana	ma·*nya*·na en la ma·*nya*·na
tomorrow afternoon	mañana en la tarde	ma·*nya*·na en la *tar*·de
tomorrow evening	mañana en la noche	ma·*nya*·na en la *no*·che
day after tomorrow	pasado mañana	pa·*sa*·do ma·*nya*·na
in (six) days	en (seis) días	en (says) *dee*·as
until (June)	hasta (junio)	*as*·ta (*khoo*·nyo)
next week	la próxima semana	la *prok*·see·ma se·*ma*·na
next month	el mes que viene	el mes ke *vye*·ne
next year	el año que viene	el *a*·nyo ke *vye*·ne

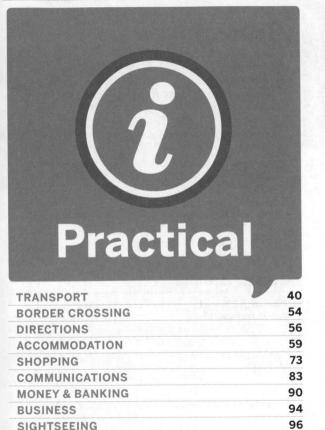

Practical

Transport

KEY PHRASES

When's the next bus?	¿A qué hora sale el próximo camión?	a ke o·ra sa·le el prok·see·mo ka·myon
A ticket to ..., please.	Un boleto a ..., por favor.	oon bo·le·to a ... por fa·vor
Can you tell me when we get to ...?	¿Me puede avisar cuando lleguemos a ...?	me pwe·de a·vee·sar kwan·do ye·ge·mos a ...
Please take me to this address.	Por favor, lléveme a esta dirección.	por fa·vor ye·ve·me a es·ta dee·rek·syon
I'd like to hire a car.	Quisiera rentar un coche.	kee·sye·ra ren·tar oon ko·che

Getting Around

Can we get there by public transport?	¿Podemos llegar en transporte público? po·de·mos ye·gar en trans·por·te poo·blee·ko
Can we get there by bicycle?	¿Podemos llegar en bicicleta? po·de·mos ye·gar en bee·see·kle·ta
I'd prefer to walk there.	Prefiero ir caminando. pre·fye·ro eer ka·mee·nan·do

What time does the ... leave?	¿A qué hora sale el ...? a ke o·ra sa·le el ...	
boat	barco	*bar*·ko
bus (city)	autobús	ow·to·*boos*
bus (intercity)	camión	ka·*myon*
metro	metro	*me*·tro
minibus	pesero	pe·*se*·ro
plane	avión	a·*vyon*
train	tren	tren
trolleybus	trolebús	tro·le·*boos*

What time's the first bus?	¿A qué hora sale el primer autobús? a ke o·ra sa·le el pree·*mer* ow·to·*boos*
What time's the last bus?	¿A qué hora sale el último autobús? a ke o·ra sa·le el *ool*·tee·mo ow·to·*boos*
What time's the next bus?	¿A qué hora sale el próximo autobús? a ke o·ra sa·le el *prok*·see·mo ow·to·*boos*
Can I have a lift in your ...?	¿Me puede dar un aventón en su ...? me *pwe*·de dar oon a·ven·*ton* en soo ...

trailer	trailer	*trai*·ler
truck	camión	ka·*myon*
ute/pick-up	camioneta	ka·myo·*ne*·ta
van	vagoneta	va·go·*ne*·ta

PRACTICAL TRANSPORT

That's my seat.	Ése es mi asiento.
	e·se es mee a·syen·to
Is this seat free?	¿Está libre este asiento?
	es·ta lee·bre es·te a·syen·to
✂ **Is it free?**	¿Está libre? · es·ta lee·bre
How long will it be delayed?	¿Cuánto tiempo habrá de retraso?
	kwan·to tyem·po a·bra de re·tra·so
When's the next flight to (Mexico City)?	¿Cuándo sale el próximo vuelo para (México)?
	kwan·do sa·le el prok·see·mo vwe·lo pa·ra (me·khee·ko)
Can you tell me when we get to (Puerto Vallarta)?	¿Me puede avisar cuando lleguemos a (Puerto Vallarta)?
	me pwe·de a·vee·sar kwan·do ye·ge·mos a (pwer·to va·yar·ta)
I want to get off here.	¡Aquí me bajo!
	a·kee me ba·kho
✂ **Getting off!**	¡Bajan! · ba·khan

Buying Tickets

Where can I buy a ticket?	¿Dónde puedo comprar un boleto?	
	don·de pwe·do kom·*prar* oon bo·*le*·to	
Do I need to book?	¿Tengo que reservar?	
	ten·go ke re·ser·*var*	
Can I get a stand-by ticket?	¿Puede ponerme en la lista de espera?	
	pwe·de po·*ner*·me en la *lees*·ta de es·*pe*·ra	
I'd like to ... my ticket, please.	Me gustaría ... mi boleto, por favor.	
	me goos·ta·*ree*·a ... mee bo·*le*·to por fa·*vor*	

cancel	cancelar	kan·se·*lar*
change	cambiar	kam·*byar*
collect	recoger	re·ko·*kher*
confirm	confirmar	kon·feer·*mar*

A ... ticket (to Oaxaca), please.	Un boleto ... (a Oaxaca), por favor.	
	oon bo·*le*·to ... (a wa·*ha*·ka) por fa·*vor*	

1st-/2nd-class	de primera/ segunda clase	de pree·*me*·ra/ se·*goon*·da *kla*·se
child's	infantil	een·fan·*teel*
one-way	de viaje sencillo	de *vya*·khe sen·*see*·yo
return	redondo	re·*don*·do
student's	de estudiante	de es·too·*dyan*·te

I'd like an aisle seat.	Quisiera un asiento de pasillo.	kee·*sye*·ra oon a·*syen*·to de pa·*see*·yo
I'd like a window seat.	Quisiera un asiento junto a la ventana.	kee·*sye*·ra oon a·*syen*·to *khoon*·to a la ven·*ta*·na
I'd like a (non-)smoking seat.	Quisiera un asiento en la sección de (no) fumar.	kee·*sye*·ra oon a·*syen*·to en la sek·*syon* de (no) foo·*mar*
Is there (a) ...?	¿Hay ...?	ai ...

air-conditioning	aire acondicionado	*ai*·re a·kon·dee·syo·*na*·do
blanket	una cobija	*oo*·na ko·*bee*·kha
toilet	sanitarios	sa·nee·*ta*·ryos
video	video	vee·*de*·o

How long does the trip take?	¿Cuánto dura el viaje?	*kwan*·to *doo*·ra el *vya*·khe
Is it a direct route?	¿Es un viaje directo?	es oon *vya*·khe dee·*rek*·to
What time do I have to check in?	¿A qué hora tengo que documentar?	a ke *o*·ra *ten*·go ke do·koo·men·*tar*

For phrases about entering and leaving countries, see **border crossing** (p54).

Luggage

My luggage has been damaged.	Se dañaron mis maletas. se da·*nya*·ron mees ma·*le*·tas

Buying a Ticket

What time is the next ...?

¿A qué hora sale el próximo ...?

a ke o·ra sa·le el prok·see·mo ...

 boat
barco
bar·ko

 bus
camión
ka·myon

 train
tren
tren

One ... ticket, please.

Un boleto ..., por favor. *oon bo·le·to ... por fa·vor*

 one-way
de viaje
sencillo
*de vya·khe
sen·see·yo*

 return
redondo
re·don·do

I'd like a/an ... seat.

Quisiera un asiento ...

kee·sye·ra oon a·syen·to ...

aisle
de pasillo
de pa·see·yo

window
junto a la
ventana
*khoon·to a la
ven·ta·na*

Which platform does it depart from?

¿De cuál andén sale?

de kwal an·den sa·le

My luggage has been lost.	Se perdieron mis maletas. se per·*dye*·ron mees ma·*le*·tas
My luggage has been stolen.	Se robaron mis maletas. se ro·*ba*·ron mees ma·*le*·tas
My luggage hasn't arrived.	Mis maletas no han llegado. mees ma·*le*·tas no an ye·*ga*·do
I'd like a luggage locker.	Quisiera un casillero. kee·*sye*·ra oon ka·see·*ye*·ro
I'd like some coins/tokens.	Quisiera unas monedas/fichas. kee·*sye*·ra oo·nas mo·*ne*·das/*fee*·chas

Bus, Trolleybus & Metro

In Mexico City, you'll probably use the *Metrobús* me·tro·*boos*, a bus line with stations (like a train) that criss-crosses the city and links up to the metro system.

Which city/intercity bus goes to ...?	¿Qué autobús/camión va a ...? ke ow·to·*boos*/ka·*myon* va a ...
How many stops (to the market)?	¿Cuántas paradas son (al mercado)? *kwan*·tas pa·*ra*·das son (al mer·*ka*·do)
Please take me to the bus terminal.	Por favor, lléveme a la central (de autobuses). por fa·*vor* ye·ve·me a la sen·*tral* (de ow·to·*boo*·ses)
This/That one.	Éste./Ése. es·te/e·se
Bus/Trolleybus number (11).	El autobús/trolebús número (once). el ow·to·*boos*/tro·le·*boos* *noo*·me·ro (*on*·se)

> **CULTURE TIP**
>
> **Mexico City**
>
> Mexico City is called 'México' if you're travelling there from anywhere else in the country. It is also very often called *DF* de·e·fe (short for *Distrito Federal* dis·*tree*·to fe·de·*ral*), a special administrative district around the national capital. Within the city, it's also spoken of as *la Ciudad de México* la syu·*dad* de *me*·khee·ko.

Train

What station is this?	¿Cuál es esta estación? kwal es *es*·ta es·ta·*syon*
What's the next station?	¿Cuál es la próxima estación? kwal es la *prok*·see·ma es·ta·*syon*
Does this train stop at (Chihuahua)?	¿Para el tren a (Chihuahua)? *pa*·ra el tren a (chee·*wa*·wa)
Do I need to change trains?	¿Tengo que cambiar de tren? *ten*·go ke kam·*byar* de tren
Which is the dining car?	¿Cuál es el vagón comedor? kwal es el va·*gon* ko·me·*dor*
Which carriage is 1st class?	¿Cuál es el vagón de primera clase? kwal es el va·*gon* de pree·*me*·ra *kla*·se
Which carriage is for (Querétaro)?	¿Cuál es el vagón para (Querétaro)? kwal es el va·*gon* pa·ra (ke·*re*·ta·ro)

PRACTICAL TRANSPORT

Bussing It

Originally, a small bus was simply called a *colectivo* ko·*lek*·tee·vo but in the '70s, small public transport vehicles (including cars and vans) came to be classified as *peseros* pe·*se*·ros – so called because the trip then cost one peso. During the '80s, the goverment began introducing new minibuses known as *microbuses* mee·kro·*boo*·ses or just *micros* mee·kros. While all these terms are widely used, the general word is still *pesero*.

There are also different terms for intercity minibuses and open-backed trucks, depending on the route and city: *combi* kom·bee, *rédila* re·dee·la, *suburban* soo·*boor*·ban etc. To keep it simple, you can just use the word *transporte* trans·*por*·te.

Taxi

I'd like a taxi now/ tomorrow.	Quisiera un taxi ahora/ mañana. kee·*sye*·ra oon *tak*·see a·o·ra/ ma·*nya*·na
I'd like a taxi at (9am).	Quisiera un taxi a las (nueve de la mañana). kee·*sye*·ra oon *tak*·see a las (*nwe*·ve de la ma·*nya*·na)
Is this taxi free?	¿Está libre este taxi? es·*ta lee*·bre es·te *tak*·see
✂ **Is it free?**	**¿Está libre?** es·*ta lee*·bre
How much is it to ...?	¿Cuánto cuesta ir a ...? *kwan*·to *kwes*·ta eer a ...
Please put the meter on.	Por favor, ponga el taxímetro. por fa·*vor pon*·ga el tak·*see*·me·tro

Please take me to (this address).	Por favor, lléveme a (esta dirección). por fa·*vor* ye·ve·me a (es·ta dee·rek·*syon*)
✂ To ...	A ... a ...
Please slow down.	Por favor vaya más despacio. por fa·*vor* va·ya mas des·*pa*·syo
Please wait here.	Por favor espere aquí. por fa·*vor* es·*pe*·re a·*kee*
Stop at the corner.	Pare en la esquina. *pa*·re en la es·*kee*·na
Stop here.	Pare aquí. *pa*·re a·*kee*

PRACTICAL TRANSPORT

ANTHONY PLUMMER / GETTY IMAGES ©

¿Por aquí se va a ...?
por a·*kee* se va a ...
Is this the road to ...?

Car & Motorbike

| I'd like to hire a/an ... | Quisiera rentar ... kee·sye·ra ren·tar ... |

4WD	un cuatro por cuatro	oon kwa·tro por kwa·tro
automatic (car)	un (coche) automático	oon (ko·che) ow·to·ma·tee·ko
manual (car)	un (coche) manual	oon (ko·che) man·wal
motorbike	una moto	oo·na mo·to

with (air-conditioning)	con (aire acondicionado) kon (ai·re a·kon·dee·syo·na·do)
without (a driver)	sin (chofer) seen (cho·fer)
How much for hourly hire?	¿Cuánto cuesta la renta por hora? kwan·to kwes·ta la ren·ta por o·ra
How much for daily hire?	¿Cuánto cuesta la renta diaria? kwan·to kwes·ta la ren·ta dya·rya

◀)) LISTEN FOR

diesel	*dee*·sel	diesel
gasolina	ga·so·*lee*·na	petrol
Magna	*mag*·na	regular unleaded
Premium	*pre*·mee·oom	premium unleaded
sin plomo	seen *plo*·mo	unleaded

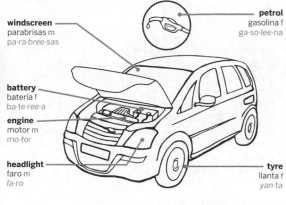

petrol
gasolina f
ga·so·*lee*·na

windscreen
parabrisas m
pa·ra·*bree*·sas

battery
batería f
ba·te·*ree*·a

engine
motor m
mo·*tor*

headlight
faro m
fa·ro

tyre
llanta f
yan·ta

How much for weekly hire?	¿Cuánto cuesta la renta semanal?
	kwan·to *kwes*·ta la *ren*·ta se·ma·*nal*
What's the speed limit in town?	¿Cuál es el límite de velocidad en las calles?
	kwal es el *lee*·mee·te de ve·lo·see·*dad* en las *ka*·yes
What's the speed limit on the highway?	¿Cuál es el límite de velocidad en las carreteras?
	kwal es el *lee*·mee·te de ve·lo·see·*dad* en las ka·re·*te*·ras
Is this the road to (Palenque)?	¿Por aquí se va a (Palenque)?
	por a·*kee* se va a (pa·*len*·ke)

🔍 LOOK FOR

Alto	*al*·to	Stop
Ceda el Paso	*se*·da el *pa*·so	Give Way
Cuota	*kwo*·ta	Toll
Entrada	en·*tra*·da	Entrance
Estacionamiento	es·ta·syo·na·*myen*·to	Parking
Peligro	pe·*lee*·gro	Danger
Prohibido el Paso	pro·ee·*bee*·do el *pa*·so	No Entry
Prohibido Estacionar	pro·ee·*bee*·do es·ta·syo·*nar*	No Parking
Salida	sa·*lee*·da	Exit
Un Sólo Sentido	oon *so*·lo sen·*tee*·do	One Way

Where's a petrol station?	¿Dónde hay una gasolinera/bomba? *don*·de ai *oo*·na ga·so·lee·*ne*·ra/*bom*·ba
Please fill it up.	Lleno, por favor. *ye*·no por fa·*vor*
I'd like (100) pesos' worth.	Quiero (cien) pesos. *kye*·ro (syen) *pe*·sos
Please check the oil/water.	Por favor, revise el nivel del aceite/agua. por fa·*vor* re·*vee*·se el nee·*vel* del a·*say*·te/*a*·gwa
Please check the tyre pressure.	Por favor, revise la presión de las llantas. por fa·*vor* re·*vee*·se la pre·*syon* de las *yan*·tas
(How long) Can I park here?	¿(Por cuánto tiempo) Puedo estacionarme aquí? (por *kwan*·to *tyem*·po) *pwe*·do es·ta·syo·*nar*·me a·*kee*

Where do I pay?	¿Dónde se paga? *don*·de se *pa*·ga
I need a mechanic.	Necesito un mecánico. ne·se·*see*·to oon me·*ka*·nee·ko
The car has broken down (at the intersection).	El coche se descompuso (en la intersección). el *ko*·che se des·kom·*poo*·so (en la een·ter·sek·*syon*)
I had an accident.	Tuve un accidente. *too*·ve oon ak·see·*den*·te

Bicycle

I have a puncture.	Se me ponchó una llanta. se me pon·*cho* oo·na *yan*·ta
Where can I buy a second-hand bike?	¿Dónde puedo comprar una bicicleta usada? *don*·de *pwe*·do kom·*prar* oo·na bee·see·*kle*·ta oo·*sa*·da
Where can I hire a bicycle?	¿Dónde puedo rentar una bicicleta? *don*·de *pwe*·do ren·*tar* oo·na bee·see·*kle*·ta
How much is it per hour?	¿Cuánto cuesta por hora? *kwan*·to *kwes*·ta por *o*·ra
How much is it per day?	¿Cuánto cuesta por día? *kwan*·to *kwes*·ta por *dee*·a

Border Crossing

KEY PHRASES

I'm here for ... days.	Voy a estar ... días.	voy a es·*tar* ... *dee*·as
I'm staying at ...	Me estoy quedando en ...	me es·*toy* ke·*dan*·do en ...
I have nothing to declare.	No tengo nada que declarar.	no *ten*·go *na*·da ke de·kla·*rar*

Border Crossing

I'm here ... Estoy aquí ...
es·*toy* a·*kee* ...

in transit	en tránsito	en *tran*·see·to
on business	de negocios	de ne·*go*·syos
on holiday	de vacaciones	de va·ka·*syo*·nes
to study	estudiando	es·too·*dyan*·do
to visit family	visitando a mi familia	vee·see·*tan*·do a mee fa·*mee*·lya

 LOOK FOR

Aduana	a·*dwa*·na	Customs
Artículos Libres de Impuestos	ar·*tee*·koo·los *lee*·bres de eem·*pwes*·tos	Duty-Free Goods
Control de Pasaportes	kon·*trol* de pa·sa·*por*·tes	Passport Control

🔊 LISTEN FOR

Su pasaporte, por favor.	soo pa·sa·*por*·te por fa·*vor* Your passport, please.
Su tarjeta de turista, por favor.	soo tar·*khe*·ta de too·*rees*·ta por fa·*vor* Your tourist card, please.
¿Está viajando en grupo?	es·*ta* vya·*khan*·do en *groo*·po Are you travelling in a group?
¿Está viajando solo/a? m/f	es·*ta* vya·*khan*·do *so*·lo/a Are you travelling on your own?

I'm here for (10) days.	Voy a estar (diez) días. voy a es·*tar* (dyes) *dee*·as
I'm here for (two) months.	Voy a estar (dos) meses. voy a es·*tar* (dos) *me*·ses
I'm here for (three) weeks.	Voy a estar (tres) semanas. voy a es·*tar* (tres) se·*ma*·nas
I'm staying at (the) ...	Me estoy quedando en (el) ... me es·*toy* ke·*dan*·do en (el) ...

For phrases about payment, see **money & banking** (p90).

At Customs

I have nothing to declare.	No tengo nada que declarar. no *ten*·go *na*·da ke de·kla·*rar*
I have something to declare.	Quisiera declarar algo. kee·*sye*·ra de·kla·*rar* al·go
I didn't know I had to declare it.	No sabía que tenía que declararlo. no sa·*bee*·a ke te·*nee*·a ke de·kla·*rar*·lo
Do you have this form in (English)?	¿Tiene este formato en (inglés)? *tye*·ne *es*·te for·*ma*·to en (een·*gles*)

Directions

KEY PHRASES

Where's ...?	¿Dónde queda ...?	don·de ke·da ...
What's the address?	¿Cuál es la dirección?	kwal es la dee·rek·syon
How far is it?	¿A qué distancia está?	a ke dees·tan·sya es·ta

I'm looking for (the cathedral).	Busco (la catedral). boos·ko (la ka·te·dral)
Which way's (the main square)?	¿Cómo se llega (al zócalo)? ko·mo se ye·ga (al so·ka·lo)
How do I get to ...?	¿Cómo llego a ...? ko·mo ye·go a ...
What's the address?	¿Cuál es la dirección? kwal es la dee·rek·syon
How far is it?	¿A qué distancia está? a ke dees·tan·sya es·ta
Can you show me (on the map)?	¿Me lo puede señalar (en el mapa)? me lo pwe·de se·nya·lar (en el ma·pa)
🔲 **Where's (the bank)?**	¿Dónde queda (el banco)? don·de ke·da (el ban·ko)
🔳 **It's ...**	Está ... es·ta ...
Turn left/right.	Dé vuelta a la izquierda/ derecha. de vwel·ta a la ees·kyer·da/ de·re·cha

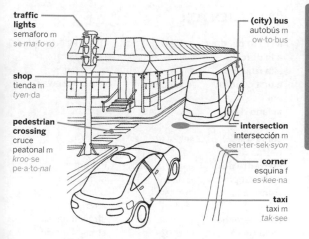

traffic lights
semáforo m
se·*ma*·fo·ro

shop
tienda m
tyen·da

pedestrian crossing
cruce peatonal m
kroo·se
pe·a·to·*nal*

(city) bus
autobús m
ow·to·bus

intersection
intersección m
een·ter·sek·*syon*

corner
esquina f
es·*kee*·na

taxi
taxi m
tak·see

Turn at the corner.	Dé vuelta en la esquina. de *vwel*·ta en la es·*kee*·na
Turn at the traffic lights.	Dé vuelta en el semáforo. de *vwel*·ta en el se·*ma*·fo·ro
It's (100) metres.	Está a (cien) metros. es·*ta* a (syen) *me*·tros
It's (two) kilometres.	Está a (dos) kilómetros. es·*ta* a (dos) kee·*lo*·me·tros
It's (30) minutes away.	Está a (treinta) minutos. es·*ta* a (*trayn*·ta) mee·*noo*·tos

PRACTICAL DIRECTIONS

🔊 LISTEN FOR

a (tres) cuadras	a (tres) *kwa*·dras	(three) blocks away
a la derecha	a la de·*re*·cha	to the right
a la izquierda	a la ees·*kyer*·da	to the left
a una cuadra	a *oo*·na *kwa*·dra	one block away
ahí	a·*ee*	there
al lado de ...	al *la*·do de ...	next to ...
aquí	a·*kee*	here
cerca (de ...)	*ser*·ka (de ...)	near (to ...)
detrás de ...	de·*tras* de ...	behind ...
en frente de ...	en *fren*·te de ...	in front of ...
en la esquina	en la es·*kee*·na	on the corner
frente a ...	*fren*·te a ...	opposite ...
lejos	*le*·khos	far away
todo derecho	*to*·do de·*re*·cho	straight ahead
todo recto	*to*·do *rek*·to	straight ahead

by bus (city)	en autobús en ow·to·*boos*
by car	en coche en *ko*·che
by metro	en metro en *me*·tro
by minibus	en pesero en pe·*se*·ro
by taxi	en taxi en *tak*·see
by train	en tren en tren
on foot	a pie a pye

Accommodation

KEY PHRASES

Where's a hotel?	¿Dónde hay un hotel?	*don*·de ai oon o·*tel*
Do you have a double room?	¿Tiene una habitación doble?	*tye*·ne *oo*·na a·bee·ta·*syon* *do*·ble
How much is it per night?	¿Cuánto cuesta por noche?	*kwan*·to *kwes*·ta por *no*·che
Is breakfast included?	¿El desayuno está incluido?	el de·sa·*yoo*·no es·*ta* een·kloo·*ee*·do
What time is checkout?	¿A qué hora hay que dejar la habitación?	a ke o·ra ai ke de·*khar* la a·bee·ta·*syon*

Finding Accommodation

Where's a ...?		¿Dónde hay ...? *don*·de ai ...

campsite	un área para acampar	oon *a*·re·a *pa*·ra a·kam·*par*
guesthouse	una pensión	*oo*·na pen·*syon*
hotel	un hotel	oon o·*tel*
lodging house	casa de huéspedes	*ka*·sa de *wes*·pe·des
room	una habitación	*oo*·na a·bee·ta·*syon*
small inn	una posada	*oo*·na po·*sa*·da
youth hostel	un albergue juvenil	oon al·*ber*·ge khoo·ve·*neel*

Can you recommend somewhere ...?	¿Puede recomendarme alojamiento ...? *pwe·de re·ko·men·dar·me a·lo·kha·myen·to ...*

cheap	barato	ba·*ra*·to
good	bueno	*bwe*·no
luxurious	lujoso	loo·*kho*·so
nearby	cercano	ser·*ka*·no
romantic	romántico	ro·*man*·tee·ko

Booking Ahead & Checking In

I'd like to book a room, please.	Quisiera reservar una habitación. *kee·sye·ra re·ser·var oo·na a·bee·ta·syon*

✂	**Are there rooms?**	¿Tiene habitaciones?	*tye*·ne a·bee·ta·*syo*·nes

Do I need to pay upfront?	¿Necesito pagar por adelantado? *ne·se·see·to pa·gar por a·de·lan·ta·do*

Do you have a ... room?	¿Tiene una habitación ...? *tye·ne oo·na a·bee·ta·syon ...*

single	sencilla	sen·*see*·ya
double	doble	*do*·ble
twin	con dos camas	kon dos *ka*·mas
triple	triple	*tree*·ple

🔊 LISTEN FOR

Lo siento, no hay vacantes.	lo *syen*·to no ai va·*kan*·tes I'm sorry, we're full.
¿Por cuántas noches?	por *kwan*·tas *no*·ches For how many nights?
Su pasaporte, por favor.	soo pa·sa·*por*·te por fa·*vor* Your passport, please.

with/without (a) ...   con/sin ...
kon/seen ...

air- conditioning	aire acondicionado	*ai*·re a·kon·dee·syo·*na*·do
bathroom	baño	*ba*·nyo
fan	ventilador	ven·tee·la·*dor*
sea view	vista al mar	*vees*·ta al mar
street view	vista a la calle	*vees*·ta a la *ka*·ye
TV	televisión	te·le·vee·*syon*

How much is it per person?	¿Cuánto cuesta por persona? *kwan*·to *kwes*·ta por per·*so*·na
How much is it per night?	¿Cuánto cuesta por noche? *kwan*·to *kwes*·ta por *no*·che
How much is it per week?	¿Cuánto cuesta por semana? *kwan*·to *kwes*·ta por se·*ma*·na
Is breakfast included?	¿El desayuno está incluido? el de·sa·*yoo*·no es·*ta* een·kloo·ee·do
I have a reservation.	Tengo una reserva. *ten*·go *oo*·na re·*ser*·va
For (three) nights/weeks.	Por (tres) noches/semanas. por (tres) *no*·ches/se·*ma*·nas

From (30 July) to (4 August).	Del (treinta de julio) al (cuatro de agosto). del (*trayn*·ta de *khoo*·lyo) al (*kwa*·tro de a·*gos*·to)
Can I see it?	¿Puedo verla? *pwe*·do *ver*·la
It's fine, I'll take it.	Está bien, la tomo. es·*ta* byen la *to*·mo

For phrases on payment, see **money & banking** (p90).

Requests & Queries

When/Where is breakfast served?	¿Cuándo/Dónde se sirve el desayuno? *kwan*·do/*don*·de se *seer*·ve el de·sa·*yoo*·no
Do you have room service?	¿Tiene servicio al cuarto? *tye*·ne ser·*vee*·syo al *kwar*·to
Please wake me at (seven).	Por favor, despiérteme a las (siete). por fa·*vor* des·*pyer*·te·me a las (*sye*·te)
Can I get (another towel)?	¿Puede darme (otra toalla)? *pwe*·de *dar*·me (o·tra to·a·ya)
Can I use the kitchen?	¿Puedo usar la cocina? *pwe*·do oo·*sar* la ko·*see*·na
Can I use the laundry?	¿Puedo usar la lavandería? *pwe*·do oo·*sar* la la·van·de·*ree*·a
Can I use the telephone?	¿Puedo usar el teléfono? *pwe*·do oo·*sar* el te·*le*·fo·no
There's no need to change my sheets.	No es necesario que cambie mis sábanas. no es ne·se·*sa*·ryo ke *kam*·bye mees *sa*·ba·nas

Finding a Room

Do you have a ... room?

¿Tiene una habitación ...?

tye·ne oo·na a·bee·ta·syon ...

 double
doble
do·ble

 single
sencilla
sen·see·ya

How much is it per ...?

¿Cuánto cuesta por ...?

kwan·to kwes·ta por ...

 night
noche
no·che

 person
persona
per·so·na

Is breakfast included?

¿El desyauno está incluído?

el de·sa·yoo·no es·ta een·kloo·ee·do

Can I see the room?

¿Puedo verla?

pwe·do ver·la

'll take it.
.a tomo.
a *to·*mo

I won't take it.
No la tomo.
no la *to·*mo

Do you have (a/an) ...?	¿Hay ...?	
	ai ...	

dry-cleaning service	servicio de tintorería	ser·*vee*·syo de teen·to·re·*ree*·a
elevator	elevador	e·le·va·*dor*
gym	gimnasio	kheem·*na*·syo
internet	internet	een·ter·*net*
laundry service	servicio de lavandería	ser·*vee*·syo de la·van·de·*ree*·a
message board	pizarrón de anuncios	pee·sa·*ron* de a·*noon*·syos
safe	caja fuerte	*ka*·kha *fwer*·te
swimming pool	alberca	al·*ber*·ka

Do you arrange tours here?	¿Aquí organizan tours? a·*kee* or·ga·*nee*·san toors
Do you change money here?	¿Aquí cambian dinero? a·*kee* kam·byan dee·*ne*·ro
Can I leave a message for someone?	¿Puedo dejar un mensaje para alguien? *pwe*·do de·*khar* oon men·*sa*·khe *pa*·ra *al*·gyen
Is there a message for me?	¿Hay algún mensaje para mí? ai al·*goon* men·*sa*·khe *pa*·ra mee
I'm locked out of my room.	Dejé la llave dentro del cuarto. de·*khe* la *ya*·ve *den*·tro del *kwar*·to
The (bathroom) door is locked.	La puerta (del baño) está cerrada con llave. la *pwer*·ta (del *ba*·nyo) es·*ta* se·*ra*·da kon *ya*·ve

🔊 LISTEN FOR

lugar de mala muerte	loo·*gar* de *ma*·la *mwer*·te	dive
lugar de moda	loo·*gar* de *mo*·da	top spot
plagado de ratas	pla·*ga*·do de *ra*·tas	rat-infested

Complaints

The room is too ...		La habitación es muy ...
		la a·bee·ta·*syon* es mooy ...

cold	fría	*free*·a
dark	oscura	os·*koo*·ra
light/bright	iluminada	ee·loo·mee·*na*·da
noisy	ruidosa	rwee·*do*·sa
small	pequeña	pe·*ke*·nya

The (air-conditioning) doesn't work.	No funciona (el aire acondicionado). no foon·*syo*·na (el *ai*·re a·kon·dee·syo·*na*·do)
This (blanket) isn't clean.	Esta (cobija) no está limpia. *es*·ta (ko·*bee*·kha) no es·*ta leem*·pya

For more things you might want in your room, see the **dictionary**.

Answering the Door

Who is it?	¿Quién es? *kyen* es
Just a moment.	Un momentito. oon mo·*men*·tee·to

Come in.	Pase.
	pa·se
Come back later, please.	¿Puede volver más tarde, por favor?
	pwe·de vol·ver mas tar·de por fa·vor

Checking Out

What time is checkout?	¿A qué hora hay que dejar la habitación?
	a ke o·ra ai ke de·khar la a·bee·ta·syon
Can I have a late checkout?	¿Puedo dejar la habitación más tarde?
	pwe·do de·khar la a·bee·ta·syon mas tar·de
How much extra to stay until (six o'clock)?	¿Cuánto cuesta quedarse hasta (las seis)?
	kwan·to kwes·ta ke·dar·se as·ta (las says)
Can I leave my luggage here?	¿Puedo dejar mis maletas aquí?
	pwe·do de·khar mees ma·le·tas a·kee
Can you call a taxi for me (for 11 o'clock)?	¿Me puede pedir un taxi (para las once)?
	me pwe·de pe·deer oon tak·see (pa·ra las on·se)
I'm leaving now.	Me voy ahora.
	me voy a·o·ra
Could I have my deposit, please?	¿Me puede dar mi depósito, por favor?
	me pwe·de dar mee de·po·see·to por fa·vor

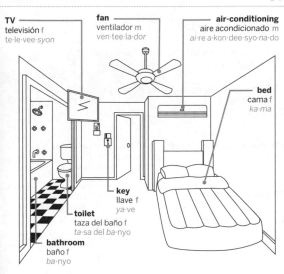

TV
televisión f
te·le·vee·*syon*

fan
ventilador m
ven·tee·la·*dor*

air-conditioning
aire acondicionado m
ai·re a·kon·dee·syo·*na*·do

bed
cama f
ka·ma

key
llave f
ya·ve

toilet
taza del baño f
ta·sa del *ba*·nyo

bathroom
baño f
ba·nyo

Could I have my passport, please?	¿Me da mi pasaporte, por favor? me da mee pa·sa·*por*·te por fa·*vor*
Could I have my valuables, please?	¿Me da mis objetos de valor, por favor? me da mees ob·*khe*·tos de va·*lor* por fa·*vor*
I'll be back in (three) days.	Volveré en (tres) días. vol·ve·*re* en (tres) *dee*·as
I'll be back on (Tuesday).	Volveré el (martes). vol·ve·*re* el (*mar*·tes)
There's a mistake in the bill.	Hay un error en la cuenta. ai oon e·*ror* en la *kwen*·ta

🔊 LISTEN FOR

La llave está en la recepción.	la *ya*·ve es·*ta* en la re·sep·*syon*
	The key is at reception.
¿Consumió algo del minibar?	kon·soo·*myo al*·go del mee·nee·*bar*
	Did you use the mini-bar?

I had a great stay, thank you.	Tuve una estancia muy agradable, gracias. *too*·ve *oo*·na es·*tan*·sya mooy a·gra·*da*·ble *gra*·syas
You've been terrific.	Han sido estupendos. **pl** an *see*·do es·too·*pen*·dos
I'll recommend it to my friends.	Se lo recomendaré a mis amigos. se lo re·ko·men·da·*re* a mees a·*mee*·gos

Camping

Where's the nearest campsite?	¿Dónde está el área para acampar más cercana? *don*·de es·*ta* el *a*·re·a *pa*·ra a·kam·*par* mas ser·*ka*·na
Who do I ask to stay here?	¿Con quién tengo que hablar para quedarme aquí? kon kyen *ten*·go ke a·*blar pa*·ra ke·*dar*·me a·*kee*
Can I camp here?	¿Se puede acampar aquí? se *pwe*·de a·kam·*par* a·*kee*
Can I park next to my tent?	¿Se puede estacionar al lado de la tienda? se *pwe*·de es·ta·syo·*nar* al *la*·do de la *tyen*·da

Do you have ...?	¿Tiene ...? *tye·ne ...*	
a site	un lugar de acampado	oon *loo·*gar de a·*kam*·pa·do
electricity	electricidad	e·lek·tree·see·*dad*
shower facilities	regaderas	re·ga·*de*·ras
tents for hire	tiendas de campaña en renta	*tyen*·das de kam·*pa*·nya en *ren*·ta

How much is it per tent?	¿Cuánto es por tienda? *kwan*·to es por *tyen*·da
How much is it per vehicle?	¿Cuánto es por vehículo? *kwan*·to es por ve·*ee*·koo·lo
Could I borrow (a mallet)?	¿Me puede prestar (un martillo)? me *pwe*·de pres·*tar* (oon mar·*tee*·yo)
Where's the nearest shop?	¿Dónde está la tienda más cercana? *don*·de es·*ta* la *tyen*·da mas ser·*ka*·na
Where's the toilet block?	¿Dónde están los sanitarios? *don*·de es·*tan* los sa·nee·*ta*·ryos
Is it coin-operated?	¿Funciona con monedas? foon·*syo*·na kon mo·*ne*·das
Is the water drinkable?	¿El agua es potable? el *a*·gwa es po·*ta*·ble

For more words related to camping, see the **dictionary**.

Renting

I'm here about the ... for rent.	Vengo por el/la ... en renta. m/f *ven*·go por el/la ... en *ren*·ta
Do you have a/an ... for rent?	¿Tiene ... en renta? *tye*·ne ... en *ren*·ta

apartment	un departamento	oon de·par·ta·*men*·to
bungalow	un búngalow	oon *boon*·ga·lo
cabin	una cabaña	*oo*·na ka·*ba*·nya
house	una casa	*oo*·na *ka*·sa
room	una recámara	*oo*·na re·*ka*·ma·ra
villa	una villa	*oo*·na *vee*·ya

(partly) furnished	(parcialmente) amueblado/a m/f (par·*syal*·men·te) a·mwe·*bla*·do/a
unfurnished	sin amueblar seen a·mwe·*blar*
How much is it for (one) week?	¿Cuánto cuesta por (una) semana? *kwan*·to *kwes*·ta por (*oo*·na) se·*ma*·na
How much is it for (two) months?	¿Cuánto cuesta por (dos) meses? *kwan*·to *kwes*·ta por (dos) me·ses
Are bills extra?	¿Los servicios se pagan aparte? los ser·*vee*·syos se *pa*·gan a·*par*·te

KARAMYSH / SHUTTERSTOCK ©

¿Se puede acampar aquí?
se pwe·de a·kam·par a·kee
Can I camp here?

Staying with Locals

Can I stay at your place?	¿Me puedo quedar en su/tu casa? pol/inf me *pwe*·do ke·*dar* en soo/too *ka*·sa
Thanks for your hospitality.	Gracias por su/tu hospitalidad. pol/inf *gra*·syas por soo/too os·pee·ta·lee·*dad*
Is there anything I can do to help?	¿Puedo ayudar en algo? *pwe*·do a·*yoo*·dar en *al*·go
I have my own hammock.	Tengo mi propia hamaca. *ten*·go mee *pro*·pya a·*ma*·ka
I have my own mattress.	Tengo mi propio colchón. *ten*·go mee *pro*·pyo kol·*chon*

PRACTICAL ACCOMMODATION

CULTURE TIP

Body Language

Be aware of sending the wrong signals with your body language. In Mexico, women are expected to initiate handshakes with men, but will greet other women or male friends with a kiss on the cheek or a pat on the forearm. Conversations take place at a close physical distance and male acquaintances often hug each other when meeting.

When paying for something, place the cash or credit card directly into the hand of the person you're dealing with, even if you're in a restaurant. Leaving payment on the counter can be interpreted as a sign that you don't respect the person enough to have contact with them.

I have my own sleeping bag.	Tengo mi propia bolsa de dormir.
	ten·go mee *pro*·pya *bol*·sa de dor·*meer*
Can I ...?	¿Puedo ...?
	pwe·do ...

bring anything for the meal	traer algo para la comida	tra·*er al*·go *pa*·ra la ko·*mee*·da
do the dishes	lavar los platos	la·*var* los *pla*·tos
set/clear the table	poner/quitar la mesa	po·*ner*/kee·*tar* la *me*·sa
take out the rubbish	sacar la basura	sa·*kar* la ba·*soo*·ra

If you're dining with your hosts, see **eating out** (p174), for additional phrases.

Shopping

KEY PHRASES

I'd like to buy ...	Quisiera comprar ...	kee·sye·ra kom·prar ...
Can I look at it?	¿Puedo verlo?	pwe·do ver·lo
Can I try it on?	¿Me lo puedo probar?	me lo pwe·do pro·bar
How much is this?	¿Cuánto cuesta esto?	kwan·to kwes·ta es·to
That's too expensive.	Es demasiado caro/a. m/f	es de·ma·sya·do ka·ro/a

Looking For ...

Where's (a supermarket)?	¿Dónde hay (un supermercado)? don·de ai (oon soo·per·mer·ka·do)
Where can I buy (locally produced) goods/souvenirs?	¿Dónde puedo comprar productos/suvenirs (locales)? don·de pwe·do kom·prar pro·dook·tos/soo·ve·neers (lo·ka·les)
What is typical of the region?	¿Qué es típico de la región? ke es tee·pee·ko de la re·khyon

For more items and shopping locations, see the **dictionary**. Want to know how to get there? See **directions** (p56).

PRACTICAL SHOPPING

Making a Purchase

I'm just looking.	Sólo estoy mirando. *so*·lo es·*toy* mee·*ran*·do
I'd like to buy ...	Quisiera comprar ... kee·*sye*·ra kom·*prar* ...
How much is this?	¿Cuánto cuesta esto? *kwan*·to *kwes*·ta es·to

✂ **How much?** ¿Cuánto cuesta? *kwan*·to *kwes*·ta

Can you write down the price?	¿Puede escribir el precio? *pwe*·de es·kree·*beer* el *pre*·syo
Can I look at it?	¿Puedo verlo? *pwe*·do *ver*·lo
I don't like it.	No me gusta. no me *goos*·ta
It's faulty/broken.	Está defectuoso/roto. es·ta de·fek·*two*·so/*ro*·to
Do you have any others?	¿Tiene otros? *tye*·ne o·tros
Does it have a guarantee?	¿Tiene garantía? *tye*·ne ga·ran·*tee*·a
Could I have it wrapped?	¿Me lo podría envolver? me lo po·*dree*·a en·vol·*ver*
Could I have a bag/box, please?	¿Podría darme una bolsa/caja, por favor? po·*dree*·a *dar*·me oo·na *bol*·sa/*ka*·kha por fa·*vor*
I don't need a bag, thanks.	No necesito una bolsa, gracias. no ne·se·*see*·to oo·na *bol*·sa *gra*·syas

For phrases about payment, see **money & banking** (p90).

Making a Purchase

I'd like to buy ...
Quisiera comprar ...
kee·sye·ra kom·prar ...

How much is it?
¿Cuánto cuesta esto?
kwan·to kwes·ta es·to

······ OR ······

Can you write down the price?
¿Puede escribir el precio?
pwe·de es·kree·beer el pre·syo

Do you accept credit cards?
¿Aceptan tarjetas de crédito?
a·sep·tan tar·khe·tas de kre·dee·to

Could I have a ..., please?
¿Podría darme ..., por favor?
po·dree·a dar·me ... por fa·vor

 receipt
un recibo
oon re·see·bo

 bag
una bolsa
oo·na bol·sa

| Could I have a receipt, please? | ¿Podría darme un recibo, por favor? po·*dree*·a *dar*·me *oon* re·*see*·bo por fa·*vor* |

| ✂ | **Receipt, please.** | Un recibo, por favor. | *oon* re·*see*·bo por fa·*vor* |

| I'd like my change, please. | Quisiera mi cambio, por favor. kee·*sye*·ra mee *kam*·byo por fa·*vor* |

| I'd like to return this, please. | Quisiera devolver esto, por favor. kee·*sye*·ra de·vol·*ver* es·to por fa·*vor* |

| I'd like my money back, please. | Quisiera que me devuelva el dinero, por favor. kee·*sye*·ra ke me de·*vwel*·va el dee·*ne*·ro por fa·*vor* |

Bargaining

That's too expensive.	Es demasiado caro/a. m/f es de·ma·*sya*·do *ka*·ro/a
Can you lower the price?	¿Podría bajar un poco el precio? po·*dree*·a ba·*khar* oon *po*·ko el *pre*·syo
Do you have something cheaper?	¿Tiene algo más barato? *tye*·ne *al*·go mas ba·*ra*·to
I'll give you ...	Le doy ... le doy ...
What's your final price?	¿Cuál es su precio final? kwal es soo *pre*·syo fee·*nal*

🔊 LISTEN FOR

cazador/cazadora de ofertas m/f	ka·sa·*dor*/ka·sa·*do*·ra de o·*fer*·tas	bargain hunter
estafa f	es·*ta*·fa	rip-off
ganga f	*gan*·ga	bargain
rebajas f pl	re·*ba*·khas	specials
venta f	*ven*·ta	sale

Books & Reading

Is there an English-language bookshop/ section?

¿Hay alguna libreria/sección con material en inglés?
ai al·*goo*·na lee·bre·*ree*·a/ sek·*syon* kon ma·te·*ryal* en een·*gles*

Do you have a book by (Rosario Castellanos)?

¿Tiene algún libro de (Rosario Castellanos)?
tye·ne al·*goon* lee·bro de (ro·*sa*·ree·o kas·te·*ya*·nos)

Can you recommend a book for me?

¿Me puede recomendar algún libro?
me *pwe*·de re·ko·men·*dar* al·*goon* lee·bro

I'd like a ...

Quisiera ...
kee·*sye*·ra ...

dictionary	un diccionario	oon deek·syo·*na*·ryo
guidebook	una guía turística	*oo*·na *gee*·a too·*rees*·tee·ka
magazine	una revista	*oo*·na re·*vees*·ta
map	un mapa	oon *ma*·pa
newspaper (in English)	un periódico (en inglés)	oon pe·*ryo*·dee·ko (en een·*gles*)

Clothes

Can I try it on?	¿Me lo puedo probar?	me lo *pwe*·do *pro*·bar
It doesn't fit.	No me queda bien.	no me *ke*·da byen
It's too (big).	Está demasiado (grande).	es·*ta* de·ma·*sya*·do (*gran*·de)
My size is ...	Soy talla ...	soy *ta*·ya ...

(40)	(cuarenta)	(kwa·*ren*·ta)
small	chica	*chee*·ka
medium	mediana	me·*dya*·na
large	grande	*gran*·de

For different types of clothes, see the **dictionary**.

Music & DVD

I'd like a CD/DVD.	Quisiera un cómpact/DVD.	kee·*sye*·ra oon *kom*·pak/ de·ve·*de*
I'd like headphones.	Quisiera unos audífonos.	kee·*sye*·ra *oo*·nos ow·*dee*·fo·nos
I heard a band called (Maná).	Escuché a un grupo que se llama (Maná).	es·koo·*che* a oon *groo*·po ke se *ya*·ma (ma·*na*)
I heard a singer called ...	Escuché a un/una cantante que se llama ... m/f	es·koo·*che* a oon/*oo*·na kan·*tan*·te ke se *ya*·ma ...

How Much?

In Mexican Spanish, there are three ways to ask about the cost of something – and therefore three possible replies. The first two options below are equally common in Mexico.

How much is it?	¿Cuánto cuesta?	*kwan·*to kwes·ta
	¿Cuánto sale?	*kwan·*to sa·le
	¿Cuánto vale?	*kwan·*to va·le
It is ...	Cuesta ...	*kwes·*ta ...
	Sale ...	*sa·*le ...
	Vale ...	*va·*le ...

What's his/her best recording?	¿Cuál es su mejor disco? kwal es soo me·*khor* dees·ko
Can I listen to this?	¿Puedo escucharlo? *pwe·*do es·koo·*char·*lo
Which region is this DVD for?	¿Para qué región es este DVD? *pa·*ra ke re·*khyon* es es·te de·ve·*de*

Photography

I need passport photos taken.	Necesito fotos tamaño pasaporte. ne·se·*see·*to *fo·*tos ta·*ma·*nyo pa·sa·*por·*te
Can you print digital photos?	¿Se puede imprimir fotos digitales? se *pwe·*de eem·pree·*meer* *fo·*tos dee·khee·*ta·*les
Can you transfer my photos to a CD?	¿Se puede pasar las fotos a un cómpact? se *pwe·*de pa·*sar* las *fo·*tos a oon *kom·*pak

🔊 LISTEN FOR

¿En qué le puedo servir?	en ke le *pwe*·do ser·*veer* Can I help you?
¿Qué desea?	ke de·*se*·a What would you like?
No, no tenemos.	no no te·*ne*·mos No, we don't have any.

Can you recharge the battery?	¿Se puede recargar esta batería? se *pwe*·de re·kar·*gar* es·ta ba·te·*ree*·ya
Do you have batteries for this camera?	¿Tiene baterías para esta cámara? *tye*·ne ba·te·*ree*·yas *pa*·ra es·ta *ka*·ma·ra
Do you have a memory card for this camera?	¿Tiene una tarjeta de memoria para esta cámara? *tye*·ne oo·na tar·*khe*·ta de me·*mo*·rya *pa*·ra es·ta *ka*·ma·ra
Can you develop this film?	¿Puede revelar este rollo? *pwe*·de re·ve·*lar* es·te *ro*·yo
How much is it to develop this film?	¿Cuánto cuesta revelar este rollo? *kwan*·to *kwes*·ta re·ve·*lar* es·te *ro*·yo
Can you load my film?	¿Puede cargar la cámara? *pwe*·de kar·*gar* la *ka*·ma·ra
I'd like glossy/matte photos.	Quisiera fotos en papel brillante/mate. kee·*sye*·ra *fo*·tos en pa·*pel* bree·*yan*·te/*ma*·te

¿Me lo puedo probar?
me lo *pwe*·do pro·*bar*
Can I try it on?

I need ... film for this camera.	Necesito un rollo ... para esta cámara. ne·se·*see*·to oon ro·yo ... *pa*·ra *es*·ta *ka*·ma·ra

(400) speed	ASA (cuatrocientos)	*a*·sa (*kwa*·tro·*syen*·tos)
a 35 mm	de treinta y cinco milímetros	de *trayn*·tai·*seen*·ko mee·*lee*·me·tros
B&W	blanco y negro	*blan*·ko y *ne*·gro
colour	de color	de ko·*lor*
slide	de transparencias	de trans·pa·*ren*·syas

CULTURE TIP Souvenirs

alebrijes m pl   a·le·*bree*·khes
wood carvings of mythical creatures, crafted in Oaxaca

hamacas f pl   a·*ma*·kas
hammocks, usually of cotton or nylon

huaraches m pl   wa·*ra*·ches
leather sandals, available all over Mexico

huipiles m pl   wee·*pee*·les
traditional women's tunics, worn mostly in the south

jipijapas m pl   khee·pee·*kha*·pas
Panama-style hats, sold in Mérida and Campeche

papel amate m   pa·*pel* a·*ma*·te
decorated bark paper, made in central Mexico

piñatas f pl   pee·*nya*·tas
traditional festive dolls filled with candy

I'm (not) happy with these photos.	(No) Estoy satisfecho/a con estas fotos. m/f (no) es·*toy* sa·tee·*fe*·cho/a kon es·tas *fo*·tos

For more photographic equipment, see the **dictionary**.

Repairs

Can I have my backpack/ camera repaired here?	¿Puede reparar mi mochila/cámara aquí? *pwe*·de re·pa·*rar* mee mo·*chee*·la/*ka*·ma·ra a·*kee*
When will it be ready?	¿Cuándo estará listo? *kwan*·do es·ta·*ra* *lees*·to

Communications

KEY PHRASES

Where's the local internet cafe?	¿Dónde hay un cibercafé por aquí?	*don*·de ai oon see·ber·ka·*fe* por a·*kee*
I'd like to check my email.	Quisiera revisar mi correo electrónico.	kee·*sye*·ra re·vee·*sar* mee ko·*re*·o e·lek·*tro*·nee·ko
I want to send a parcel.	Quisiera enviar un paquete.	kee·*sye*·ra en·*vyar* oon pa·*ke*·te
I want to make a call to ...	Quiero hacer una llamada a ...	*kye*·ro a·*ser* oo·na ya·*ma*·da a ...
I'd like a SIM card.	Quiero un chip.	*kye*·ro oon cheep

The Internet

Where's the local internet cafe?	¿Dónde hay un cibercafé por aquí? *don*·de ai oon see·ber·ka·*fe* por a·*kee*
Is there internet access here?	¿Hay acceso al internet aquí? ai ak·*se*·so al een·ter·*net* a·*kee*
Is there wireless internet access here?	¿Hay acceso al internet inalámbrico aquí? ai ak·*se*·so al een·ter·*net* ee·na·*lam*·bree·ko a·*kee*

I'd like to ...
Quisiera ...
kee·sye·ra ...

check my email	revisar mi correo electrónico	re·vee·sar mee ko·re·o e·lek·tro·nee·ko
download my photos	descargar mis fotos	des·kar·gar mees fo·tos
get internet access	usar el internet	oo·sar el een·ter·net
use a printer	usar una impresora	oo·sar oo·na eem·pre·so·ra
use a scanner	usar un escáner	oo·sar oon es·ka·ner
use Skype	utilizar el Skype	oo·tee·lee·sar el es·kai·pe

How much per ...?
¿Cuánto cuesta por ...?
kwan·to kwes·ta por ...

CD	cómpact	kom·pak
hour	hora	o·ra
(five) minutes	(cinco) minutos	(seen·ko) mee·noo·tos
page	hoja	o·kha

Can I connect my laptop here?
¿Se puede enchufar mi laptop aquí?
se pwe·de en·choo·far mee lap·top a·kee

Do you have a Zip drive?
¿Tiene una unidad de Zip?
tye·ne oo·na oo·nee·dad de seep

Do you have Macs/PCs?
¿Tiene Macs/PCs?
tye·ne maks/pe·ses

Do you have headphones (with a microphone)?	¿Tiene audífonos (con micrófono)? *tye*·ne ow·*dee*·fo·nos (kon mee·*kro*·fo·no)
I need help with the computer.	Necesito ayuda con la computadora. ne·se·*see*·to a·*yoo*·da kon la kom·poo·ta·*do*·ra
How do I log on?	¿Cómo entro al sistema? *ko*·mo *en*·tro al sees·*te*·ma
How do I log off?	¿Cómo salgo del sistema? *ko*·mo *sal*·go del sees·*te*·ma
It's crashed.	Se trabó. se tra·*bo*
I've finished.	Ya terminé. ya ter·mee·*ne*

Mobile/Cell Phone

I'd like a/an ...	Quisiera ... kee·*sye*·ra ...

adaptor plug	un adaptador	oon a·dap·ta·*dor*
charger for my phone	un cargador para mi celular	oon kar·ga·*dor* *pa*·ra mee se·loo·*lar*
mobile/cell phone for hire	rentar un celular	ren·*tar* oon se·loo·*lar*
prepaid mobile/cell phone	un celular con tarjetas prepagadas	oon se·loo·*lar* kon tar·*khe*·tas pre·pa·*ga*·das
SIM card for your network	una chip para su red	oon cheep *pa*·ra soo red

What are the rates?	¿Cuáles son las tarifas? *kwa*·les son las ta·*ree*·fas

PRACTICAL COMMUNICATIONS

(Cinco pesos) por minuto.	(seen·ko pe·sos) por mee·noo·to (Five pesos) per minute.

Phone

Q What's your phone number?	¿Cuál es su número de teléfono? kwal es soo noo·me·ro de te·le·fo·no
A The number is ...	El número es ... el noo·me·ro es ...
Where's the nearest public phone?	¿Dónde hay un teléfono público? don·de ai oon te·le·fo·no poo·blee·ko
I want to make a call to ...	Quiero hacer una llamada a ... kye·ro a·ser oo·na ya·ma·da a ...
I want to make a reverse charge/collect call.	Quiero hacer una llamada por cobrar. kye·ro a·ser oo·na ya·ma·da por ko·brar
I want to buy a phone card.	Quiero comprar una tarjeta telefónica. kye·ro kom·prar oo·na tar·khe·ta te·le·fo·nee·ka
What's the area/country code for ...?	¿Cuál es la clave Lada de ...? kwal es la kla·ve la·da de ...
It's engaged.	Está llamando. es·ta ya·man·do

ANTHONY PLUMMER / GETTY IMAGES ©

¿Hay acceso al internet aquí?
ai ak·*se*·so al een·ter·*net* a·*kee*

Is there internet access here?

I've been cut off.	Se cortó la línea. se kor·*to* la *lee*·ne·a
The connection's bad.	La conexión es mala. la ko·nek·*syon* es *ma*·la
Hello. (when making a call)	¡Hola! o·la
It's ... (when introducing yourself)	Habla ... *a*·bla ...
Can I speak to ..., please?	¿Me comunica con..., por favor? me ko·moo·*nee*·ka kon ... por fa·*vor*
Can I leave a message?	¿Puedo dejar un mensaje? *pwe*·do de·*khar* oon men·*sa*·khe

🔊 LISTEN FOR

¿Bueno?	*bwe*·no Hello! (answering a call)
¿De parte de quién?	de *par*·te de kyen Who's calling?
¿Con quién quiere hablar?	kon kyen *kye*·re a·*blar* Who do you want to speak to?
Ahorita no está.	a·o·*ree*·ta no es·*ta* I'm sorry, he's/she's not here.
Sí, aquí está.	see a·*kee* es·*ta* Yes, he's/she's here.
Con él/ella. m/f	kon el/*e*·ya You're speaking to him/her.
No puedo oírte.	no *pwe*·do o·*eer*·te I can't hear you.
Tiene el número equivocado.	*tye*·ne el *noo*·me·ro e·*kee*·vo·*ka*·do Sorry, wrong number.

Please tell him/her I called.	Por favor, dile que le llamé. por fa·*vor* *dee*·le ke le ya·*me*
I'll call back (later).	Llamaré (más tarde). ya·ma·*re* (mas *tar*·de)
What time should I call?	¿A qué hora debería llamar? a ke o·ra de·be·*ree*·a ya·*mar*
I don't have a contact number.	No tengo teléfono. no *ten*·go te·*le*·fo·no
My number is ...	Mi número es ... mee *noo*·me·ro es ...

Post Office

I want to buy an envelope.	Quisiera comprar un sobre. kee·*sye*·ra kom·*prar* oon *so*·bre

I want to buy some stamps.	Quisiera comprar unas estampillas. kee·*sye*·ra kom·*prar* oo·nas es·tam·*pee*·yas
I want to send a ...	Quisiera enviar ... kee·*sye*·ra en·*vyar* ...

letter	una carta	oo·na *kar*·ta
money order	un giro	oon *khee*·ro
parcel	un paquete	oon pa·*ke*·te
postcard	una postal	oo·na pos·*tal*

Please send it by air/ regular mail to (France).	Por favor, mándelo por vía aérea/terrestre a (Francia). por fa·*vor* man·de·lo por *vee*·a a·e·re·a/te·*res*·tre a (*fran*·sya)
It contains ...	Contiene ... kon·*tye*·ne ...

 LISTEN FOR

correo m aéreo	ko·*re*·o a·e·re·o	airmail
correo m certificado	ko·*re*·o ser·tee·fee·*ka*·do	registered mail
correo m expreso	ko·*re*·o ek·*spre*·so	express mail
correo m ordinario	ko·*re*·o or·dee·*na*·ryo	regular mail
declaración f de aduana	de·kla·ra·*syon* de a·*dwa*·na	customs declaration

PRACTICAL MONEY & BANKING

Money & Banking

KEY PHRASES

How much is it?	¿Cuánto cuesta esto?	*kwan·*to *kwes·*ta *es·*to
What's the exchange rate?	¿Cuál es el tipo de cambio?	kwal es el *tee·*po de *kam·*byo
Where's the nearest ATM?	¿Dónde está el cajero automático más cercano?	*don·*de es*·ta* el ka*·khe·*ro ow·to·*ma·*tee·ko mas ser·*ka·*no
I'd like to change money.	Me gustaría cambiar dinero.	me goos·ta·*ree·*a kam·*byar* dee·*ne·*ro
Can I have smaller notes?	¿Me lo puede dar en billetes más pequeños?	me lo *pwe·*de dar en bee·*ye·*tes mas pe·*ke·*nyos

Paying the Bill

Q How much is it?	¿Cuánto cuesta esto? *kwan·*to *kwes·*ta *es·*to
A It's free.	Es gratis. es *gra·*tees
A It's (10) pesos.	Cuesta (diez) pesos. *kwes·*ta (dyes) *pe·*sos
Can you write down the price?	¿Puede escribir el precio? *pwe·*de es·kree·*beer* el *pre·*syo
Can I pay cash?	¿Puedo pagar en efectivo? *pwe·*do pa·*gar* en e·fek·*tee·*vo

Do you accept credit cards?	¿Aceptan tarjetas de crédito? a·*sep*·tan tar·*khe*·tas de *kre*·dee·to
Do you accept debit cards?	¿Aceptan tarjetas de débito? a·*sep*·tan tar·*khe*·tas de *de*·bee·to
Do you accept travellers cheques?	¿Aceptan cheques de viajero? a·*sep*·tan *che*·kes de vya·*khe*·ro
Do I need to pay upfront?	¿Necesito pagar por adelantado? ne·se·*see*·to pa·*gar* por a·de·lan·*ta*·do
I'd like a receipt, please.	Quisiera un recibo, por favor. kee·*sye*·ra oon re·*see*·bo por fa·*vor*
I'd like my change, please.	Quisiera mi cambio, por favor. kee·*sye*·ra mee *kam*·byo por fa·*vor*
There's a mistake in the bill.	Hay un error en la cuenta. ai oon e·*ror* en la *kwen*·ta

Banking

Where's the nearest ATM?	¿Dónde está el cajero automático más cercano? *don*·de es·*ta* el ka·*khe*·ro ow·to·*ma*·tee·ko mas ser·*ka*·no
Where's the nearest foreign exchange office?	¿Dónde está la casa de cambio más cercana? *don*·de es·*ta* la ka·sa de *kam*·byo mas ser·*ka*·na

What time does the bank open?	¿A qué hora abre el banco?
	a ke *o*·ra *a*·bre el *ban*·ko
I'd like to ...	Me gustaría ...
	me goos·ta·*ree*·a ...

arrange a transfer	hacer una transferencia	a·ser *oo*·na trans·fe·*ren*·sya
cash a cheque	cambiar un cheque	kam·*byar* oon *che*·ke
change money	cambiar dinero	kam·*byar* dee·*ne*·ro
get a cash advance	obtener un adelanto	ob·te·*ner* oon a·de·*lan*·to
use internet banking	usar la banca por internet	oo·*sar* la *ban*·ka por een·ter·*net*
withdraw money	sacar dinero	sa·*kar* dee·*ne*·ro

Do you change money here?	¿Se cambia dinero aquí?
	se *kam*·bya dee·*ne*·ro a·*kee*
The ATM took my card.	El cajero automático se tragó mi tarjeta.
	el ka·*khe*·ro ow·to·*ma*·tee·ko se tra·*go* mee tar·*khe*·ta
I've forgotten my PIN.	Se me olvidó mi NIP.
	se me ol·vee·*do* mee neep
Can I use my credit card to withdraw money?	¿Puedo usar mi tarjeta de crédito para sacar dinero?
	pwe·do oo·*sar* mee tar·*khe*·ta de *kre*·dee·to *pa*·ra sa·*kar* dee·*ne*·ro
What's the exchange rate?	¿Cuál es el tipo de cambio?
	kwal es el *tee*·po de *kam*·byo
What's the commission?	¿Cuál es la comisión?
	kwal es la ko·mee·*syon*

🔊 LISTEN FOR

¿Puede escribirlo?	*pwe*·de es·kree·*beer*·lo Can you write it down?
Su identificación.	soo ee·den·tee·fee·ka·*syon* Your ID.
Firme aquí.	*feer*·me a·*kee* Sign here.
En (cinco) días hábiles.	en (*seen*·ko) *dee*·as a·bee·les In (five) working days.
En (dos) semanas.	en (dos) se·*ma*·nas In (two) weeks.
Hay un problema con su cuenta.	ai oon pro·*ble*·ma kon soo *kwen*·ta There's a problem with your account.
No podemos hacer eso.	no po·*de*·mos a·*ser* e·so We can't do that.

What's the charge for that?	¿Cuánto hay que pagar por éso? *kwan*·to ai ke pa·*gar* por *e*·so
Can I have smaller notes?	¿Me lo puede dar en billetes más pequeños? me lo *pwe*·de dar en bee·*ye*·tes mas pe·*ke*·nyos
Has my money arrived yet?	¿Ya llegó mi dinero? ya ye·*go* mee dee·*ne*·ro
How long will it take to arrive?	¿Cuánto tiempo tardará en llegar? *kwan*·to *tyem*·po tar·da·*ra* en ye·*gar*
Where do I sign?	¿Dónde firmo? *don*·de *feer*·mo

Business

KEY PHRASES

I'm attending a conference.	Estoy asistiendo a un congreso.	es·*toy* a·sees·*tyen*·do a oon kon·*gre*·so
I have an appointment with ...	Tengo una cita con ...	*ten*·go *oo*·na *see*·ta kon ...
Can I have your business card?	¿Me dará su tarjeta de presentación?	me da·*ra* soo tar·*khe*·ta de pre·sen·ta·*syon*

Where's the business centre?
¿Dónde es el centro de conferencias?
don·de es el *sen*·tro de kon·fe·*ren*·syas

I'm attending a/an ...
Estoy asistiendo a ...
es·*toy* a·sees·*tyen*·do a ...

conference	un congreso	oon kon·*gre*·so
convention	una convención	*oo*·na kon·ven·*syon*
course	un curso	oon *koor*·so
exhibition	una exhibición	*oo*·na ek·see·bee·*syon*
meeting	una reunión	*oo*·na re·oo·*nyon*
trade fair	una feria de negocios	*oo*·na *fe*·rya de ne·*go*·syos

I'm with my company.
Estoy con mi compañía.
es·*toy* kon mee kom·pa·*nyee*·a

I'm with my colleague(s).	Estoy con mi(s) colega(s). es·*toy* kon mee(s) ko·*le*·ga(s)
I'm alone.	Estoy solo/a. **m/f** es·*toy* so·lo/a
I have an appointment with ...	Tengo una cita con ... *ten*·go oo·na *see*·ta kon ...
Let me introduce my colleague.	Le/Te presento a mi colega. **pol/inf** le/te pre·*sen*·to a mee ko·*le*·ga
Q Can I have your business card?	¿Me dará su tarjeta de presentación? me da·*ra* soo tar·*khe*·ta de pre·sen·ta·*syon*
A Here's my business card.	Aquí tiene mi tarjeta de presentación. a·*kee* tye·ne mee tar·*khe*·ta de pre·sen·ta·*syon*
I'm expecting a call.	Estoy esperando una llamada. es·*toy* es·pe·*ran*·do oo·na ya·*ma*·da
I need ...	Necesito ... ne·se·*see*·to ...

an internet connection	una conexión al internet	oo·na ko·nek·*syon* al een·ter·*net*
an interpreter	un/una intérprete **m/f**	oon/oo·na een·*ter*·pre·te
to make photocopies	sacar fotocopias	sa·*kar* fo·to·*ko*·pyas
to use a computer	usar una computadora	oo·*sar* oo·na kom·poo·ta·*do*·ra

For equipment you might need at a conference, see the **dictionary**.

Sightseeing

KEY PHRASES

I'd like a guide.	Quisiera un guía.	kee·sye·ra oon gee·a
Can I take a photo?	¿Puedo tomar una foto?	pwe·do to·mar oo·na fo·to
When's the museum open?	¿A qué hora abre el museo?	a ke o·ra a·bre el moo·se·o
I'm interested in ...	Me interesa ...	me een·te·re·sa ...
When's the next tour?	¿Cuándo es el próximo tour?	kwan·do es el prok·see·mo toor

I'd like a/an ...   Quisiera ...
kee·sye·ra ...

audio set	una audioguía	oo·na ow·dyo·gee·a
catalogue	un catálogo	oon ka·ta·lo·go
guide (person)	un guía	oon gee·a
guidebook (in English)	una guía turística (en inglés)	oo·na gee·a too·rees·tee·ka (en een·gles)
(local) map	un mapa (de la zona)	oon ma·pa (de la so·na)

I'd like to see ...   Me gustaría ver ...
me goos·ta·ree·a ver ...

Do you have information on ... sights?	¿Tiene información sobre atracciones ... *tye*·ne een·for·ma·*syon* *so*·bre a·trak·*syo*·nes ...
cultural	culturales kool·too·*ra*·les
local	locales lo·*ka*·les
religious	religiosas re·lee·*khyo*·sas
historic	históricas ees·*to*·ree·kas

What's that?	¿Qué es eso? ke es *e*·so
Who made it?	¿Quién lo hizo? kyen lo *ee*·so
How old is it?	¿De cuándo es? de *kwan*·do es
Could you take a photograph of me?	¿Me puede tomar una foto? me *pwe*·de to·*mar* oo·na *fo*·to
Can I take a photograph (of you)?	¿Puedo tomar(le) una foto? *pwe*·do to·*mar*(le) oo·na *fo*·to

Getting In

What time does it open/close?	¿A qué hora abren/cierran? a ke *o*·ra *a*·bren/*sye*·ran
What's the admission charge?	¿Cuánto cuesta la entrada? *kwan*·to *kwes*·ta la en·*tra*·da
Is there a discount for ...?	¿Hay descuento para ...? ai des·*kwen*·to *pa*·ra ...

children	niños	*nee*·nyos
groups	grupos	*groo*·pos
retirees	jubilados	khoo·bee·*la*·dos
students	estudiantes	es·too·*dyan*·tes

Museums & Galleries

When does the (museum) open?	¿A qué hora abre el (museo)?	a ke *o*·ra *a*·bre el (moo·*se*·o)
When does the (gallery) close?	¿A qué hora cierra la (galería)?	a ke *o*·ra *sye*·ra la (ga·le·*ree*·a)
Q What kind of art are you interested in?	¿Qué tipo de arte le/te interesa? pol/inf	ke *tee*·po de *ar*·te le/te een·te·*re*·sa
A I'm interested in (Mexican muralism).	Me interesa (el muralismo mexicano).	me een·te·*re*·sa (el moo·ra·*lees*·mo me·khee·*ka*·no)
A I like the works of ...	Me gusta la obra de ...	me *goos*·ta la *o*·bra de ...
Q What's in the collection?	¿Qué hay en la colección?	ke ai en la ko·lek·*syon*
A It's a (cartoon) exhibition.	Hay una exposición de (historieta).	ai *oo*·na ek·spo·see·*syon* de (ees·to·*rye*·ta)
What do you think of ...?	¿Qué piensa/piensas de ...? pol/inf	ke *pyen*·sa/pyen·sas de ...
... art	arte m ...	*ar*·te ...

Aztec	azteca	as·*te*·ka
Mayan	maya	*ma*·ya
prehispanic	prehispánico	pre·ees·*pa*·nee·ko
revolutionary	revolucionario	re·vo·loo·syo·*na*·ryo

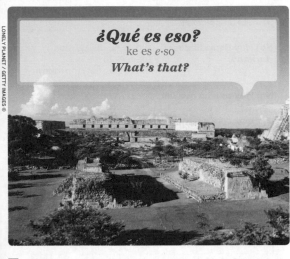

LONELY PLANET / GETTY IMAGES ©

¿Qué es eso?
ke es *e*·so
What's that?

Tours

Can you recommend a boat trip?	¿Puede recomendar algún paseo en lancha? *pwe*·de re·ko·men·*dar* al·*goon* pa·*se*·o en *lan*·cha
Can you recommend a tour?	¿Puede recomendar algún tour? *pwe*·de re·ko·men·*dar* al·*goon* toor
When's the next tour?	¿Cuándo es el próximo tour? *kwan*·do es el *prok*·see·mo toor
When's the next day trip?	¿Cuándo es la próxima excursión de un día? *kwan*·do es la *prok*·see·ma ek·skoor·*syon* de oon *dee*·a

PRACTICAL SIGHTSEEING

🔊 LISTEN FOR

(No) Hay demasiados turistas.	(no) ai de·ma·sya·dos too·rees·tas There are (not) too many tourists.
(No) Hay mucho que ver.	(no) ai moo·cho ke ver There's (not) a lot to see.
La mejor época para ir es ...	la me·khor e·po·ka pa·ra eer es ... The best time to go is ...
Hay una muy buena vida nocturna.	ai oo·na mooy bwe·na vee·da nok·toor·na There's a fabulous nightlife.

Is accommodation/ transport included?	¿Incluye alojamiento/ transporte? een·kloo·ye a·lo·kha·myen·to/ trans·por·te
Do I need to take food?	¿Necesito llevar comida? ne·se·see·to ye·var ko·mee·da
Can we hire a (local) guide?	¿Podemos contratar un guía (local)? po·de·mos kon·tra·tar oon gee·a (lo·kal)
How long is the tour?	¿Cuánto dura el tour? kwan·to doo·ra el toor
What time should I be back?	¿A qué hora tengo que regresar? a ke o·ra ten·go ke re·gre·sar
I'm with them.	Estoy con ellos. es·toy kon e·yos
I've lost my group.	He perdido a mi grupo. e per·dee·do a mee groo·po

Senior & Disabled Travellers

KEY PHRASES

I need assistance.	Necesito asistencia.	ne·se·*see*·to a·sees·*ten*·sya
Is there wheelchair access?	¿Hay acceso para la silla de ruedas?	ai ak·*se*·so *pa*·ra la *see*·ya de *rwe*·das
Are there toilets for people with a disability?	¿Hay baños para discapacitados?	ai *ba*·nyos *pa*·ra dees·ka·pa·see·*ta*·dos

I need assistance.	Necesito asistencia. ne·se·*see*·to a·sees·*ten*·sya
I have a disability.	Soy discapacitado/a. **m/f** soy dees·ka·pa·see·*ta*·do/a
What services do you have for people with a disability?	¿Qué servicios tienen para discapacitados? ke ser·*vee*·syos *tye*·nen *pa*·ra dees·ka·pa·see·*ta*·dos
Are guide dogs permitted?	¿Se permite la entrada a los perros guía? se per·*mee*·te la en·*tra*·da a los *pe*·ros *gee*·a
Is there wheelchair access?	¿Hay acceso para la silla de ruedas? ai ak·*se*·so *pa*·ra la *see*·ya de *rwe*·das
How wide is the entrance?	¿Qué tan ancha es la entrada? ke tan *an*·cha es la en·*tra*·da

Is there a lift?	¿Hay elevador? ai e·le·va·*dor*
How many steps are there?	¿Cuántos escalones hay? *kwan*·tos es·ka·*lo*·nes ai
Is there somewhere I can sit down?	¿Hay algún lugar donde me pueda sentar? ai al·*goon* loo·*gar* don·de me *pwe*·da sen·*tar*
Are there toilets for people with a disability?	¿Hay baños para discapacitados? ai *ba*·nyos *pa*·ra dees·ka·pa·see·*ta*·dos
Could you call me a taxi for the disabled, please?	¿Me puede llamar un taxi para discapacitados? me *pwe*·de ya·*mar* oon *tak*·see *pa*·ra dees·ka·pa·see·*ta*·dos
Could you help me cross this street?	¿Me puede ayudar a cruzar la calle? me *pwe*·de a·yoo·*dar* a kroo·*sar* la *ka*·ye
access for the disabled	acceso m para discapacitados ak·*se*·so *pa*·ra dees·ka·pa·see·*ta*·dos
guide dog	perro m guía *pe*·ro *gee*·a
person with a disability	persona f discapacitada per·*so*·na dees·ka·pa·see·*ta*·da
ramps	rampas f pl *ram*·pas
wheelchair	silla f de ruedas *see*·ya de *rwe*·das

Travel with Children

KEY PHRASES

Are children allowed?	¿Se admiten niños?	se ad·*mee*·ten nee·*nyos*
Is there a family discount?	¿Hay un descuento familiar?	ai oon des·*kwen*·to fa·mee·*lyar*
Is there a baby change room?	¿Hay una sala para cambiarle el pañal al bebé?	ai *oo*·na *sa*·la *pa*·ra kam·*byar*·le el pa·*nyal* al be·*be*

I need (a) ...   Necesito ...
ne·se·*see*·to ...

baby seat	un asiento de seguridad para bebé	oon a·*syen*·to de se·goo·ree·*dad pa*·ra be·*be*
booster seat	un asiento de seguridad para niños	oon a·*syen*·to de se·goo·ree·*dad pa*·ra nee·nyos
bottle	una mamila	*oo*·na ma·*mee*·la
crib	una cuna	*oo*·na *koo*·na
diapers/ nappies	unos pañales	*oo*·nos pa·*nya*·les
dummy	un chupón	oon choo·*pon*
potty	una bacinica	*oo*·na ba·see·*nee*·ka
stroller	una carreola	*oo*·na ka·re·o·la

Is there a/an ...?	**¿Hay ...?** ai ...

baby change room	una sala para cambiarle el pañal al bebé	oo·na sa·la pa·ra kam·byar·le el pa·nyal al be·be
child-minding service	club para niños	kloob pa·ra nee·nyos
children's menu	menú infantil	me·noo een·fan·teel
creche	guardería	gwar·de·ree·a
(English-speaking) babysitter	niñera (que hable inglés)	nee·nye·ra (ke a·ble een·gles)
family discount	descuento familiar	des·kwen·to fa·mee·lyar
highchair	silla para bebé	see·ya pa·ra be·be
park	un parque	oon par·ke
playground nearby	juegos por aquí	khwe·gos por a·kee
theme park	una feria	oo·na fe·rya
toyshop	una juguetería	oo·na joo·ge·te·ree·a

Do you mind if I breastfeed here?	¿Le molesta que dé el pecho aquí? le mo·les·ta ke de el pe·cho a·kee
Are children allowed?	¿Se admiten niños? se ad·mee·ten nee·nyos
Is this suitable for (four)-year-old children?	¿Es apto para niños de (cuatro) años? es ap·to pa·ra nee·nyos de (kwa·tro) a·nyos

If your child is sick, see **health** (p158).

Social

Meeting People

SOCIAL MEETING PEOPLE

KEY PHRASES

My name is ...	Me llamo ...	me *ya*·mo ...
I'm from ...	Soy de ...	soy de ...
I work in ...	Trabajo en ...	tra·*ba*·kho en ...
I'm ... years old.	Tengo ... años.	*ten*·go ... *a*·nyos
And you?	¿Y Usted? pol	ee oos·*ted*
	¿Y tú? inf	ee too

Basics

Yes.	Sí. see
No.	No. no
Please.	Por favor. por fa·*vor*
Thank you (very much).	(Muchas) Gracias. (*moo*·chas) *gra*·syas
You're welcome.	De nada. de *na*·da No hay de qué. no ai de ke
Sorry. (regret)	Lo siento. lo *syen*·to
Sorry. (apology)	Perdón. per·*don*
Excuse me. **(attention, apology)**	Disculpe. dees·*kool*·pe

Pardon? **(misunderstanding)**	¿Mande? *man·de*

Greetings

Hi.	¡Hola! *o·la*
Hello./Good day.	Buen día. *bwen dee·a* ¡Buenas! inf *bwe·nas*
Good morning.	Buenos días. *bwe·nos dee·as*
Good afternoon.	Buenas tardes. *bwe·nas tar·des*
Good evening/night.	Buenas noches. *bwe·nas no·ches*
See you later.	Hasta luego. *as·ta lwe·go*
Goodbye.	Adiós. *a·dyos*
💬 **How are you?**	¿Cómo está? sg pol *ko·mo es·ta* ¿Cómo estás? sg inf *ko·mo es·tas* ¿Cómo están? pl *ko·mo es·tan*
🅰 **Fine, thanks.** **And you?**	Bien, gracias. ¿Y Usted/tú? pol/inf *byen gra·syas ee oos·ted/too*
💬 **What's your name?**	¿Cómo se llama Usted? pol *ko·mo se ya·ma oos·ted* ¿Cómo te llamas? inf *ko·mo te ya·mas*

A My name is ...	Me llamo ... me *ya*·mo ...
I'm pleased to meet you.	Mucho gusto. *moo*·cho *goos*·to
I'd like to introduce you to ...	Le/Te presento a ... **pol/inf** le/te pre·*sen*·to a ...
This is ...	Éste/Ésta es ... **m/f** *es*·te/*es*·ta es ...

Titles & Addressing People

The terms *Don* don (Sir) and *Doña do*·nya (Madam) are sometimes used to address older men and women in rural areas or local neighbourhoods, but are rare elsewhere. Use the word *Señor* se·*nyor* to show politeness towards a man and *Señora* se·*nyo*·ra towards a woman. You might also hear children address their godfather as *padrino* pa·*dree*·no and godmother as *madrina* ma·*dree*·na.

Mr	Señor se·*nyor*
young man	jóven *kho*·ven
Mrs	Señora se·*nyo*·ra
Miss/Ms	Señorita se·nyo·*ree*·ta
Doctor	Doctor(a) **m/f** dok·*tor*/dok·*to*·ra

Making Conversation

| **Do you live here?** | ¿Vive/Vives aquí? **pol/inf**
vee·ve/*vee*·ves a·*kee* |
| **Where are you going?** | ¿A dónde va/vas? **pol/inf**
a *don*·de va/vas |

LANGUAGE TIP

Polite & Informal

Remember that there are two ways of saying 'you'. When addressing a stranger, an older person or someone in a position of authority, use the polite form *Usted* oos·*ted*. When talking to children or people who are familiar to you, use the informal form *tú* too. In this book we have used the most appropriate form for each phrase, but where you see pol/inf you have both options.

What are you doing?	¿Qué hace/haces? pol/inf ke *a*·se/*a*·ses
Are you waiting (for a bus)?	¿Está/Estás esperando (el autobús)? pol/inf es·*ta*/es·*tas* es·pe·*ran*·do (el ow·to·*boos*)
Can I have a light?	¿Tiene/Tienes encendedor? pol/inf *tye*·ne/*tye*·nes en·sen·de·*dor*
What's this called?	¿Cómo se llama ésto? *ko*·mo se *ya*·ma *es*·to
What a beautiful baby!	¡Qué bebé tan hermoso/a! m/f ke be·*be* tan er·*mo*·so/a
I'm here ...	Estoy aquí ... es·*toy* a·*kee* ...

with my family	con mi familia	kon mee fa·*mee*·lya
with my friends	con mis amigos/as m/f	kon mees a·*mee*·gos/as
with my partner	con mi pareja m&f	kon mee pa·*re*·kha

CULTURE TIP

Chicanismos

Americans with a Mexican background often identify themselves as *chicanos/as* chee·ka·nos/chee·ka·nas m/f, a label derived from the word *mexicano* (formerly pronounced me·shee·ka·no). Though originally a derogatory term, it now denotes an empowered Mexican-American cultural identity, which has also led to a greater recognition of Chicano Spanish. Chicanos may use older words that have disappeared from 'standard' Spanish, eg *semos* se·mos for *somos* so·mos (we are), or new words influenced by English, eg *cookiar* koo·kee·ar (cook). Here are some other common *chicanismos* (with their standard Spanish equivalents given in the third column):

ansina an·see·na	like this	*así* a·see
dispués dees·pwes	after	*después* des·pwes
leyer le·yer	read	*leer* le·er
muncho moon·cho	much/a lot	*mucho* moo·cho
naiden nai·den	nobody	*nadie* na·dye
nejecitar ne·khe·see·tar	need	*necesitar* ne·se·see·tar
ónde on·de	where	*dónde* don·de
parkiar par·kyar	park	*estacionar* es·ta·syo·nar
pos pos	since	*pués* pwes
prebar pre·bar	try	*probar* pro·bar
watchar wa·char	watch	*mirar* mee·rar

Q How long are you here for?	¿Cuánto tiempo va/vas a estar aquí? pol/inf kwan·to tyem·po va/vas a es·tar a·kee
A I'm here for ... weeks/days.	Voy a estar ... semanas/días. voy a es·tar ... se·ma·nas/dee·as
Q Do you like it here?	¿Le/Te gusta este lugar? pol/inf le/te goos·ta es·te loo·gar
A I love it here.	Me encanta este lugar. me en·kan·ta es·te loo·gar
I'm here for a holiday.	Estoy aquí de vacaciones. es·toy a·kee de va·ka·syo·nes
I'm here on business.	Estoy aquí en viaje de negocios. es·toy a·kee en vya·khe de ne·go·syos

Nationalities

Q Where are you from?	¿De dónde es/eres? pol/inf de don·de es/e·res
A I'm from (Japan).	Soy de (Japón). soy de (kha·pon)

For more countries, see the **dictionary**.

Age

Q How old are you?	¿Cuántos años tiene/tienes? pol/inf kwan·tos a·nyos tye·ne/tye·nes

🔊 LISTEN FOR

¡De ninguna manera!	de neen·*goo*·na ma·*ne*·ra	No way!
Está bien.	es·*ta* byen	It's OK.
Estoy bien.	es·*toy* byen	I'm OK.
No hay problema.	no ai pro·*ble*·ma	No problem.
¡Padrísimo!	pa·*dree*·see·mo	Great!
¡Qué chido!	ke *chee*·do	How cool!
¿Qué hubo?	*kyoo*·bo	What's up?
Seguro.	se·*goo*·ro	Sure.
Tal vez.	tal ves	Maybe.

🅐 I'm ... years old.	Tengo ... años. *ten*·go ... *a*·nyos	
🇶 How old is your daughter?	¿Cuántos años tiene su/tu hija? **pol/inf** *kwan*·tos *a*·nyos *tye*·ne soo/too ee·*kha*	
🇶 How old is your son?	¿Cuántos años tiene su/tu hijo? **pol/inf** *kwan*·tos *a*·nyos *tye*·ne soo/too ee·*kho*	
🅐 He/She is ... years old.	Tiene ... años. *tye*·ne ... *a*·nyos	
Too old!	¡Demasiados! de·ma·*sya*·dos	
I'm younger than I look.	Soy más joven de lo que parezco. soy mas *kho*·ven de lo ke pa·*res*·ko	

For your age, see **numbers & amounts** (p32).

Occupations & Studies

Q What's your occupation?	¿A qué se dedica? **pol** a ke se de·*dee*·ka ¿A qué te dedicas? **inf** a ke te de·*dee*·kas
A I'm a (teacher).	Soy (maestro/a). **m/f** soy (ma·*es*·tro/a)
A I work in communications.	Trabajo en comunicaciones. tra·*ba*·kho en ko·moo·nee·ka·*syo*·nes
A I work in education.	Trabajo en educación. tra·*ba*·kho en e·doo·ka·*syon*
A I work in hospitality.	Trabajo en hotelería. tra·*ba*·kho en o·te·le·*ree*·a
A I'm retired.	Estoy jubilado/a. **m/f** es·*toy* khoo·bee·*la*·do/a
A I'm unemployed.	Estoy desempleado/a. **m/f** es·*toy* des·em·ple·*a*·do/a

---

CULTURE TIP **Gringo Lingo**

So are you a *gringo green*·go? In Mexico the word *gringo/a green*·go/*green*·ga **m/f** generally describes a person from the USA, although it may also refer to any European-looking foreigner. Americans needn't be offended by the term, which is rarely derogatory. It can be used to describe anything that has come from over the northern border, be it people, cars or films.

A popular myth is that the term originated during the war between Mexico and the USA (1846–48). American soldiers, who wore green uniforms, were supposedly taunted with the slogan 'Green, go home!'. The most likely theory, though, is that *gringo* is derived from the Spanish *griego grye*·go (meaning 'Greek').

SOCIAL MEETING PEOPLE

LANGUAGE TIP

Addressing Friends

The most common word for friend is *amigo/a* a·*mee*·go/a·*mee*·ga m/f, but Mexican Spanish has an abundance of fun alternatives. You may hear people call each other *mano* m *ma*·no or *mana* f *ma*·na, an abbreviation of *hermano/a* er·*ma*·no/a (brother/sister). Young people may call each other *güey* gway (buddy), while in the north friends sometimes address each other as *batos* *ba*·tos (youngsters). Here are some other colloquial Mexican words for 'friend':

cuate m&f	*kwa*·te	(from 'twin' in Náhuatl)
chavo/a m/f	*cha*·vo/a	(lit: kid)
maestro/a m/f	ma·*es*·tro/a	(lit: teacher)

A	I'm self-employed.	Trabajo por mi cuenta. tra·*ba*·kho por mee *kwen*·ta
Q	What are you studying?	¿Qué estudia/estudias? pol/inf ke es·*too*·dya/es·*too*·dyas
A	I'm studying business.	Estudio economía. es·*too*·dyo e·ko·no·*mee*·a
A	I'm studying history.	Estudio historia. es·*too*·dyo ees·*to*·rya
A	I'm studying languages.	Estudio idiomas. es·*too*·dyo ee·*dyo*·mas

For more occupations and studies, see the **dictionary**.

Family

Q	Do you have (children)?	¿Tiene/Tienes (hijos)? pol/inf *tye*·ne/*tye*·nes (ee·khos)
A	I have (a partner).	Tengo (pareja). *ten*·go (pa·*re*·kha)

Q Do you live with (your family)?	¿Vive/Vives con (su/tu familia)? pol/inf *vee*·ve/*vee*·ves kon (soo/too fa·*mee*·lya)
A I live with (my parents).	Vivo con (mis papás). *vee*·vo kon (mees pa·*pas*)
Q Are you married?	¿Está casado/a? m/f pol es·*ta* ka·*sa*·do/a ¿Estás casado/a? m/f inf es·*tas* ka·*sa*·do/a
A I'm married.	Soy casado/a. m/f soy ka·*sa*·do/a
A I live with someone.	Vivo con alguien. *vee*·vo kon al·gyen
A I'm separated.	Soy separado/a. m/f soy se·pa·*ra*·do/a
A I'm single.	Soy soltero/a. m/f soy sol·*te*·ro/a

For more kinship terms, see the **dictionary**.

Talking with Children

When's your birthday?	¿Cuándo es tu cumpleaños? *kwan*·do es too koom·ple·*a*·nyos
Do you go to school?	¿Vas a la primaria? vas a la pree·*ma*·rya
What grade are you in?	¿En qué grado estás? en ke *gra*·do es·*tas*
Do you like school?	¿Te gusta la escuela? te *goos*·ta la es·*kwe*·la
Do you like sport?	¿Te gusta el deporte? te *goos*·ta el de·*por*·te

Do you learn (English)?	¿Aprendes (inglés)? a·*pren*·des (een·*gles*)	
What do you do after school?	¿Qué haces después de la escuela? ke *a*·ses des·*pwes* de la es·*kwe*·la	
Show me how to play.	Dime cómo se juega. *dee*·me *ko*·mo se *khwe*·ga	
Well done!	¡Muy bien! mooy byen	

Farewells

Tomorrow is my last day here.	Mañana es mi último día aquí. ma·*nya*·na es mee *ool*·tee·mo *dee*·a a·*kee*
Q What's your ...?	¿Cuál es tu ...? kwal es too ...
A Here's my ...	Éste/a es mi ... **m/f** *es*·te/a es mee ...

address	dirección **f**	dee·rek·*syon*
email address	dirección **f** de email	dee·rek·*syon* de ee·*mayl*
mobile/cell phone number	número **m** de celular	*noo*·me·ro do se·loo·*lar*
work number	número **m** de trabajo	*noo*·me·ro de tra·*ba*·kho

If you ever visit (the United States), come and visit us.	Si algún día visitas (los Estados Unidos), ven a visitarnos. see al·*goon dee*·a vee·*see*·tas (los es·*ta*·dos oo·*nee*·dos) ven a vee·see·*tar*·nos

LANGUAGE TIP

Pronouncing the Letter 'x'

Beware of the letter x in Mexican Spanish, as it can be pronounced in four different ways. In words such as *México* me·khee·ko it's pronounced kh (as in the Scottish 'loch') and in words like *exacto* ek·*sak*·to it's pronounced ks. In some words of indigenous origin, such as *mixiotes* mee·*shyo*·tes and *xcatic* shka·*teek* (types of food) it sounds like sh, but in place names like *Xóchitl* so·cheel and *Xochicalco* so·chee·*kal*·ko it's pronounced s. Don't get too confused by this – just check our coloured phonetic guides for the correct pronunciation, and, of course, listen to Mexicans!

See also **pronunciation** (p11).

If you ever visit (Australia), you can stay with me.	Si algún día visitas (Australia), te puedes quedar conmigo. see al·*goon* dee·avee·*see*·tas (ow·*stra*·lya) te *pwe*·des ke·*dar* kon·*mee*·go
I'll send you copies of the photos.	Te mandaré copias de las fotos. te *man*·da·re *ko*·pyas de las *fo*·tos
Keep in touch!	¡Mantente en contacto! man·*ten*·te en kon·*tak*·to
It's been great meeting you.	Ha sido un placer conocerte. a *see*·do oon pla·*ser* ko·no·*ser*·te
I'm going to miss you!	¡Te voy a extrañar! te voy a ek·stra·*nyar*

For addresses, see also **directions** (p56).

Interests

KEY PHRASES

What do you do in your spare time?	¿Qué te gusta hacer en tu tiempo libre?	ke te *goos*·ta a·*ser* en too *tyem*·po *lee*·bre
Do you like ...?	¿Te gusta ...? sg ¿Te gustan ...? pl	te *goos*·ta ... te *goos*·tan ...
I (don't) like ...	(No) Me gusta ... sg (No) Me gustan ... pl	(no) me *goos*·ta ... (no) me *goos*·tan ...

Common Interests

What do you do in your spare time?	¿Qué te gusta hacer en tu tiempo libre? ke te *goos*·ta a·*ser* en too *tyem*·po *lee*·bre
Q Do you like ...?	¿Te gusta/gustan ...? sg/pl te *goos*·ta/*goos*·tan ...
A I (don't) like ...	(No) Me gusta ... sg (no) me *goos*·ta ... (No) Me gustan ... pl (no) me *goos*·tan ...

cooking	cocinar sg	ko·see·*nar*
dancing	bailar sg	bai·*lar*
gardening	la jardinería sg	la khar·dee·ne·*ree*·a
sport	los deportes pl	los de·*por*·tes
travelling	viajar sg	vya·*khar*

For more hobbies and types of sports, see **sports** (p140), and the **dictionary**.

Music

Do you like to ...?		Te gusta ...? te *goos*·ta ...
dance	bailar	bai·*lar*
go to concerts	ir a conciertos	eer a kon·*syer*·tos
listen to music	escuchar música	es·koo·*char* *moo*·see·ka
play an instrument	tocar un instrumento	to·*kar* oon een·stroo·*men*·to
sing	cantar	kan·*tar*

Which bands do you like?	¿Qué grupos te gustan? ke *groo*·pos te *goos*·tan
What music do you like?	¿Qué música te gusta? ke *moo*·see·ka te *goos*·ta
... music	música ... *moo*·see·ka ...

electronic	electrónica	e·lek·*tro*·nee·ka
Spanish- language	en español	en es·pa·*nyol*
traditional	tradicional	tra·dee·syo·*nal*
world	folklórica	fol·*klo*·ree·ka

Planning to go to a concert? See **buying tickets** (p43), and
going out (p129).

Cinema & Theatre

I feel like going to a movie.	Tengo ganas de ir a ver una película. *ten*·go *ga*·nas de eer a ver *oo*·na pe·*lee*·koo·la

SOCIAL INTERESTS

CULTURE TIP — **Mexican Music Styles**
From Latin rhythms blaring from bus stereos to wandering mariachis and live salsa bands, music is absolutely everywhere in Mexico. Here are some unique styles to listen for:

corridos m pl   ko·*ree*·dos
narrative ballads influenced by polka and waltz styles

huapango m   wa·*pan*·go
a fast, indigenous dance-song from the Huastec region

música f **tropical**   moo·*see*·ka tro·pee·*kal*
slow-paced rhythmic music of Caribbean origin including *danzón* (Cuba) and *cumbia* (Colombia)

norteña f   nor·*te*·nya
country ballad and dance music from northern Mexico

ranchera f   ran·*che*·ra
very cheesy, very popular, country-style big-band music

son m   son
a folk fusion of African, Spanish and indigenous music styles, combining guitar, violin and voice

trova f   *tro*·va
poetic troubadour-style folk music

I feel like going to a play.	Tengo ganas de ir a ver una obra de teatro. *ten*·go *ga*·nas de eer a ver oo·na o·bra de te·a·tro
What's showing at the cinema/theatre tonight?	¿Qué dan en el cine/teatro esta noche? ke dan en el *see*·ne/te·a·tro es·ta *no*·che

Is it in English/Spanish?	¿Es en inglés/español?	es en een·*gles*/es·pa·*nyol*
Does it have subtitles?	¿Tiene subtítulos?	*tye*·ne soob·*tee*·too·los
Have you seen ...?	¿Has visto ...?	as *vees*·to ...
🄠 **Who's in it?**	¿Quién actúa?	kyen ak·*too*·a
🄰 **It stars ...**	Actúa(n) ... sg/pl	ak·*too*·a(n) ...
🄠 **Did you like (the film)?**	¿Te gustó (la película)?	te goos·*to* (la pe·*lee*·koo·la)
🄰 **I thought it was ...**	Pienso que fue ...	*pyen*·so ke fwe ...

excellent	excelente	ek·se·*len*·te
long	largo/a m/f	*lar*·go/a
OK	regular	re·goo·*lar*
very bad	malísimo/a m/f	ma·*lee*·see·mo/a

animated films	dibujos m pl animados dee·*boo*·khos a·nee·*ma*·dos
(Mexican) cinema	cine m (mexicano) *see*·ne (me·khee·*ka*·no)
documentaries	documentales m pl do·koo·men·*ta*·les
film noir	cine m negro *see*·ne *ne*·gro
horror movies	películas f pl de terror pe·*lee*·koo·las de te·*ror*
sci-fi	películas f pl de ciencia ficción pe·*lee*·koo·las de *syen*·sya feek·*syon*

short films	cortos m pl *kor*·tos
thrillers	películas f pl de suspenso pe·*lee*·koo·las de soos·*pen*·so

Books & Reading

Q What kind of books do you read?	¿Qué tipo de libros lees? ke *tee*·po de *lee*·bros *le*·es
Q Have you read ...?	¿Has leído ...? as le·*ee*·do ...
Q On this trip I'm reading...	En este viaje estoy leyendo ... en *es*·te *vya*·khe es·*toy* le·*yen*·do ...
A I normally read ...	Suelo leer ... *swe*·lo le·*er* ...
Q Which (Mexican) author do you recommend?	¿Qué autor (mexicano) me recomiendas? ke ow·*tor* (me·khee·*ka*·no) me re·ko·*myen*·das
A I recommend ...	Te recomiendo a ... te re·ko·*myen*·do a ...

CULTURE TIP **Mexican Literature**

Mexico has a very lively literary scene. Much of the activity centres on Mexico City, though Latin America's most prestigious book fair, *La Feria Internacional del Libro* (International Book Fair) is held in Guadalajara in late November each year. Good city bookshops will stock English translations of famous authors such as Carlos Fuentes, Rosario Castellanos, Mariano Azuela, Elena Poniatowska and Nobel Prize winner Octavio Paz. Newer Mexican writers to look out for include Jorge Volpi, Pedro Ángel Palou and Ignacio Padilla.

LANGUAGE TIP

Likes & Dislikes

In Spanish, in order to say you like something, you say *me gusta* me goos·ta (lit: me it-pleases). If it's a plural noun, use *me gustan* me goos·tan (lit: me they-please). If you're referring to an activity, eg cooking or travelling, use *me gusta* followed by the verb. You can negate any of these sentences by adding *no* no (not) to the beginning of a phrase.

I like this song.	Me gusta esta canción. me goos·ta es·ta kan·syon
I like tacos.	Me gustan los tacos. me goos·tan los ta·kos
I like singing.	Me gusta cantar. me goos·ta kan·tar
I don't like dancing.	No me gusta bailar. no me goos·ta bai·lar

Where can I exchange books?	¿Dónde puedo intercambiar libros? don·de pwe·do een·ter·kam·byar lee·bros

Volunteering

I'd like to volunteer my skills.	Me gustaría ser voluntario. me goos·ta·ree·a ser vo·loon·ta·ryo
Are there any volunteer programs available in the area?	¿Hay algún programa para voluntarios en esta región? ai al·goon pro·gra·ma pa·ra vo·loon·ta·ryos en es·ta re·khyon

SOCIAL — FEELINGS & OPINIONS

Feelings & Opinions

KEY PHRASES

Are you ...?	¿Está ...? pol	es·ta ...
	¿Estás ...? inf	es·tas ...
	¿Tiene ...? pol	tye·ne ...
	¿Tienes ...? inf	tye·nes ...
I'm (not) ...	(No) Estoy ...	(no) es·toy ...
	(No) Tengo ...	(no) ten·go ...
What did you think of it?	¿Qué pensó/ pensaste de eso? pol/inf	ke pen·so/ pen·sas·te de e·so
I thought it was OK.	Pienso que fue regular.	pyen·so ke fwe re·goo·lar
How do people feel about ...?	¿Cómo se siente la gente acerca de ...?	ko·mo se syen·te la khen·te a·ser·ka de ...

Feelings

Feelings are described with either nouns or adjectives: the nouns use the verb *tener* te·ner (have) – eg 'I have hunger' – and the adjectives use the verbs *ser* ser or *estar* es·tar (be), like in English.

Q Are you (happy)?	¿Está/Estás (feliz)? pol/inf es·ta/es·tas (fe·lees)
A I'm (sick).	Estoy (enfermo/a). m/f es·toy (en·fer·mo/a)
A I'm not (bored).	No estoy (aburrido/a). m/f no es·toy (a·boo·ree·do/a)
Q Are you ...?	¿Tiene/Tienes ...? pol/inf tye·ne/tye·nes ...

A I'm (not) ...	(No) Tengo ... (no) *ten*·go ...	
cold	frío	*free*·o
hungry	hambre	*am*·bre
sleepy	sueño	*swe*·nyo
thirsty	sed	sed

I'm a little (sad).	Estoy un poco (triste). es·*toy* oon *po*·ko (*trees*·te)
I'm quite (disappointed).	Estoy bastante (decepcionado/a). **m/f** es·*toy* bas·*tan*·te (de·sep·syo·*na*·do/a)
I'm very (happy).	Estoy muy (feliz). es·*toy* mooy (fe·*lees*)

For more feelings, see the **dictionary**.

Opinions

Q Did you like it?	¿Le/Te gustó? **pol/inf** le/te goos·*to*
Q What did you think of it?	¿Qué pensó/pensaste de eso? **pol/inf** ke pen·*so*/pen·*sas*·te de *e*·so
A I thought it was ...	Pienso que fue ... *pyen*·so ke fwe ...
A It's ...	Es ... es ...

beautiful	hermoso/a **m/f**	er·*mo*·so/a
crazy	loco/a **m/f**	*lo*·ko/a
excellent	excelente	ek·se·*len*·te
horrible	horrible	o·*ree*·ble

Politics & Social Issues

While Mexicans are very critical of their leaders, they can be fiercely patriotic at the same time. Visitors should try to pick the mood, and ask questions before offering opinions. Mexican history, art and culture are fruitful subjects of conversation. As a rule, avoid topics such as the Mexican–American war and undocumented migration.

Q Who do you vote for?
¿Por quién vota/votas? pol/inf
por kyen vo·ta/vo·tas

A I support the ... party.
Apoyo al partido ...
a·po·yo al par·tee·do ...

A I'm a member of the ... party.
Soy miembro del partido ...
soy myem·bro del par·tee·do ...

communist	comunista	ko·moo·nees·ta
conservative	conservador	kon·ser·va·dor
green	verde	ver·de
labour	laborista	la·bo·rees·ta
liberal (progressive)	progresista	pro·gre·sees·ta
social democratic	social-demócrata	so·syal·de·mo·kra·ta
socialist	socialista	so·sya·lees·ta

Q Are you against ...?
¿Está/Estás en contra de ...? pol/inf
es·ta/es·tas en kon·tra de ...

Q Are you in favour of ...?
¿Está/Estás a favor de ...? pol/inf
es·ta/es·tas a fa·vor de ...

A I (don't) agree with ...
(No) estoy de acuerdo con ...
(no) es·toy de a·kwer·do kon ...

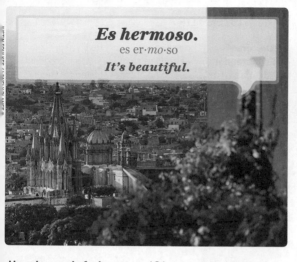

Es hermoso.
es er·*mo*·so

It's beautiful.

How do people feel about ...?	¿Cómo se siente la gente acerca de ...? *ko·mo se syen·te la khen·te a·ser·ka de ...*
In my country we are concerned about ...	En mi país nos preocupamos por ... *en mi pa·ees nos pre·o·koo·pa·mos por ...*
organised crime	crimen m organizado *kree·men or·ga·nee·sa·do*
the economy	economía f *e·ko·no·mee·a*
the environment	medio m ambiente *me·dyo am·byen·te*
the war in ...	la guerra f en ... *la ge·ra en ...*

🔊 LISTEN FOR

¿De veras?	de *ve*·ras	Really?
¡Es increíble!	es een·kre·*ee*·ble	That's incredible!
¡Escucha (esto)!	es·*koo*·cha (*es*·to)	Listen (to this)!
¡Mira!	*mee*·ra	Look!
¡No me digas!	no me *dee*·gas	You don't say!
¡Por supuesto!	por soo·*pwes*·to	Of course!
¡Ya lo creo!	ya lo *kre*·o	You bet!

The Environment

Is there a/an (environmental) problem here?	¿Aquí hay problemas con (el medio ambiente)? a·*kee* ai pro·*ble*·mas kon (el *me*·dyo am·*byen*·te)
Where can I recycle this?	¿En dónde puedo reciclar ésto? en *don*·de *pwe*·do re·see·*klar* *es*·to
climate change	cambio m climático *kam*·byo klee·*ma*·tee·ko
pollution	contaminación f kon·ta·mee·na·*syon*
recycling programmes	programas m pl de reciclaje pro·*gra*·mas de re·see·*kla*·khe
Is this forest/park protected?	¿Está protegido este bosque/parque? es·*ta* pro·te·*khee*·do *es*·te *bos*·ke/*par*·ke
Is this species protected?	¿Está protegida esta especie? es·*ta* pro·te·*khee*·da *es*·ta es·*pe*·sye

Going Out

KEY PHRASES

What's on tonight?	¿Qué hay esta noche?	ke ai *es*·ta *no*·che
Where are the clubs?	¿Dónde hay antros?	*don*·de ai *an*·tros
Would you like to go for a coffee?	¿Te gustaría tomar un café?	te goos·ta·*ree*·a to·*mar* oon ka·*fe*
What time shall we meet?	¿A qué hora nos vemos?	a ke *o*·ra nos *ve*·mos
Where will we meet?	¿Dónde nos vemos?	*don*·de nos *ve*·mos

Where to Go

What's there to do in the evenings?	¿Qué se puede hacer en las noches? ke se *pwe*·de a·*ser* en las *no*·ches
What's on ...?	¿Qué hay ...? ke ai ...

locally	en la zona	en la *so*·na
today	hoy	oy
tonight	esta noche	*es*·ta *no*·che
this weekend	este fin de semana	*es*·te feen de se·*ma*·na

Is there a local ... guide?	¿Hay una guía de ... de la zona?	ai *oo*·na *gee*·a de ... de la *so*·na

entertainment	entretenimiento	en·tre·te·nee·*myen*·to
film	cines	*see*·nes
gay	los lugares gay	los loo·*ga*·res gay
music	de música	de *moo*·see·ka

Where are the ...?	¿Dónde hay ...?	*don*·de ai ...

bars	bares	*ba*·res
cafes	cafeterías	ka·fe·te·*ree*·as
clubs	antros	*an*·tros
gay venues	lugares gay	loo·*ga*·res gay
places to eat	lugares donde comer	loo·*ga*·res *don*·de ko·*mer*

I feel like going to ...	Tengo ganas de ir ...	*ten*·go *ga*·nas de eer ...

a cafe	a una cafetería	a *oo*·na ka·fe·te·*ree*·a
a concert	a un concierto	a oon kon·*syer*·to
a party	a una fiesta	a *oo*·na *fyes*·ta
a restaurant	a un restaurante	a oon res·tow·*ran*·te
the movies	al cine	al *see*·ne
the theatre	al teatro	al te·*a*·tro

Do you know a good restaurant?	¿Conoces algún buen restaurante? ko·*no*·ses al·*goon* bwen res·tow·*ran*·te

Where can we go (salsa) dancing?	¿Dónde podemos ir a bailar (salsa)? *don·de po·de·mos eer a bai·lar (sal·sa)*
What's the cover charge?	¿Cuánto cuesta el cover? *kwan·to kwes·ta el ko·ver*

Invitations

What are you doing ...?		¿Qué vas a hacer ...? *ke vas a a·ser ...*
right now	ahorita	*a·o·ree·ta*
this evening	esta noche	*es·ta no·che*
tomorrow	mañana	*ma·nya·na*
this weekend	este fin de semana	*es·te feen de se·ma·na*

Would you like to go (out somewhere)?	¿Te gustaría salir (a algún lado)? *te goos·ta·ree·a sa·leer (a al·goon la·do)*
I feel like going for a ...	Me gustaría ir a ... *me goos·ta·ree·a eer a ...*

coffee	tomar un café	*to·mar oon ka·fe*
dance	bailar	*bai·lar*
drink	tomar algo	*to·mar al·go*
meal	comer	*ko·mer*
walk	caminar	*ka·mee·nar*

My round.	Yo invito. *yo een·vee·to*

SOCIAL — GOING OUT

CULTURE TIP

Mexican Bars

From rowdy rum-soaked saloons to cosy, romantic lounge-bars, Mexico has it all.

antro m *an·*tro
bar or nightclub – word formerly used to describe a dive

bar m bar
a place for drinking and talking, rather than dancing or listening to live music

cantina f kan·*tee·*na
a uniquely Mexican establishment, where tequila, mezcal, beer, rum and brandy are the order of the day; some *cantinas* are men-only zones, but most others are more relaxed

peña f *pe·*nya
a place to go for either a drink or a meal, usually with live romantic Mexican music

We're having a party.	Vamos a hacer una fiesta. *va·*mos a a·*ser* oo·na *fyes·*ta
You should come.	¿Por qué no vienes? por ke no *vye·*nes

Responding to Invitations

Sure!	¡Claro que sí, gracias! *kla·*ro ke see *gra·*syas
Yes, I'd love to.	Sí, me encantaría. see me en·kan·ta·*ree·*a
Where shall we go?	¿Adónde vamos? a·*don·*de *va·*mos
Thanks, but I'm afraid I can't.	Gracias, pero no puedo. *gra·*syas *pe·*ro no *pwe·*do

What about tomorrow?	¿Qué tal mañana? ke tal ma·*nya*·na
Sorry, I can't sing/dance.	Perdón, no sé cantar/bailar. per·*don* no se kan·*tar*/bai·*lar*

Arranging to Meet

Q	**What time shall we meet?**	¿A qué hora nos vemos? a ke *o*·ra nos *ve*·mos
A	**Let's meet at (eight o'clock).**	Nos vemos a (las ocho). nos *ve*·mos a (las *o*·cho)
Q	**Where will we meet?**	¿Dónde nos vemos? *don*·de nos *ve*·mos
A	**Let's meet at (the entrance).**	Nos vemos en (la entrada). nos *ve*·mos en (la en·*tra*·da)
	I'll pick you up.	Paso por tí. *pa*·so por *tee*
	I'll be coming later.	Te alcanzo más tarde. te al·*kan*·so mas *tar*·de
	I'll see you then.	Nos vemos. nos *ve*·mos
	I'm looking forward to it.	Tengo muchas ganas de ir. *ten*·go *moo*·chas *ga*·nas de eer

Drugs

I don't take drugs.	No consumo drogas. no kon·*soo*·mo *dro*·gas
I have ... occasionally.	Consumo ... de vez en cuando. kon·*soo*·mo ... de ves en *kwan*·do
Do you want to have a smoke?	¿Nos fumamos un churro? nos foo·*ma*·mos oon *choo*·ro

Romance

KEY PHRASES

Would you like to do something?	¿Quieres hacer algo?	*kye*·res a·*ser al*·go
I love you.	Te quiero.	te *kye*·ro
Leave me alone.	Déjame en paz.	*de*·kha·me en pas

Asking Someone Out

Q Would you like to do something (tonight)?
¿Quieres hacer algo (esta noche)?
kye·res a·*ser al*·go (*es*·ta *no*·che)

A Yes, I'd love to.
Sí, me encantaría.
see me en·kan·ta·*ree*·a

A No, I'm afraid I can't.
Gracias, pero no puedo.
gra·syas *pe*·ro no *pwe*·do

Pick-up Lines

Would you like a drink?	¿Te invito una copa? te een·*vee*·to oo·na *ko*·pa
Do you have a light?	¿Tienes encendedor? *tye*·nes en·sen·de·*dor*
What star sign are you?	¿De qué signo eres? de ke *seeg*·no *e*·res
Shall we get some fresh air?	¿Vamos afuera? *va*·mos a·*fwe*·ra

You have (a) beautiful ...	Tienes ...	
	tye·nes ...	
body	un muy buen cuerpo	oon mooy bwen *kwer*·po
eyes	unos ojos preciosos	*oo*·nos o·khos pre·*syo*·sos
laugh	una risa preciosa	*oo*·na *ree*·sa pre·*syo*·sa
personality	una gran personalidad	*oo*·na gran per·so·na·lee·*dad*

Rejections

I'm here with my boyfriend/girlfriend.	Estoy aquí con mi novio/a. es·*toy* a·*kee* kon mee *no*·vyo/a
I have a boyfriend/girlfriend.	Tengo novio/a. *ten*·go *no*·vyo/a
Excuse me, I have to go now.	Lo siento, pero me tengo que ir. lo *syen*·to *pe*·ro me *ten*·go ke eer
I'm not interested.	No estoy interesado/a. m/f no es·*toy* een·te·re·*sa*·do/a
Leave me alone!	Déjame en paz. *de*·kha·me en pas
Piss off!	¡Vete a la mierda! *ve*·te a la *myer*·da

Getting Closer

You're very nice.	Eres muy simpático/a. m/f *e*·res mooy seem·*pa*·tee·ko/a

You're very attractive.	Eres muy atractivo/a. **m/f** e·res mooy a·trak·*tee*·vo/a
Do you like me?	¿Te caigo bien? te *kai*·go byen
I like you very much.	Me gustas mucho. me *goos*·tas *moo*·cho
Can I kiss you?	¿Te puedo besar? te *pwe*·do be·*sar*
Will you take me home?	¿Te puedo acompañar a tu casa? te *pwe*·do a·kom·*pa*·nyar a too *ka*·sa
Do you want to come inside for a while?	¿Quieres pasar un rato? *kye*·res pa·*sar* oon *ra*·to

Sex

I want to make love to you.	Quiero hacerte el amor. *kye*·ro a·*ser*·te el a·*mor*
I won't do it without protection.	No lo haré sin protección. no lo a·*re* seen pro·tek·*syon*
Let's use a condom.	Usemos condón. oo·*se*·mos kon·*don*
I think we should stop now.	Pienso que deberíamos parar. *pyen*·so ke de·be·*ree*·a·mos pa·*rar*
Let's go to bed!	¡Vamos a la cama! *va*·mos a la *ka*·ma
Kiss me!	¡Bésame! *be*·sa·me
I want you.	Te deseo. te de·*se*·o

Take this off.	Quítate ésto.
	kee·ta·te es·to
Q Do you like this?	¿Te gusta ésto?
	te goos·ta es·to
A I (don't) like that.	Esto (no) me gusta.
	es·to (no) me goos·ta
Touch me here.	Tócame aquí.
	to·ka·me a·kee
That's great.	Eso es genial.
	e·so es khe·nyal
Please stop!	¡Para!
	pa·ra
Please don't stop!	¡No pares!
	no pa·res
That was amazing.	Eso fue increíble.
	e·so fwe een·kre·ee·ble
Can I stay over?	¿Puedo quedarme?
	pwe·do ke·dar·me
When can I see you again?	¿Cuándo nos vemos de nuevo?
	kwan·do nos ve·mos de nwe·vo

Love

I'm in love with you.	Estoy enamorado/a de tí. **m/f**
	es·toy e·na·mo·ra·do/a de tee
Q Do you love me?	¿Me quieres?
	me kye·res
A I love you.	Te quiero.
	te kye·ro
I think we're good together.	Creo que hacemos buena pareja.
	kre·o ke a·se·mos bwe·na pa·re·kha

SOCIAL | BELIEFS & CULTURE

Beliefs & Culture

KEY PHRASES

What's your religion?	¿Cuál es su/tu religión? pol/inf	kwal es soo/too re·lee·*khyon*
I'm ...	Soy ...	soy ...
I'm sorry, it's against my beliefs.	Perdón, pero eso va en contra de mis creencias.	per·*don* pe·ro e·so va en *kon*·tra de mees kre·*en*·syas

Religion

Q What's your religion?   ¿Cuál es su/tu religión? pol/inf
kwal es soo/too re·lee·*khyon*

A I'm (not) ...   (No) Soy ...
(no) soy ...

agnostic	agnóstico/a m/f	ag·*nos*·tee·ko/a
atheist	ateo/a m/f	a·*te*·o/a
Buddhist	budista m&f	boo·*dees*·ta
Catholic	católico/a m/f	ka·*to*·lee·ko/a
Christian	cristiano/a m/f	krees·*tya*·no/a
Hindu	hindú m&f	een·*doo*
Jewish	judío/a m/f	khoo·*dee*·o/a
Muslim	musulmán m	moo·sool·*man*
	musulmana f	moo·sool·*ma*·na
practising	practicante m&f	prak·tee·*kan*·te
Protestant	protestante m&f	pro·tes·*tan*·te

I'd like to go to (the) ...	Me gustaría ir a ... me goos·ta·*ree*·a ...

church	la iglesia	la ee·*gle*·sya
mosque	la mezquita	la mes·*kee*·ta
synagogue	la sinagoga	la see·na·*go*·ga
temple	el templo	el *tem*·plo

Can I (pray) here?	¿Puedo (rezar) aquí? *pwe*·do (re·*sar*) a·*kee*
Where can I (attend mass)?	¿Dónde puedo (ir a misa)? *don*·de *pwe*·do (eer a *mee*·sa)

Cultural Differences

Is this a local custom?	¿Es una costumbre local? es *oo*·na kos·*toom*·bre lo·*kal*
I'm not used to this.	No estoy acostumbrado/a a ésto. **m/f** no es·*toy* a·kos·toom·*bra*·do/a a *es*·to
Sorry, I didn't mean to say/ do something wrong.	Perdón, lo dice/hice sin querer. per·*don* lo *dee*·se/*ee*·se seen ke·*rer*
I'm sorry, it's against my beliefs.	Perdón, pero eso va en contra de mis creencias. per·*don* pe·ro e·so va en *kon*·tra de mees kre·*en*·syas
I don't mind watching, but I'd rather not join in.	No me importa mirar, pero prefiero no participar. no me eem·*por*·ta mee·*rar* pe·ro pre·*fye*·ro no par·tee·see·*par*

Sports

SOCIAL SPORTS

Which sport do you play?	¿Qué deporte practicas?	ke de·*por*·te prak·*tee*·kas
Who's your favourite team?	¿Cuál es tu equipo favorito?	kwal es too e·*kee*·po fa·vo·*ree*·to
What's the score?	¿Cómo van?	*ko*·mo van

Sporting Interests

Q Do you like (tennis)?	¿Te gusta (el tenis)?	te *goos*·ta (el *te*·nees)
A Yes, very much.	Sí, mucho.	see *moo*·cho
A Not really.	En realidad, no mucho.	en re·a·lee·*dad* no *moo*·cho
A I like watching it.	Me gusta ver.	me *goos*·ta ver
Q Which sport do you play?	¿Qué deporte practicas?	ke de·*por*·te prak·*tee*·kas
A I play (basketball).	Practico (el balconcesto).	prak·*tee*·ko (el ba·lon·*ses*·to)
Q Which sport do you follow?	¿A qué deporte eres aficionado/a? **m/f**	a ke de·*por*·te e·res a·fee·syo·*na*·do/a
A I follow (football/ soccer).	Soy aficionado/a al (fútbol). **m/f**	soy a·fee·syo·*na*·do/a al (*foot*·bol)

Who's your favourite sportsman/woman?	¿Quién es tu deportista favorito/a? m/f kyen es too de·por·*tees*·ta fa·vo·*ree*·to/a
What's your favourite team?	¿Cuál es tu equipo favorito? kwal es too e·*kee*·po fa·vo·*ree*·to

For more sports, see the **dictionary**.

Going to a Game

Would you like to go to a match?	¿Te gustaría ir a un partido? te goos·ta·*ree*·a eer a oon par·*tee*·do
Who's playing?	¿Quién juega? kyen *khwe*·ga
Who are you supporting?	¿A qué equipo te vas? a ke e·*kee*·po te vas
Who's winning?	¿Quién va ganando? kyen va ga·*nan*·do
What's the score?	¿Cómo van? *ko*·mo van
How much time is left?	¿Cuánto tiempo queda (de partido)? *kwan*·to *tyem*·po *ke*·da (de par·*tee*·do)
🅠 **What was the final score?**	¿Cómo terminó el partido? *ko*·mo ter·mee·*no* el par·*tee*·do
🅐 **It was a draw.**	Fue un empate. fwe oon em·*pa*·te
That was a boring game!	¡Fue un partido aburridísimo! fwe oon par·*tee*·do a·boo·ree·*dee*·see·mo

CULTURE TIP **Traditional Sports**

Bullfighting and cockfighting are both popular in Mexico. You might see posters advertising the following:

corridas f pl **de toros**   ko·*ree*·das de *to*·ros
bullfighting, especially popular in major towns

lucha f **libre**   *loo*·cha *lee*·bre
theatrical free-style Mexican wrestling in which competitors are masked

peleas f pl **de gallos**   pe·*le*·as de *ga*·yos
cockfights – two roosters fight to the death using blades attached to their feet

pelota f **mixteca**   pe·lo·ta mee·*ste*·ka
a five-a-side ball game reconstructed from a pre-Hispanic version that often ended with human sacrifice

That was a bad game!	¡Fue un partido malo! fwe oon par·*tee*·do *ma*·lo
That was a great game!	¡Fue un partido buenísimo! fwe oon par·*tee*·do bwe·*nee*·see·mo
What a ...!	¡Qué ...! ke ...

goal	gol	gol
hit	tiro	*tee*·ro
kick	chute	*choo*·te
pass	pase	*pa*·se

Playing Sport

Q	**Do you want to play?**	¿Quieres jugar? *kye·*res khoo·*gar*
Q	**Can I join in?**	¿Puedo jugar? *pwe·*do khoo·*gar*
A	**Yes, that'd be great.**	Sí, me encantaría. see me en·kan·ta·*ree·*a
A	**Not at the moment, thanks.**	Ahorita no, gracias. a·o·*ree·*ta no *gra·*syas
A	**I have an injury.**	Estoy lastimado/a. m/f es·*toy* las·tee·*ma·*do/a

Where's the nearest ...?	¿Dónde queda ...? *don·*de *ke·*da ...

gym	el gimnasio más cercano	el kheem·*na·*syo mas ser·*ka·*no
park	el parque más cercano	el *par·*ke mas ser·*ka·*no
sports club	el club deportivo más cercano	el kloob de·por·*tee·*vo mas ser·*ka·*no
swimming pool	la alberca más cercana	la al·*ber·*ka mas ser·*ka·*na
tennis court	la cancha de tenis más cercana	la *kan·*cha de *te·*nees mas ser·*ka·*na

Where's the best place to jog around here?	¿Cuál es el mejor sitio para correr por aquí cerca? kwal es el me·*khor* see·*tyo *pa·*ra ko·*rer* por a·*kee* ser·*ka*
Can I hire a ball?	¿Puedo rentar una pelota? *pwe·*do ren·*tar* oo·na pe·*lo·*ta

Can I hire a court?	¿Puedo rentar una cancha?	*pwe·do ren·tar oo·na kan·cha*
Can I hire a racquet?	¿Puedo rentar una raqueta?	*pwe·do ren·tar oo·na ra·ke·ta*
What's the charge per ...?	¿Cúanto cobran por ...?	*kwan·to ko·bran por ...*

day	día	*dee·a*
game	juego	*khwe·go*
hour	hora	*o·ra*
visit	visita	*vee·see·ta*

◀)) LISTEN FOR

delantero m	de·lan·te·ro	striker
gol m	gol	goal (scored)
fuera de lugar	*fwe·ra de loo·gar*	offside
medio-campista m	me·dyo·kam·pees·ta	mid-fielder
pelota f	pe·lo·ta	ball
penalty m	pe·nal·tee	penalty
portería f	por·te·ree·a	goal (place)
portero m	por·te·ro	goalkeeper
tarjeta f **amarilla**	tar·khe·ta a·ma·ree·ya	yellow card
tarjeta f **roja**	tar·khe·ta ro·kha	red card
tiro m **de esquina**	*tee·ro de es·kee·na*	corner (kick)
tiro m **libre**	*tee·ro lee·bre*	free kick

Do I have to be a member to attend?	¿Hay que ser socio/a para entrar? m/f ai ke ser *so*·syo/a *pa*·ra en·*trar*
Is there a women-only pool?	¿Hay alguna alberca sólo para mujeres? ai al·*goo*·na al·*ber*·ka *so*·lo *pa*·ra moo·*khe*·res
Where are the changing rooms?	¿Dónde están los vestidores? *don*·de es·*tan* los ves·tee·*do*·res
Can I have a locker?	¿Puedo usar un casillero? *pwe*·do oo·*sar* oon ka·see·*ye*·ro

Football/Soccer

Who plays for (the Pumas)?	¿Quién juega en (los Pumas)? kyen *khwe*·ga en (los *poo*·mas)
He's a great (player).	Es un gran (jugador). es oon gran (khoo·ga·*dor*)
Which team is at the top of the league?	¿Qué equipo está primero en la liga? ke e·*kee*·po es·*ta* pree·*me*·ro en la *lee*·ga
He/She played brilliantly in the match against (Venezuela).	Jugó excelente en el partido contra (Venezuela). khoo·*go* ek·se·*len*·te en el par·*tee*·do *kon*·tra (ve·ne·*swe*·la)
What a terrible team!	¡Qué equipo más malo! ke e·*kee*·po mas *ma*·lo

Off to see a match? Check out **buying tickets** (p43), and **going to a game** (p141).

Outdoors

KEY PHRASES

Where can I buy supplies?	¿Dónde puedo comprar provisiones?	*don*·de *pwe*·do kom·*prar* pro·vee·*syo*·nes
Do we need a guide?	¿Necesitamos un guía?	ne·se·see·*ta*·mos oon *gee*·a
Is it safe?	¿Es seguro?	es se·*goo*·ro
I'm lost.	Estoy perdido/a. **m/f**	es·*toy* per·*dee*·do/a
What's the weather like?	¿Cómo está el clima?	*ko*·mo es·*ta* el *klee*·ma

Hiking

Where can I ...? ¿Dónde puedo ...?
don·de *pwe*·do ...

buy supplies	comprar provisiones	kom·*prar* pro·vee·*syo*·nes
find someone who knows the area	encontrar a alguien que conozca la zona	en·kon·*trar* a *al*·gyen ke ko·*nos*·ka la *so*·na
get a map	obtener un mapa	ob·te·*ner* oon *ma*·pa
hire hiking gear	rentar equipo para excursionismo	ren·*tar* e·*kee*·po *pa*·ra ek·skoor·syo·*nees*·mo

Do we need to take bedding?	¿Necesitamos llevar algo en que dormir? ne·se·see·*ta*·mos ye·*var* al·go en ke dor·*meer*
Do we need to take food/water?	¿Necesitamos llevar comida/agua? ne·se·see·*ta*·mos ye·*var* ko·*mee*·da/a·gwa
Which is the easiest route?	¿Cuál es la ruta más fácil? kwal es la *roo*·ta mas *fa*·seel
Which is the shortest/ longest route?	¿Cuál es la ruta más corta/ larga? kwal es la *roo*·ta mas *kor*·ta/ *lar*·ga
Is the track (well-)marked?	¿El sendero está (bien) marcado? el sen·*de*·ro es·*ta* (byen) mar·*ka*·do
Is the track open?	¿El sendero está abierto? el sen·*de*·ro es·*ta* a·*byer*·to
Is the track scenic?	¿Es escénico el sendero? es e·se·*nee*·ko el sen·*de*·ro
How high is the climb?	¿A qué altura se escala? a ke al·*too*·ra se es·*ka*·la
How long is the trail?	¿Qué tan larga es la ruta? ke tan *lar*·ga es la *roo*·ta
How long does the hike take?	¿Cuánto dura la caminata? *kwan*·to *doo*·ra la ka·mee·*na*·ta
Do we need a guide?	¿Necesitamos un guía? ne·se·see·*ta*·mos oon *gee*·a
Are there guided treks?	¿Hay escaladas guiadas? ai es·ka·*la*·das gee·*a*·das

Is it safe?	¿Es seguro? es se·*goo*·ro
Is there a hut?	¿Hay alguna cabaña? ai al·*goo*·na ka·*ba*·nya
When does it get dark?	¿A qué hora oscurece? a ke *o*·ra os·koo·*re*·se
Where have you come from?	¿De dónde vienes/ vienen? **sg inf/pl** de *don*·de *vye*·nes/ *vye*·nen
How long did it take?	¿Cuánto tardaste? *kwan*·to tar·*das*·te
Does this path go to (Morelia)?	¿Este camino va a (Morelia)? es·te ka·*mee*·no va a (mo·*re*·lya)
Can we go through here?	¿Podemos atravesar por aquí? po·*de*·mos a·tra·ve·*sar* por a·*kee*
Is the water OK to drink?	¿Se puede tomar el agua? se *pwe*·de to·*mar* el *a*·gwa
Where's the nearest village?	¿Dónde está pueblo más cercano? *don*·de es·*ta* el *pwe*·blo mas ser·*ka*·no
Where's a campsite?	¿Dónde hay un lugar para acampar? *don*·de ai oon loo·*gar* pa·ra a·kam·*par*

🔍 LOOK FOR

Prohibido Nadar	pro·ee·*bee*·do na·*dar*	No Swimming

¿Es seguro?
es se·*goo*·ro
Is it safe?

Where are the showers/ toilets?	¿Dónde hay regaderas/ sanitarios? *don*·de ai re·ga·*de*·ras/ sa·nee·*ta*·ryos
I'm lost.	Estoy perdido/a. **m/f** es·*toy* per·*dee*·do/a

Beach

Where's the best beach?	¿Dónde está la mejor playa? *don*·de es·*ta* la me·*khor* pla·ya
Where's the nearest beach?	¿Dónde está la playa más cercana? *don*·de es·*ta* la *pla*·ya mas ser·*ka*·na

Where's the nudist beach?	¿Dónde está la playa nudista?
	don·de es·ta la pla·ya noo·dees·ta
Is it safe to dive here?	¿Es seguro echarse clavados aquí?
	es se·goo·ro e·char·se kla·va·dos a·kee
Is it safe to scuba dive here?	¿Es seguro bucear aquí?
	es se·goo·ro boo·se·ar a·kee
Is it safe to swim here?	¿Es seguro nadar aquí?
	es se·goo·ro na·dar a·kee
What time is high/low tide?	¿A qué hora es la marea alta/baja?
	a ke o·ra es la ma·re·a al·ta/ba·kha
How much for a chair/hut?	¿Cuánto cuesta rentar una silla/palapa?
	kwan·to kwes·ta ren·tar oo·na see·ya/pa·la·pa
How much for an umbrella (for sun)?	¿Cuánto cuesta rentar una sombrilla?
	kwan·to kwes·ta ren·tar oo·na som·bree·ya
Are there any reefs?	¿Hay arrecifes?
	ai a·re·see·fes

🔊 LISTEN FOR

Cuidado con la resaca.	*kwee·da·do kon la re·sa·ka*
	Be careful of the undertow.
¡Es peligroso!	*es pe·lee·gro·so*
	It's dangerous!

Are there any rips?	¿Hay corrientes?
	ai ko·*ryen*·tes

Are there any water hazards?	¿Hay peligros en el agua?
	ai pe·*lee*·gros en el *a*·gwa

Weather

Q What's the weather like?	¿Cómo está el clima?
	ko·mo es·*ta* el *klee*·ma

A It's raining.	Llueve.
	ywe·ve

A It's (cold).	Hace (frío).
	a·se (*free*·o)

Q Will it be (hot) tomorrow?	Mañana hará (calor)?
	ma·*nya*·na a·*ra* (ka·*lor*)

A Tomorrow it will be raining.	Mañana lloverá.
	ma·*nya*·na yo·ve·*ra*

Q Will it be ... tomorrow?	¿Estará ... mañana?
	es·ta·*ra* ... (ma·*nya*·na)

A It's ...	Está ...
	es·*ta* ...

cloudy	nublado	noo·*bla*·do
sunny	soleado	so·le·*a*·do
warm	cálido	*ka*·lee·do
windy	ventoso	ven·*to*·so

Where can I buy an umbrella (for rain)?	¿Dónde puedo comprar un paraguas?
	don·de *pwe*·do kom·*prar* oon pa·*ra*·gwas

Where can I buy a rain jacket?	¿Dónde puedo comprar un impermeable?
	don·de *pwe*·do kom·*prar* oon eem·per·me·*a*·ble

dry season	temporada f seca	tem·po·*ra*·da *se*·ka
hail	granizo m	gra·*nee*·so
rainy season	temporada f de lluvias	tem·po·*ra*·da de *yoo*·vyas
storm	tormenta f	tor·*men*·ta

Flora & Fauna

What ... is that?	¿Qué ... es ése/a? m/f	ke ... es *e*·se/a

animal	animal m	a·nee·*mal*
flower	flor f	flor
plant	planta f	*plan*·ta
tree	árbol m	*ar*·bol

What's it used for?	¿Para qué se usa?	*pa*·ra ke se *oo*·sa
Can you eat it?	¿Se puede comer?	se *pwe*·de ko·*mer*
Is it ...?	¿Es ...?	es ...

common	común	ko·*moon*
dangerous	peligroso/a m/f	pe·lee·*gro*·so/a
endangered	en peligro de extinción	en pe·*lee*·gro de ek·steen·*syon*
poisonous	venenoso/a m/f	ve·ne·*no*·so/a
protected	protegido/a m/f	pro·te·*khee*·do/a

For names of plants and animals, see the **dictionary**.

Safe Travel

Emergencies

KEY PHRASES

Help!	¡Socorro!	so·*ko*·ro
There's been an accident.	Ha habido un accidente.	a a·*bee*·do oon ak·see·*den*·te
It's an emergency.	Es una emergencia.	es *oo*·na e·mer·*khen*·sya

Help!	¡Socorro! so·*ko*·ro
Stop!	¡Pare! *pa*·re
Go away!	¡Váyase! *va*·ya·se
Thief!	¡Ladrón! la·*dron*
Fire!	¡Fuego! *fwe*·go
Watch out!	¡Cuidado! kwee·*da*·do
Call the police!	¡Llame a la policía! *ya*·me a la po·lee·*see*·a
Call a doctor!	¡Llame a un médico! *ya*·me a oon *me*·dee·ko
Call an ambulance!	¡Llame a una ambulancia! *ya*·me a *oo*·na am·boo·*lan*·sya
It's an emergency.	Es una emergencia. es *oo*·na e·mer·*khen*·sya

Could you help me, please?	¿Me puede ayudar, por favor?	me *pwe*·de a·*yoo*·dar por *fa*·vor
I have to use the telephone.	Necesito usar el teléfono.	ne·se·*see*·to oo·*sar* el te·*le*·fo·no
We've had a (traffic) accident.	Tuvimos un accidente (de tráfico).	too·*vee*·mos oon ak·see·*den*·te (de *tra*·fee·ko)
There's been an accident.	Ha habido un accidente.	a a·*bee*·do oon ak·see·*den*·te
I'm lost.	Estoy perdido/a. m/f	es·*toy* per·*dee*·do/a
Where are the toilets?	¿Dónde están los baños?	*don*·de es·*tan* los *ba*·nyos
Is it safe ...?	¿Es seguro ...?	es se·*goo*·ro ...

at night	de noche	de *no*·che
for foreigners	para los extranjeros	*pa*·ra los ek·stran·*khe*·ros
for gay travellers	para viajeros gay	*pa*·ra vya·*khe*·ros gay
for women travellers	para viajeras	*pa*·ra vya·*khe*·ras
to go alone	para ir solo/a m/f	*pa*·ra eer *so*·lo/a
to hitchhike	pedir aventón	pe·*deer* a·ven·*ton*

Police

KEY PHRASES

Where's the police station?	¿Dónde está la estación de policía?	*don*·de es·*ta* la es·ta·*syon* de po·lee·*see*·a
I want to contact my consulate/ embassy.	Quiero ponerme en contacto con mi consulado/ embajada.	*kye*·ro po·*ner*·me en kon·*tak*·to kon mee kon·soo·*la*·do/ em·ba·*kha*·da
My bag was stolen.	Mi bolso fue robado.	mee *bol*·so fwe ro·*ba*·do

Where's the police station?	¿Dónde está la estación de policía? *don*·de es·*ta* la es·ta·*syon* de po·lee·*see*·a
I want to report an offence.	Quiero denunciar un delito. *kye*·ro de·noon·*syar* oon de·*lee*·to
I've lost (my wallet).	Perdí (mi billetera). per·*dee* (mee bee·ye·*te*·ra)
My bag was stolen.	Mi bolso fue robado. mee *bol*·so few ro·*ba*·do
My money was stolen.	Mi dinero fue robado. mee dee·*ne*·ro fwe ro·*ba*·do
I've been robbed.	Me han robado. me an ro·*ba*·do
I've been raped.	Me violaron. me vyo·*la*·ron

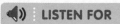

LISTEN FOR

agresión f	a·gre·*syon* assault
alterar el orden público	al·te·*rar* el *or*·den *poo*·blee·ko disturbing the peace
exceso m **de velocidad**	ek·se·so de ve·lo·see·*dad* speeding
faltas f pl **a la moral**	*fal*·tas a la mo·*ral* indecent behaviour
robo m	*ro*·bo theft

I want to contact my consulate/embassy.	Quiero ponerme en contacto con mi consulado/embajada. *kye*·ro po·*ner*·me en kon·*tak*·to kon mee kon·soo·*la*·do/em·ba·*kha*·da
Can I call someone?	¿Puedo llamar a alguien? *pwe*·do ya·*mar* a *al*·gyen
Can I have a lawyer (who speaks English)?	Quisiera un abogado (que hable inglés). kee·*sye*·ra oon a·bo·*ga*·do (ke *a*·ble een·*gles*)
I have a prescription for this drug.	Tengo receta para esta medicina. *ten*·go re·*se*·ta *pa*·ra es·ta me·dee·*see*·na
What am I accused of?	¿De qué me acusan? de ke me a·*koo*·san
I'm innocent.	Soy inocente. soy ee·no·*sen*·te
I didn't do it.	No lo hice. no lo *ee*·se

Health

KEY PHRASES

Where's the nearest hospital?	¿Dónde está el hospital más cercano?	don·de es·ta el os·pee·tal mas ser·ka·no
I'm sick.	Estoy enfermo/a. m/f	es·toy en·fer·mo/a
I need a doctor.	Necesito un doctor.	ne·se·see·to oon dok·tor
I'm on medication for ...	Estoy bajo tratamiento médico contra ...	es·toy ba·kho tra·ta·myen·to me·dee·ko kon·tra ...
I'm allergic to ...	Soy alérgico/a a ... m/f	soy a·ler·khee·ko/a a ...

Doctor

Where's the nearest ...?	¿Dónde está ... más cercano/a? m/f
	don·de es·ta ... mas ser·ka·no/a

(night) chemist	la farmacia f (de guardia)	la far·ma·sya (de gwar·dya)
dentist	el dentista m	el den·tees·ta
doctor	el médico m	el me·dee·ko
hospital	el hospital m	el os·pee·tal
medical centre	la clínica f	la klee·nee·ka
optometrist	el optometrista m	el op·to·me·trees·ta

I need a doctor (who speaks English).	Necesito un doctor (que hable inglés). ne·se·*see*·to oon dok·*tor* (ke *a*·ble een·*gles*)
Could I see a female doctor?	¿Puede revisarme una doctora? *pwe*·de re·vee·*sar*·me *oo*·na dok·*to*·ra
Can the doctor come here?	¿Puede visitarme el doctor? *pwe*·de vee·see·*tar*·me el dok·*tor*
I've been vaccinated against ...	Estoy vacunado/a contra ... **m/f** es·*toy* va·koo·*na*·do/a *kon*·tra ...

hepatitis A/B/C	hepatitis A/B/C	e·pa·*tee*·tees a/be/se
tetanus	tétanos	*te*·ta·nos
typhoid	tifoidea	tee·foy·*de*·a
yellow fever	fiebre amarilla	*fye*·bre a·ma·*ree*·ya

I need new contact lenses.	Necesito lentes de contacto nuevos. ne·se·*see*·to *len*·tes de kon·*tak*·to *nwe*·vos
I need new glasses.	Necesito lentes nuevos. ne·se·*see*·to *len*·tes *nwe*·vos
I've run out of my medication.	Se me terminaron mis medicinas. se me ter·mee·*na*·ron mees me·dee·*see*·nas
This is my usual medicine.	Esta es mi medicina habitual. *es*·te es mee me·dee·*see*·na a·bee·*twal*

SAFE TRAVEL **HEALTH**

Can I have a receipt for my insurance?	¿Puede darme un recibo para mi seguro médico? *pwe·de dar·me oon re·see·bo pa·ra mee se·goo·ro me·dee·ko*

Symptoms & Conditions

I'm sick.	Estoy enfermo/a. **m/f** *es·toy en·fer·mo/a*
My friend is sick.	Mi amigo está enfermo. **m** *mee a·mee·go es·ta en·fer·mo* Mi amiga está enferma. **f** *mee a·mee·ga es·ta en·fer·ma*
It hurts here.	Me duele aquí. *me dwe·le a·kee*
I've been injured.	He sido lastimado/a. **m/f** *e see·do las·tee·ma·do/a*
I've been vomiting.	He estado vomitando. *e es·ta·do vo·mee·tan·do*
I'm dehydrated.	Estoy deshidratado/a. **m/f** *es·toy des·ee·dra·ta·do/a*
I'm all hot and cold.	Tengo escalofríos. *ten·go es·ka·lo·free·os*
I can't sleep.	No puedo dormir. *no pwe·do dor·meer*

◀⊙ LISTEN FOR

¿Usted bebe?	*oos·ted be·be* Do you drink?
¿Usted fuma?	*oos·ted foo·ma* Do you smoke?
¿Usted consume drogas?	*oos·ted kon·soo·me dro·gas* Do you take drugs?

🔊 LISTEN FOR

¿Dónde le duele?	*don*·de le *dwe*·le Where does it hurt?
¿Está tomando algún medicamento?	es·*ta* to·*man*·do al·*goon* me·dee·ka·*men*·to Are you on medication?
¿Desde cuándo se siente así?	des·de *kwan*·do se *syen*·te a·*see* How long have you been like this?
¿Ha tenido ésto antes?	a te·*nee*·do *es*·to *an*·tes Have you had this before?

I feel ...	Me siento ... me *syen*·to ...

anxious	ansioso/a m/f	an·*syo*·so/a
dizzy	mareado/a m/f	ma·re·a·do/a
nauseous	con náuseas	kon *now*·se·as
shivery	destemplado/a m/f	des·tem·*pla*·do/a
weak	débil	*de*·beel

I've (recently) had ...	(Hace poco) Tuve ... (*a*·se *po*·ko) *too*·ve ...
I'm on medication for ...	Estoy bajo tratamiento médico contra ... es·*toy ba*·kho tra·ta·*myen*·to *me*·dee·ko kon·tra ...
I'm asthmatic.	Soy asmático/a. m/f soy as·*ma*·tee·ko/a
I'm diabetic.	Soy diabético/a. m/f soy dya·*be*·tee·ko/a

I'm epileptic.	Soy epiléptico/a. **m/f** soy e·pee·*lep*·tee·ko/a

For more symptoms and conditions, see the **dictionary**.

Women's Health

(I think) I'm pregnant.	(Creo que) Estoy embarazada. (*kre*·o ke) es·*toy* em·ba·ra·*sa*·da
I haven't had my period for (three) days/weeks.	Hace (tres) días/semanas que no tengo mi período. *a*·se (tres) *dee*·as/se·*ma*·nas ke no *ten*·go mee pe·*ree*·o·do
I'm on the Pill.	Tomo pastillas anticonceptivas. *to*·mo pas·*tee*·yas an·tee·kon·sep·*tee*·vas

 **LISTEN FOR**

¿Está menstruando?	es·*ta* men·*strwan*·do Are you menstruating?
¿Cuándo tuvo su último período?	*kwan*·do *too*·vo soo *ool*·tee·mo pe·*ree*·o·do When did you last have your period?
¿Usa anticonceptivos?	*oo*·sa an·tee·kon·sep·*tee*·vos Are you using contraception?
¿Está embarazada?	es·*ta* em·ba·ra·*sa*·da Are you pregnant?
Está embarazada.	es·*ta* em·ba·ra·*sa*·da You're pregnant.

I need contraception.	Necesito algún método anticonceptivo.
	ne·se·*see*·to al·*goon me*·to·do an·tee·kon·sep·*tee*·vo
I need the morning-after pill.	Necesito tomar la pastilla del día siguiente.
	ne·se·*see*·to to·*mar* la pas·*tee*·ya del *dee*·a see·*gyen*·te
I need a pregnancy test.	Necesito una prueba del embarazo.
	ne·se·*see*·to *oo*·na *prwe*·ba de em·ba·*ra*·so
I've noticed a lump here.	He notado que tengo una bola aquí.
	e no·*ta*·do ke *ten*·go *oo*·na *bo*·la a·*kee*

Allergies

I have a skin allergy.	Tengo alergia en la piel.
	ten·go a·*ler*·gya en la pyel
I'm allergic to ...	Soy alérgico/a a ... m/f
	soy a·*ler*·khee·ko/a a ...

antihistamines	los antihistamínicos	los an·tee·ees·ta·*mee*·nee·kos
antiinflammatories	los antiinflamatorios	los an·tee·een·fla·ma·*to*·ryos
inhalers	los inhaladores	los ee·na·la·*do*·res
penicillin	la penicilina	la pe·nee·see·*lee*·na

For food-related allergies, see **vegetarian & special meals** (p186).

Parts of the Body

My (stomach) hurts.	Me duele (el estómago). me *dwe*·le (el es·*to*·ma·go)
I can't move my (ankle).	No puedo mover (el tobillo). no *pwe*·do mo·*ver* (el to·*bee*·yo)
I have a cramp in my (foot).	Tengo calambres en (el pie). *ten*·go ka·*lam*·bres en (el pye)
My ... is swollen.	Mi ... está hinchado/a. **m/f** mee ... es·*ta* een·*cha*·do/a

For more parts of the body, see the **dictionary**.

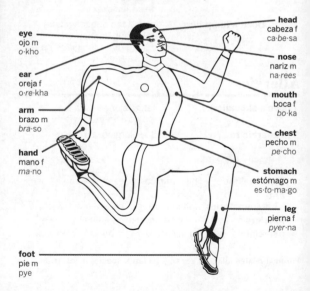

eye
ojo m
o·kho

ear
oreja f
o·*re*·kha

arm
brazo m
bra·so

hand
mano f
ma·no

foot
pie m
pye

head
cabeza f
ca·*be*·sa

nose
nariz m
na·*rees*

mouth
boca f
bo·ka

chest
pecho m
pe·cho

stomach
estómago m
es·*to*·ma·go

leg
pierna f
pyer·na

🔊 LISTEN FOR

¿Ha tomado ésto antes?	a to·*ma*·do es·to *an*·tes Have you taken this before?
Debe terminar el tratamiento.	*de*·be ter·mee·*nar* el tra·ta·*myen*·to You must complete the course.
Dos veces al día (con la comida).	dos *ve*·ses al *dee*·a (kon la ko·*mee*·da) Twice a day (with food).

Chemist

I need something for (fever).	Necesito algo para (la fiebre). ne·se·*see*·to *al*·go *pa*·ra (la *fye*·bre)
Do I need a prescription for (antihistamines)?	¿Necesito una receta para (antihistamínicos)? ne·se·*see*·to *oo*·na re·*se*·ta *pa*·ra (an·tee·ees·ta·*mee*·nee·kos)
How many times a day?	¿Cuántas veces al día? *kwan*·tas *ve*·ses al *dee*·a
Will it make me drowsy?	¿Me dará sueño? me da·*ra* swe·nyo

For more chemist items, see the **dictionary**.

Dentist

I have a toothache.	Tengo dolor de muelas. *ten*·go do·*lor* de *mwe*·las
I have a cavity.	Tengo una caries. *ten*·go *oo*·na *ka*·ryes

🔊 LISTEN FOR

Abra grande.	a·bra *gran*·de	Open wide.
Muerda ésto.	*mwer*·da *es*·to	Bite down on this.
No se mueva.	no se *mwe*·va	Don't move.
Esto no le dolerá.	*es*·to no le do·le·*ra*	This won't hurt a bit.
Enjuáguese.	en·*khwa*·ge·se	Rinse.

I have a broken tooth.	Tengo un diente roto. *ten*·go oon *dyen*·te *ro*·to
I've lost a filling.	Se me cayó una amalgama. se me ka·*yo* oo·na a·mal·*ga*·ma
My dentures are broken.	Se me rompió la dentadura postiza. se me rom·*pyo* la den·ta·*doo*·ra pos·*tee*·sa
I need a filling.	Necesito una amalgama. ne·se·*see*·to oo·na a·mal·*ga*·ma
I need a crown.	Necesito una corona. ne·se·*see*·to oo·na ko·*ro*·na
My gums hurt.	Me duelen las encías. me *dwe*·len las en·*see*·as
I don't want it extracted.	No quiero que me lo saque. no *kye*·ro ke me lo *sa*·ke
I need an anaesthetic.	Necesito una anestesia. ne·se·*see*·to oo·na a·nes·*te*·sya

Food

Eating Out

KEY PHRASES

Can you recommend a restaurant?	¿Me puede recomendar un restaurante?	me *pwe*·de re·ko·men·*dar* oon res·tow·*ran*·te
A table for (two), please.	Una mesa para (dos), por favor.	*oo*·na *me*·sa *pa*·ra (dos) por fa·*vor*
I'd like the menu, please.	Quisiera la carta, por favor.	kee·*sye*·ra la *kar*·ta por fa·*vor*
I'd like a beer, please.	Quisiera una cerveza, por favor.	kee·*sye*·ra·oo·na ser·*ve*·sa por fa·*vor*
Please bring us the bill.	Por favor, nos trae la cuenta.	por fa·*vor* nos *tra*·e la *kwen*·ta

Basics

breakfast	desayuno m de·sa·*yoo*·no
lunch	comida f ko·*mee*·da
dinner	cena f *se*·na
eat	comer ko·*mer*
drink	beber be·*ber*
I'm starving!	¡Me muero de hambre! me *mwe*·ro de *am*·bre
Enjoy the meal!	¡Buen provecho! bwen pro·*ve*·cho

Finding a Place to Eat

Can you recommend a ...?	¿Me puede recomendar ...? me *pwe*·de re·ko·men·*dar* ...

bar	un bar	oon bar
cafe	un café	oon ka·*fe*
coffee bar	una cafetería	*oo*·na ka·fe·te·te·*ree*·a
eatery	un comedor	oon ko·me·*dor*
restaurant	un restaurante	oon res·tow·*ran*·te
stall (market/ street)	un puesto	oon *pwes*·to

Where would you go for a celebration?	¿Dónde se puede ir para festejar? *don*·de se *pwe*·de eer *pa*·ra fes·te·*khar*

Where would you go for a cheap meal?	¿Dónde se puede comer barato? *don*·de se *pwe*·de ko·*mer* ba·*ra*·to

Where would you go for local specialities?	¿Adónde se va para comida típica? a·*don*·de se va *pa*·ra ko·*mee*·da *tee*·pee·ka

I'd like to reserve a table for (five) people.	Quisiera reservar una mesa para (cinco). kee·*sye*·ra re·ser·*var oo*·na *me*·sa *pa*·ra (*seen*·ko)

I'd like to reserve a table for (eight) o'clock.	Quisiera reservar una mesa para las (ocho). kee·*sye*·ra re·ser·*var oo*·na *me*·sa *pa*·ra las (*o*·cho)

> **CULTURE TIP**
>
> **Tacos**
> Fresh tacos are cheap, tasty and you can find them absolutely everywhere in Mexico. Don't leave without trying these three favourites:
>
> **tacos** m pl **al pastor**   ta·kos al pas·tor
> tacos with thinly-sliced pork, pineapple, onions and coriander
>
> **tacos** m pl **de carne asada** ta·kos de kar·ne a·sa·da
> tacos with marinated minced steak, fresh onions and coriander
>
> **tacos** m pl **de carnitas**   ta·kos de kar·nee·tas
> tacos with finely-diced pork, onions and coriander

Are you still serving food?	¿Siguen sirviendo comida? see·gen seer·vyen·do ko·mee·da
How long is the wait?	¿Cuánto hay que esperar? kwan·to ai ke es·pe·rar

At the Restaurant

In any *comedor* ko·me·dor, or run-of-the-mill restaurant, Mexicans greet all the other diners when they walk past them (coming in or going out) by saying *¡Provecho!* pro·ve·cho (short for *¡Buen provecho!* bwen pro·ve·cho, or 'Enjoy the meal!'). You also say it if you start talking to someone and they're in the middle of eating, even just a snack.

I'd like a table for (two), please.	Quisiera una mesa para (dos), por favor. kee·sye·ra oo·na me·sa pa·ra (dos) por fa·vor

✂	**For two, please.**	Para dos, por favor.	pa·ra dos por fa·vor

I'd like the (non)smoking section, please.	Quisiera el área de (no) fumar, por favor. kee·*sye*·ra el a·re·a de (no) foo·*mar* por fa·*vor*
We're just having drinks.	Sólo queremos tomar algo. so·lo ke·*re*·mos to·*mar* al·go
Just drinks.	Sólo bebidas. so·lo be·*bee*·das
I'd like the drinks list, please.	Quisiera la carta de bebidas, por favor. kee·*sye*·ra la *kar*·ta de be·*bee*·das por fa·*vor*
I'd like the menu, please.	Quisiera la carta, por favor. kee·*sye*·ra la *kar*·ta por fa·*vor*
Menu, please.	La carta, por favor. la *kar*·ta por fa·*vor*
Do you have a menu (in English)?	¿Tienen una carta (en inglés)? *tye*·nen oo·na *kar*·ta (en een·*gles*)

🔊 LISTEN FOR

No tenemos mesas.	no te·*ne*·mos *me*·sas We have no tables.
Estamos llenos.	es·*ta*·mos *ye*·nos We're fully booked.
Ya cerramos.	ya se·*ra*·mos We're closed.
¿Dónde le gustaría sentarse?	*don*·de le goos·ta·*ree*·a sen·*tar*·se Where would you like to sit?

FOOD EATING OUT

Do you have children's meals?	¿Tienen menú infantil? *tye*·nen me·*noo* een·fan·*teel*
What would you recommend?	¿Qué recomienda? ke re·ko·*myen*·da
What's in that dish?	¿Qué tiene ese platillo? ke *tye*·ne *e*·se pla·*tee*·yo
Does it take long to prepare?	¿Se tarda mucho en prepararlo? se *tar*·da *moo*·cho en pre·pa·*rar*·lo

For dishes and ingredients, see the **menu decoder** (p189).

Requests

Please bring us (a serviette).	Por favor, nos trae (una servilleta). por fa·*vor* nos *tra*·e (*oo*·na ser·vee·*ye*·ta)

🔊 LISTEN FOR

¿Quiere tomar algo?	*kye*·re to·*mar al*·go Would you like a drink?
¿Qué desea ordenar?	ke de·*se*·a or·de·*nar* What can I get for you?
¿Cómo lo quiere preparado?	*ko*·mo lo *kye*·re pre·pa·*ra*·do How would you like that cooked?
¿Le gusta ...?	le *goos*·ta ... Do you like ...?
Le recomiendo ...	le re·ko·*myen*·do ... I suggest the ...
Aquí tiene.	a·*kee tye*·ne Here you go!

Eating Out

Can I see the menu, please?

¿Puedo ver la carta, por favor?
pwe·do ver la kar·ta por fa·vor

What would you recommend for ...?

¿Qué recomienda para ...?
ke re·ko·myen·da pa·ra ...

 the main meal
el plato fuerte
el *pla·*to *fwer·*te

 dessert
postre
*pos·*tre

 drinks
beber
be·*ber*

Can you bring me some ..., please?

Por favor me trae ...
por fa·*vor* me *tra·*e ...

I'd like the bill, please.

Quisiera la cuenta, por favor.
*kee·sye·*ra la *kwen·*ta por fa·*vor*

Is there any (chilli sauce)?	¿Hay (salsa picante)? ai (*sal*·sa pee·*kan*·te)
I'd like it ...	Lo quiero ... lo *kye*·ro ...
I don't want it ...	No lo quiero ... no lo *kye*·ro ...

boiled	hervido/a **m/f**	er·*vee*·do/a
broiled	asado/a a la parrilla **m/f**	a·*sa*·do/a a la pa·*ree*·ya
deep-fried	sumergido/a en aceite **m/f**	soo·mer·*khee*·do/a en a·*say*·te
fried	frito/a **m/f**	*free*·to/a
grilled	a la parilla	a la pa·*ree*·ya
medium	término medio	*ter*·mee·no *me*·dyo
rare	roja	*ro*·kha
reheated	recalentado/a **m/f**	re·ka·len·*ta*·do/a
steamed	al vapor	al va·*por*
well done	bien cocido/a **m/f**	byen ko·*see*·do/a
with (the dressing on the side)	con (el aderezo aparte)	kon (el a·de·*re*·so a·*par*·te)
without (chilli)	sin (chile)	seen (*chee*·le)

Compliments & Complaints

That was delicious!	¡Estaba delicioso! es·*ta*·ba de·lee·*syo*·so
I love this dish.	Me encanta este platillo. me en·*kan*·ta es·te pla·*tee*·yo
I love the local cuisine.	Me encanta la comida típica. me en·*kan*·ta la ko·*mee*·da *tee*·pee·ka

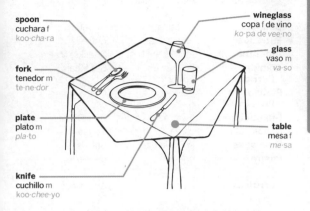

spoon
cuchara f
koo·*cha*·ra

fork
tenedor m
te·ne·*dor*

plate
plato m
pla·to

knife
cuchillo m
koo·*chee*·yo

wineglass
copa f de vino
ko·pa de *vee*·no

glass
vaso m
va·so

table
mesa f
me·sa

FOOD EATING OUT

| I'm full. | Estoy satisfecho/a. m/f |
| | es·*toy* sa·tees·*fe*·cho/a |

| My compliments to the chef. | Mis felicitaciones al chef. |
| | mees fe·lee·see·ta·*syo*·nes al chef |

| This is ... | Esto está ... |
| | *es*·to es·*ta* ... |

burnt	quemado	ke·*ma*·do
cold	frío	*free*·o
hot	caliente	kal·*yen*·te
(too) spicy	(muy) picante	(mooy) pee·*kan*·te
superb	exquisito	es·kee·*see*·to

🔍 LOOK FOR

Botanas	bo·*ta*·nas	Appetisers
Entradas	en·*tra*·das	Entrees
Antojitos	an·to·*khee*·tos	Snacks/Meals
Comida Corrida	ko·*mee*·da ko·*ree*·da	Set Meals
Platillo Principal	pla·*tee*·yo preen·see·*pal*	Main Course
Guarniciones	gwar·nee·*syo*·nes	Side Dishes
Sopas	*so*·pas	Soups
Ensaladas	en·sa·*la*·das	Salads
Postre	*pos*·tre	Desserts
Aperitivos	a·pe·ree·*tee*·vos	Aperitifs
Bebidas	be·bee·*das*	Drinks
Aguas Frescas	*a*·gwas *fres*·kas	Fruit Drinks
Refrescos	re·*fres*·kos	Soft Drinks
Licores	lee·*ko*·res	Spirits
Cervezas	ser·*ve*·sas	Beers
Vinos Blancos	*vee*·nos *blan*·kos	White Wines
Vinos Dulces	*vee*·nos *dool*·ses	Dessert Wines
Vinos Espumosos	*vee*·nos es·poo·*mo*·sos	Sparkling Wines
Vinos Tintos	*vee*·nos *teen*·tos	Red Wines
Digestivos	dee·khes·*tee*·vos	Digestifs

Paying the Bill

Please bring us the bill.	Por favor, nos trae la cuenta.	por fa·*vor* nos *tra*·e la *kwen*·ta

✂	**Bill, please.**	La cuenta, por favor.	la *kwen*·ta por fa·*vor*

Is service included in the bill?	¿La cuenta incluye el servicio? la *kwen*·ta een·*kloo*·ye el ser·*vee*·syo
There's a mistake in the bill.	Hay un error en la cuenta. ai oon e·*ror* en la *kwen*·ta

For more on paying bills, see **money & banking** (p90).

Nonalcoholic Drinks

coffee	café m ka·*fe*
juice	jugo m *khoo*·go
lemonade	limonada f lee·mo·*na*·da
milk	leche f *le*·che
milkshake	malteada f mal·te·*a*·da licuado m lee·*kwa*·do
orangeade	naranjada f na·ran·*kha*·da
rice water	horchata f or·*cha*·ta
soft drink (general)	refresco m re·*fres*·ko
soft drink (north Mexico)	soda f *so*·da
tea	té m te
with (milk)	con (leche) kon (*le*·che)
without (sugar)	sin (azúcar) seen (a·*soo*·kar)

CULTURE TIP

Tex-Mex Cuisine
Some foods that you may have thought were Mexican – such as fajitas, burritos and nachos – are actually all from Texas. Some say these dishes are a pale imitation of Mexican food, while others claim Tex-Mex cuisine belongs in a class of its own. Homesick Texans should order *tacos dorados ta·kos do·ra·dos* (deep-fried tacos) if they need a bit of crunch.

... water	agua ...	
	a·gwa ...	
boiled	hervida	er·*vee*·da
fruit mixed with	de fruta	de *froo*·ta
hibiscus-flower	de jamaica	de kha·*may*·ka
lime	de limón	de lee·*mon*
mineral	mineral	mee·ne·*ral*
sparkling	con gas	kon gas
still	sin gas	seen gas
tamarind	de tamarindo	de ta·ma·*reen*·do

Alcoholic Drinks

a shot of (gin)	un shot de (ginebra)
	oon shot de (khee·*ne*·bra)
champagne	champán **m**
	cham·*pan*
cocktail	coctel **m**
	kok·*tel*
rum	ron **m**
	ron

FOOD EATING OUT

a bottle/glass of ... wine	una botella/copa de vino ...
	oo·na bo·te·ya/ko·pa de vee·no ...

dessert	dulce	*dool*·se
red	tinto	*teen*·to
rose	rosado	ro·*sa*·do
sparkling	espumoso	es·poo·*mo*·so
white	blanco	*blan*·ko

a ... of beer	... de cerveza
	... de ser·*ve*·sa

glass	un tarro	oon *ta*·ro
jug	una jarra	oo·na *kha*·ra
large bottle (940ml)	una caguama	oo·na ka·*gwa*·ma
small bottle (325ml)	una botella	oo·na bo·*te*·ya

In the Bar

Excuse me!	¡Oiga!
	oy·ga
I'm next.	Sigo yo.
	see·go yo
I'll buy you a drink.	Te invito una copa.
	te een·*vee*·to oo·na *ko*·pa
Q What would you like?	¿Qué quieres tomar?
	ke *kye*·res to·*mar*
A I'll have (a shot of tequila).	Quiero (un caballo de tequila).
	kye·ro (oon ka·*ba*·yo de te·*kee*·la)

CULTURE TIP Mexican Spirits

mezcal m — mes·*kal*
liquor distilled from agave

posh/pox m — posh
sugar-cane liquor flavoured with herbs

pulque m — *pool*·ke
alcohol from fermented agave sap

rompope m — rom·*po*·pe
eggnog with sugar-cane alcohol and cinnamon

tepache m — te·*pa*·che
alcohol from fermented pineapple rinds

tequila f — te·*kee*·la
popular spirit distilled from the *maguey* plant

A I'd like a beer, please.	Quisiera una cerveza, por favor. kee·*sye*·ra oo·na ser·*ve*·sa por fa·*vor*
Same again, please.	Otro igual, por favor. o·tro ee·*gwal* por fa·*vor*
No ice, please.	Sin hielo, por favor. seen *ye*·lo por fa·*vor*
It's my round.	Yo invito esta ronda. yo een·*vee*·to *es*·ta *ron*·da
You can get the next one.	Tu invitas la que sigue. too een·*vee*·tas la ke *see*·ge
Do you serve meals here?	¿Sirven comidas aquí? *seer*·ven ko·*mee*·das a·*kee*

Drinking Up

Cheers!	¡Salud! sa·*lood*
Thanks, but I don't feel like it.	Gracias, pero no se me antoja. *gra*·syas *pe*·ro no se me an·*to*·kha
I don't drink alcohol.	No bebo. no *be*·bo
This is hitting the spot.	Es justo lo que necesitaba. es *khoo*·sto lo ke ne·se·see·*ta*·ba
I think I've had one too many.	Creo que he tomado demasiado. *kre*·o ke e to·*ma*·do de·ma·*sya*·do
I'm feeling drunk.	Se me está subiendo mucho. se me es·*ta* soo·*byen*·do *moo*·cho
I'm pissed.	Estoy pedo. es·*toy pe*·do
I feel ill.	Me siento mal. me *syen*·to mal

🔎 LOOK FOR

In Mexico, toilets are widely known as *baños ba*·nyos, while public toilets may also advertise themselves as *sanitarios* sa·nee·*ta*·ryos or *servicios* ser·*vee*·syos.

Caballeros	ka·ba·*ye*·ros	Gentlemen
Damas	*da*·mas	Ladies
Hombres	*om*·bres	Men
Mujeres	moo·*khe*·res	Women
Señores	sen·*yo*·res	Sirs
Señoras	sen·*yo*·ras	Madams

Self-Catering

KEY PHRASES

What's the local speciality?	¿Cuál es la especialidad de la zona?	kwal es la es·pe·sya·lee·*dad* de la *so*·na
Where can I find the ... section?	¿Dónde está la sección de ...?	*don*·de es·*ta* la sek·*syon* de ...
I'd like some ...	Quisiera algunos/as ... m/f	kee·*sye*·ra al·*goo*·nos/as ...

Buying Food

How much is (a kilo of cheese)?	¿Cuánto vale (un kilo de queso)? *kwan*·to *va*·le (oon *kee*·lo de *ke*·so)
Do you sell locally produced food?	¿Vende productos de la región? *ven*·de pro·*dook*·tos de la re·*khyon*
What's the local speciality?	¿Cuál es la especialidad de la zona? kwal es la es·pe·sya·lee·*dad* de la *so*·na
Do you sell organic produce?	¿Vende productos biológicos? *ven*·de pro·*dook*·tos bee·o·*lo*·khee·kos
Can I taste it?	¿Puedo probarlo? *pwe*·do pro·*bar*·lo

I'd like ... Quisiera ...
kee·sye·ra ...

(100) grams	(cien) gramos	(syen) gra·mos
a kilo	un kilo	oon kee·lo
(two) kilos	(dos) kilos	(dos) kee·los
a bottle	una botella	oo·na bo·te·ya
a dozen	una docena	oo·na do·sen·a
a jar	una jarra	oo·na kha·ra
a packet	un paquete	oon pa·ke·te
a piece	una pieza	oo·na pye·sa
(three) pieces	(tres) piezas	(tres) pye·sas
a slice	una rebanada	oo·na re·ba·na·da
(six) slices	(seis) rebanadas	(says) re·ba·na·das
a tin	una lata	oo·na la·ta
that one	ése/ésa m/f	e·se/e·sa
this one	ésto	es·to
a bit more	un poco más	oon po·ko mas
less	menos	me·nos

| That's enough, thanks. | Así está bien, gracias. |
| | a·see es·ta byen gra·syas |

| Do you have anything cheaper? | ¿Tiene algo más barato? |
| | tye·ne al·go mas ba·ra·to |

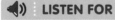 **LISTEN FOR**

| Se me terminó. | se me ter·mee·no | There's none left. |
| ¿Algo más? | al·go mas | Anything else? |

FOOD SELF-CATERING

Do you have any other kinds?	¿Tiene otros tipos?
	tye·ne o·tros tee·pos
Where can I find the ... section?	¿Dónde está la sección de ...?
	don·de es·ta la sek·syon de ...

dairy	lácteos	lak·te·os
fish and seafood	pescados y mariscos	pes·ka·dos ee ma·rees·kos
frozen goods	productos congelados	pro·dook·tos kon·khe·la·dos
fruit and vegetable	frutas y verduras	froo·tas ee ver·doo·ras
meat	carnes	kar·nes
poultry	aves	a·ves

Cooking

Could I please borrow (a)?	¿Me puede prestar ...?
	me pwe·de pres·tar ...

chopping board	una tabla para picar	oo·na ta·bla pa·ra pee·kar
corkscrew	un sacacorchos	oon sa·ka·kor·chos
saucepan	una olla	oo·na o·ya

CULTURE TIP

Market Munchies

The glory of fresh food in a Mexican market can really work up your appetite. For a cheap local meal in a rowdy atmosphere, grab a seat at a *comedor* ko·me·dor (lit: eatery) usually found in the centre of the market.

GREG ELMS / GETTY IMAGES ©

¿Puedo probarlo?
pwe·do pro·bar·lo
Can I taste it?

FOOD SELF-CATERING

Where's (a frying pan)?	¿Dónde hay (un sartén)? *don·de ai (oon sar·ten)*
cooked	cocido/a m/f *ko·see·do/a*
dried	seco/a m/f *se·ko/a*
fresh	fresco/a m/f *fres·ko/a*
frozen	congelado/a m/f *kon·khe·la·do/a*
raw	crudo/a m/f *kroo·do/a*

For more cooking implements, see the **dictionary**.

Vegetarian & Special Meals

KEY PHRASES

Do you have vegetarian food?	¿Tienen comida vegetariana?	tye·nen ko·mee·da ve·khe·ta·rya·na
Could you prepare a meal without ...?	¿Me puede preparar una comida sin ...?	me pwe·de pre·pa·rar oo·na ko·mee·da seen ...
I'm allergic to ...	Soy alérgico/a a ... m/f	soy a·ler·khee·ko/a a ...

Special Diets & Allergies

Is there a (vegetarian) restaurant near here?	¿Hay un restaurante (vegetariano) por aquí? ai oon res·tow·ran·te (ve·khe·ta·rya·no) por a·kee
Do you have vegetarian food?	¿Tienen comida vegetariana? tye·nen ko·mee·da ve·khe·ta·rya·na
Do you have halal/kosher food?	¿Tienen comida halal/kosher? tye·nen ko·mee·da kha·lal/ko·sher
I'm (vegan).	Soy (vegetariano/a estricto/a). m/f soy (ve·khe·ta·rya·no/a es·treek·to/a)
I'm on a special diet.	Estoy a dieta especial. es·toy a dye·ta es·pe·syal

I don't eat (meat).	No como (carne).	no *ko*·mo (*kar*·ne)
I'm allergic to ...	Soy alérgico/a ... m/f	soy a·*ler*·khee·ko/a ...

dairy produce	a los productos lácteos	a los pro·*dook*·tos *lak*·te·os
eggs	a los huevos	a los *we*·vos
gelatin	a la gelatina	a la khe·la·*tee*·na
gluten	al gluten	al *gloo*·ten
nuts	a las nueces	a las *nwe*·ses
peanuts	a los cacahuates	a los ka·ka·*wa*·tes
seafood	a los mariscos	a los ma·*rees*·kos
shellfish	a los moluscos	a los mo·*loos*·kos
wheat products	a los productos de trigo	a los pro·*dook*·tos de *tree*·go

Ordering Food

Is it cooked in/with (oil)?	¿Está cocinado en/con (aceite)?	es·*ta* ko·see·*na*·do en/con (a·*say*·te)

🔊 LISTEN FOR

¿Puede comer ...?	*pwe*·de ko·*mer* ...	
	Can you eat ...?	
Le preguntaré al cocinero.	le pre·goon·ta·*re* al ko·see·*ne*·ro	
	I'll check with the cook.	
Todo tiene (carne).	*to*·do *tye*·ne (*kar*·ne)	
	It all has (meat) in it.	

Is this ...?   ¿Esto es ...?
                                    es·to es ...

decaffeinated	descafeinado	des·ka·fay·*na*·do
free of animal produce	sin productos animales	seen pro·*dook*·tos a·nee·*ma*·les
free range	de corral	de ko·*ral*
genetically modified	transgénico	trans·*khe*·nee·ko
gluten-free	sin gluten	seen *gloo*·ten
low-fat	bajo en grasas	*ba*·kho en *gra*·sas
low in sugar	bajo en azúcar	*ba*·kho en a·*soo*·kar
organic	biológico	bee·o·*lo*·khee·ko
salt-free	sin sal	seen sal

Could you prepare a meal without ...?   ¿Me puede preparar una comida sin ...?
                                            me pwe·de pre·pa·rar oo·na ko·mee·da seen ...

butter	mantequilla	man·te·*kee*·ya
chicken stock	caldo de gallina	*kal*·do de ga·*yee*·na
eggs	huevos	*we*·vos
fish	pescado	pes·*ka*·do
lard	manteca	man·*te*·ka
(red) meat	carne (roja)	*kar*·ne (*ro*·kha)
meat/fish stock	consomé de carne/pescado	kon·so·*me* de *kar*·ne/pes·*ka*·do
pork	cerdo	*ser*·do
poultry	aves	*a*·ves

Menu
~ DECODER ~
léxico culinario

This miniguide to Mexican cuisine lists dishes and ingredients in Spanish alphabetical order (see **alphabet**, p12). Spanish nouns have their gender indicated by ⓜ or ⓕ. If it's a plural noun, you'll also see pl.

A

~ A ~

abulón ⓜ a·boo·*lon* abalone

aceite ⓜ a·*say*·te oil

— de girasol de khee·ra·*sol* sunflower oil

— de oliva de o·*lee*·va olive oil

— vegetal ve·khe·*tal* vegetable oil

aceituna ⓕ a·say·*too*·na olive

— negra ne·gra black olive

— verde ver·de green olive

acitrón ⓜ a·see·*tron* cactus prepared as a candy but also used in savoury dishes

acocil ⓜ a·ko·*seel* small red shrimp

achiote ⓜ a·*chyo*·te red, musky-flavoured spice used as a colouring agent in **mole** & other foods (also called **annatto**)

adobo ⓜ a·*do*·bo paste of garlic, vinegar, herbs & chillies – can be used as a sauce, marinade or pickling agent

agave ⓜ a·*ga*·ve American aloe, also known as 'century plant' – source of alcoholic beverages such as **pulque**, **mezcal** & **tequila**

— azul a·*sool* blue agave – used to produce **tequila** & **mezcal**

agua ⓕ a·gwa water

— caliente ka·*lyen*·te hot water

— con gas kon gas soda water · carbonated water

— de Jamaica de kha·*mai*·ka drink made by steeping dried hibiscus flowers in warm water – served chilled

— de la llave de la ya·ve tap water

— de manantial de ma·nan·*tyal* spring water

— embotellada em·bo·te·*ya*·da bottled water

— fresca fres·ka fruit-flavoured water

— fría free·a cold water

— mineral mee·ne·*ral* mineral water

— purificada poo·ree·fee·*ka*·da purified water

— quina kee·na tonic water

— sin gas seen gas still mineral water

— tónica to·*nee*·ka tonic water

aguacate ⓜ a·gwa·ka·te avocado

aguamiel ⓜ a·gwa·*myel* agave juice

aguardiente ⓜ a·gwar·*dyen*·te sugar cane alcohol

ajo ⓜ a·kho garlic

ajonjolí ⓜ a·khon·kho·*lee* sesame seeds

B

albahaca ① *al·ba·*ka sweet basil
albóndigas ① pl al·*bon·*dee·gas meatballs
alcachofa ① al·ka·cho·fa artichoke
alcaparras ① al·ka·*pa·*ras capers
alegrías ① pl a·le·*gree·*as sweet cake made of amaranth seeds & molasses
alfajor de coco al·fa·*khor* de *ko·*ko pastry filled with jam & sprinkled with grated coconut
algodón de azúcar al·go·*don* de a·*soo·*kar fairy floss • cotton candy
alimentos ⑩ pl a·lee·*men·*tos food
almeja ① al·*me·*kha clam • scallop
almendra ① al·*men·*dra almond
almuerzo ⑩ al·*mwer·*so brunch, also translated as 'lunch' – a late-morning snack typically consisting of a quick plate of **tacos** or a sandwich
alubia ① a·*loo·*bya haricot bean
amaranto ⑩ a·ma·*ran·*to amaranth (a native plant similar to spinach)
anchoa ① an·*cho·*a anchovy
anguila ① an·*gee·*la eel
anís ⑩ a·*nees* anise • aniseed (used in desserts, liqueurs & breads)
annatto a·*na·*to see **achiote**
antojitos ⑩ pl an·to·*khee·*tos 'little whimsies' – small portions of classic Mexican dishes, such as **quesadillas**, **sopes** & **tostadas**, served as snack food for street eating or as appetisers
añejo/a ⑩/① a·*nye·*kho/a 'aged' – describes cheeses, meat & **tequila**
apio ⑩ a·*pyo* celery
arándano ⑩ a·*ran·*da·no bilberry
— agrio a·gryo cranberry
arenque ⑩ a·*ren·*ke herring • kipper
arroz ⑩ a·*ros* rice
— a la Mexicana a la me·khee·*ka·*na 'Mexican rice' – may be coloured red with tomatoes & cooked with diced carrots & peas
— a la poblana a la po·*bla·*na pilaf with **chile poblano**, corn & melted cheese

— con leche kon *le·*che rice pudding
— de grano corto de *gra·*no *kor·*to short-grain rice
— glutinoso gloo·tee·*no·*so glutinous rice
— integral een·te·*gral* brown rice
— salvaje sal·*va·*khe wild rice
— verde *ver·*de green rice, made with **chile poblano**
asadero ⑩ a·sa·*de·*ro white cheese used in **quesadillas**
atole ⑩ a·*to·*le thin porridge or gruel of maize flour or cornflour, usually served hot for breakfast
— de chocolate de cho·ko·*la·*te chocolate **atole**
— de fresa de *fre·*sa strawberry **atole**
— de nuez de *nwes* nut **atole**
— de vainilla de vai·*nee·*ya vanilla **atole**
atún ⑩ a·*toon* tuna
avellana ① a·ve·*ya·*na hazelnut
avena ① a·*ve·*na rolled oats – a breakfast staple usually served with milk
azafrán ⑩ a·sa·*fran* saffron
azúcar ⑩ a·*soo·*kar sugar
— blanca *blan·*ka white sugar
— morena mo·*re·*na brown sugar

~ B ~

bacalao ⑩ ba·ka·*la·*o cod – usually dried
balché ⑩ bal·*che* Mayan alcoholic drink made from the fermented bark of the balché tree
banderillas ① pl ban·de·*ree·*yas long flaky pastries
barbacoa ① bar·ba·*ko·*a Mexican-style barbecue – a lamb, goat or chicken is steamed with vegetables, then baked in the ground
bebida ① be·*bee·*da drink
— alcohólica al·ko·*lee·*ka alcoholic drink

berenjena ⓕ be·ren·*khe*·na
aubergine • eggplant
betabel ⓜ be·ta·*bel* beet • beetroot
birria ⓕ *bee*·rya soupy stew made
with meat (usually goat) in a tomato-
based broth
bistec ⓜ bees·*tek* steak (beef)
blanquillos ⓜ pl blan·*kee*·yos eggs
(also **huevos**)
bolillo ⓜ bo·*lee*·yo large, French-style
bread roll, served with most meals
borrego ⓜ bo·*re*·go lamb (see also
cordero)
botana ⓕ bo·*ta*·na appetiser
botella ⓕ bo·*te*·ya bottle
brocheta ⓕ bro·*che*·ta skewer •
kebab
brócoli ⓜ *bro*·ko·lee broccoli
buey ⓜ bway ox
buñuelo ⓜ boo·*nywe*·lo tortilla-
sized fritter sprinkled with sugar &
cinnamon

~ **C** ~

cabra ⓕ *ka*·bra goat
cabrito ⓜ ka·*bree*·to milk-fed kid
rubbed with butter or oil & seasoned
with salt, pepper & lime, then roasted
whole on a spit
cacahuates ⓜ pl ka·ka·*wa*·tes
peanuts
— japoneses kha·po·*ne*·ses
Japanese-style peanuts, covered with
a crunchy coating
cacao ⓜ ka·*ka*·o cocoa
café ⓜ ka·*fe* cafe • coffee
— con leche kon *le*·che coffee with
milk
— de olla de *o*·ya coffee flavoured
with cinnamon & sweetened with
piloncillo
— expresso ek·*spre*·so espresso
cajeta ⓕ ka·*khe*·ta goat's milk
caramel
calabacita ⓕ ka·la·ba·*see*·ta zuc-
chini • courgette • vegetable marrow

calabaza ⓕ ka·la·*ba*·sa pumpkin •
squash
calamar ⓜ ka·la·*mar* squid
calaveras ⓕ pl ka·la·*ve*·ras
confectionery skulls eaten to
celebrate the Day of the Dead
— de azúcar de a·*soo*·kar skulls
made from sugar
— de chocolate de cho·ko·*la*·te
skulls made from chocolate
caldo ⓜ *kal*·do broth
— tlalpeño tlal·*pe*·nyo vegetable
soup
— xóchitl so·cheetl fiery hot soup
with serrano peppers on top
camarón ⓜ ka·ma·*ron* prawn •
shrimp
— para pelar *pa*·ra pe·*lar* whole
shrimp boiled in a very weak broth,
milled & then served with lime
camote ⓜ ka·*mo*·te sweet potato
canela ⓕ ka·*ne*·la cinnamon
cangrejo ⓜ kan·*gre*·kho crab (also
jaiba)
— moro *mo*·ro stone crab
caña ⓕ **de azúcar** *ka*·nya de
a·*soo*·kar sugar cane
capeado ⓜ ka·pe·*a*·do fried,
battered meat or vegetables
capirotada ⓕ ka·pee·ro·*ta*·da
Mexican-style bread pudding
capulines ⓜ pl ka·poo·*lee*·nes black
cherries
cardo ⓜ *kar*·do cardoon (vegetable
similar to an artichoke)
carne ⓕ *kar*·ne meat
— asada a·*sa*·da thinly cut, broiled
tenderloin or steak, served with
sliced onion & grilled sweet pepper
strips, rice, beans & **guacamole**
— a la Tampiqueña a la
tam·pee·*ke*·nya plate piled with a
small piece of meat, **chile poblano**,
a **taco** or **enchilada**, beans,
guacamole & shredded lettuce
— de cerdo de *ser*·do pork

C

C

— **de res** de res beef

— **de vaca** de *va*·ka beef

— **molida** mo·*lee*·da mince meat

— **para asar** *pa*·ra a·*sar* brisket

— **para taquear** *pa*·ra ta·*ke*·ar meat for use in **tacos**

carnero ⓜ kar·*ne*·ro mutton

carnitas ⓕ pl kar·*nee*·tas slow-simmered chunks of seasoned pork served on **tortillas** with salsa, chopped onion & fresh coriander

cáscara ⓕ *kas*·ka·ra rind • shell • husk

castaña ⓕ kas·*ta*·nya chestnut

cátsup ⓜ *kat*·soop tomato sauce • ketchup

caza ⓕ *ca*·sa game (animals)

cebada ⓕ se·*ba*·da barley

cebolla ⓕ se·*bo*·ya onion

— **blanca** *blan*·ka white onion

— **de Cambray** de kam·*bray* spring onion

— **morada** mo·*ra*·da red onion • Spanish onion

cena ⓕ *se*·na supper • dinner

cerdo ⓜ *ser*·do pig • pork

cereal ⓜ se·re·*al* cereal

cerveza ⓕ ser·*ve*·sa beer

— **amarga** a·*mar*·ga bitter

— **clara** *kla*·ra blonde beer • light beer

— **de barril** de ba·*reel* draught beer

— **oscura** os·*koo*·ra stout

ceviche ⓜ se·*vee*·che cocktail with fish, shrimp, oysters or crab, mixed with onion, coriander & tomato

chabacano ⓜ cha·ba·*ka*·no apricot

chalote ⓜ cha·*lo*·te shallot onion

chalupas ⓕ pl cha·*loo*·pas small **tortillas** made with cornflour, chilli, beans & cheese

chamorro ⓜ cha·*mo*·ro leg of pork marinated in **adobo** then oven-roasted at a very low heat

champiñones ⓜ pl cham·pee·*nyo*·nes mushrooms

champurrado ⓜ cham·poo·*ra*·do similar to **atole** but made with chocolate, water & cornflour

chapulín ⓜ cha·poo·*leen* grasshopper

charal ⓜ cha·*ral* sardine-like fish

chaya ⓕ *cha*·ya type of spinach

chayote ⓜ cha·*yo*·te popular type of squash, stuffed & baked or used raw in salad

chícharo ⓜ *chee*·cha·ro pea

— **seco** *se*·ko green split pea

— **verde** *ver*·de snap pea

chicharra ⓕ chee·*cha*·ra cricket

chicharrones ⓜ pl chee·cha·*ro*·nes deep-fried pork rinds, usually sold by street vendors with a topping • flour-based fried snack

chilaquiles ⓜ pl chee·la·*kee*·les crisp **tortillas** topped with chicken, onion, cream, fresh cheese & salsa; sometimes made with scrambled eggs & **chorizo**

chile ⓜ *chee*·le chilli – a huge variety of fresh & dried chillies is available at markets, sometimes pickled

— **ancho** *an*·cho 'broad chilli' – has wrinkled, reddish-brown skin & is the most common form of dried **chile poblano**

— **cayena** ka·*ye*·na cayenne

— **chipotles** chee·*pot*·les smoke-dried version of **chile jalapeño**

— **dulce en adobo** *dool*·se en a·*do*·bo sweet, non-spicy pickled chilli

— **en nogada** en no·*ga*·da a green **chile poblano** stuffed with a stew of beef & fruits, topped with **nogada** & decorated with pomegranate seeds

— **guajillo** gwa·*khee*·yo very hot, dried chilli, almost black in colour

— **habanero** a·ba·*ne*·ro extremely hot type of chilli

— **jalapeño** kha·la·*pe*·nyo Jalapeno pepper, often eaten in pickled form

— **mulato** moo·*la*·to dried **chile**

poblano – its almost-black colour means it can be substituted for **chilhuacle negro** in the dish **mole negro**

— pasilla pa·see·ya dark, dried & very spicy chile used in **mole** and marinades

— poblano po·bla·no medium-green to purple-black chilli, sometimes dried to produce **chile ancho** & **chile mulato** – this mildly hot, arrow-shaped chilli is also used for making stuffed peppers

— relleno re·ye·no green **chile poblano** stuffed with cheese, covered in egg batter & fried

— serrano se·ra·no fiery green chilli used in **moles** & **salsa**

chilhuacle ⓜ **negro** cheel·wa·kle ne·gro very dark, spicy strain of **chilhuacle**, a chilli about the shape & size of a small bell pepper

chilpachole ⓜ **de Jaiba** cheel·pa·cho·le de khai·ba a soup made with crab

chirimoya ⓕ chee·ree·mo·ya custard apple • cherimoya

chocolate ⓜ **oaxaqueño** cho·ko·la·te wa·ha·ke·nyo chocolate from Oaxaca mixed with hot milk

chongos ⓜ pl **zamoranos** chon·gos sa·mo·ra·nos popular dessert of curdled milk, sugar, cinnamon & egg yolks

choriqueso ⓜ cho·ree·ke·so **chorizo** & melted cheese

chorizo cho·ree·so spicy pork sausage, fried with eggs as breakfast, or cooked with potatoes as a filling for **tacos**

chuletas ⓕ choo·le·tas chops

— de cerdo de ser·do pork chops

— de res de res small beef steaks

churro ⓜ choo·ro long doughnut covered with sugar

cidra ⓕ see·dra cider

cilantro ⓜ see·lan·tro coriander • cilantro

ciruela ⓕ see·rwe·la plum

— pasa pa·sa prune

clayuda ⓕ kla·yoo·da large, crisp **tortilla** with toppings (also **tlayuda**)

cocada ⓕ ko·ka·da traditional candy made with coconut, eggs, milk, almonds & sugar

coco ⓜ ko·ko coconut

coctel ⓜ kok·tel cocktail

— de camarón de ka·ma·ron shrimp cocktail

cochinita ⓕ **pibil** ko·chee·nee·ta pee·beel pork cooked with **achiote**, red onions & orange juice

codorniz ⓕ ko·dor·nees quail

col ⓕ kol cabbage

cola ⓕ ko·la tail

coles ⓕ pl **de Bruselas** ko·les de broo·se·las Brussels sprouts

coliflor ⓕ ko·lee·flor cauliflower

comida ⓕ ko·mee·da food • lunch (the biggest meal of the day, taken between 1pm and 4pm)

comino ⓜ ko·mee·no cumin

conchas ⓕ pl **de vainilla** kon·chas de vay·nee·ya mini loaves topped with vanilla icing

conchas ⓕ pl **de chocolate** kon·chas de cho·ko·la·te mini loaves topped with chocolate icing

conejillo ⓜ **de indias** ko·ne·khee·yo de een·dyas guinea pig

conejo ⓜ ko·ne·kho rabbit

consomé kal·do meat broth • stock

— de camarón de ka·ma·ron prawn soup

— de pollo de po·yo chicken broth • soup with chicken, vegetables & sometimes rice & chickpeas

— de res de res beef & vegetable soup

corazón ⓜ ko·ra·son heart

cordero ⓜ kor·de·ro lamb • mutton

corundas ⓕ pl ko·roon·das little **tamales**

D

costillas ⓕ pl kos·*tee*·yas ribs
crema ⓕ *kre*·ma cream
— **ácida** a·*see*·da sour cream
— **batida** ba·*tee*·da whipping cream
— **chantilly** chan·tee·*yee* chantilly
— **espesa** es·*pe*·sa clotted cream
crepas ⓕ pl *kre*·pas crepes
croqueta ⓕ kro·*ke*·ta croquette
Cuba ⓕ **libre** koo·ba *lee*·bre rum &
cola (also simply called 'Cuba')
cubierta ⓕ koo·*byer*·ta topping
cubiertos ⓜ pl koo·*byer*·tos cutlery
cuerno ⓜ *kwer*·no croissant
cuitlacoche ⓜ kwee·tla·ko·che black
corn fungus (also **huitlacoche**)
culebra ⓕ koo·*le*·bra snake
cúrcuma ⓕ *koor*·koo·ma turmeric
curry ⓜ *koo*·ree curry
— **en polvo** en *pol*·vo curry powder
cus cus ⓜ koos koos cous cous

~ **D** ~

dátiles ⓜ pl *da*·tee·les dates
desayuno ⓜ de·sa·*yoo*·no breakfast
– Mexicans usually eat eggs or meat
for breakfast, including one or more
staples such as **tortillas**, beans,
chillies & **atole**
diente ⓜ **de ajo** *dyen*·te de a·*kho*
clove of garlic
dona ⓕ *do*·na doughnut
dulce ⓜ *dool*·se sweet • candy
durazno ⓜ doo·*ras*·no peach

~ **E** ~

elote ⓜ e·*lo*·te maize • corn
— **tierno** *tyer*·no sweet corn
empanada ⓕ em·pa·*na*·da pastry
turnover with a savoury meat &
vegetable filling, baked or fried, or
filled with fruit & served as a dessert
encebollado en·se·bo·*ya*·do served
with onion

encurtidos ⓜ pl en·koor·*tee*·dos
table condiment consisting of a
bowl of chillies marinated in vinegar,
combined with onions, carrots &
other vegetables
enchiladas ⓕ pl en·chee·*la*·das
meat or cheese wrapped in **tortillas**
& smothered in red or green salsa,
cream & melted cheese
— **adobadas** a·do·*ba*·das beef or
chicken **enchiladas** in **adobo** sauce
— **queretanas** ke·re·*ta*·nas fresh
enchiladas topped with shredded
lettuce & other raw vegetables
— **rojas** *ro*·khas meat or cheese
enchiladas with a red **chile ancho
sauce**, the most popular **enchiladas**
on menus
— **suizas** *swee*·sas mild & creamy
Swiss-style **enchiladas** filled with
chicken or cheese, served with
creamy green tomato sauce
— **verdes** *ver*·des served with a
delicate green **tomatillo** sauce
endivia ⓕ en·*dee*·vya endive
enebro ⓜ e·*ne*·bro juniper
eneldo ⓜ e·*nel*·do dill
enfrijolado/a ⓜ/ⓕ
en·free·kho·*la*·do/a anything cooked
in a bean sauce, most commonly
corn **tortillas** in a smooth black bean
sauce & topped with thinly sliced
onions, cream & crumbed cheese
enmolado/a ⓜ/ⓕ en·mo·*la*·do/a
anything cooked in a **mole** sauce
ensalada ⓕ en·sa·*la*·da salad
— **César** *se*·sar Caesar salad, named
after its inventor César Cardini, an
Italian immigrant to Mexico
— **de verduras** de ver·*doo*·ras salad
of cooked vegetables, a mix of fresh
vegetables, or a combination of
the two
— **mixta** *meek*·sta mix of lettuce, red
tomatoes, cucumber, peas, avocado
& fresh onion rings

entrada ⓕ en·tra·da entree

entremés ⓜ en·tre·mes appetiser

epazote ⓜ e·pa·so·te wormseed, a pungent herb similar to coriander, used in sauces, beans & **quesadillas**

escabeche ⓜ es·ka·be·che a brine used as a pickling agent or as a fish marinade

escamoles ⓜ pl es·ka·mo·les ant eggs, a delicacy that looks like rice – usually sauteed in butter & wine, served as an accompaniment to meat or with **tortillas**, avocado & salad

espárragos ⓜ pl es·pa·ra·gos asparagus

especias ⓕ pl es·pe·syas spices

espinaca ⓕ es·pee·na·ka spinach

esquites ⓜ pl es·kee·tes fresh corn grains boiled with butter, **epazote** & onions, served with fresh lime juice, chilli powder & grated cheese

estofado ⓜ es·to·fa·do stew • Oaxacan **mole** served over chicken or pork, prepared with tomatoes, almonds, bread, raisins, cloves & ground **chile guajillo**

estragón ⓜ es·tra·gon tarragon

esturión ⓜ es·too·ryon sturgeon

~ F ~

faisán ⓜ fay·san pheasant

filete ⓜ fee·le·te fillet

filete ⓜ **a la Mexicana** fee·le·te a la me·khee·ka·na grilled white fish with a tomato-based sauce

flan ⓜ flan a caramel egg custard flavoured with vanilla & covered in a syrupy topping

— napolitano na·po·lee·ta·no whiter & thicker than the custard-style flan, sometimes flavoured with liqueur

flautas ⓕ pl flow·tas tube-shaped **tacos** topped with chicken meat, deep-fried & served with cream, cheese & green or red sauce

flor ⓕ **de calabaza** flor de ka·la·ba·sa large squash flowers used in soups & other dishes

frambuesa ⓕ fram·bwe·sa raspberry

fresa ⓕ fre·sa strawberry

fideos ⓜ pl fee·de·os noodles

frijoles ⓜ pl free·kho·les beans, of which nearly 100 varieties are included in the Mexican cuisine

— borrachos bo·ra·chos 'drunken beans', made as **frijoles charros** but flavoured with flat beer

— charros cha·ros 'cowboy beans' – pork rind, fried tomatoes, onion & coriander, served as a soup

— molidos mo·lee·dos ground beans

— negros ne·gros 'black beans' – served mashed & refried, pureed as a soup or whole, usually seasoned with **epazote**

— refritos re·free·tos mashed beans fried in lard or vegetable oil

frutas ⓕ pl froo·tas fruits

— cristalizadas krees·ta·lee·sa·das different fruits cooked with sugar & water until crunchy

— secas se·kas dried fruit

~ G ~

galleta ⓕ ga·ye·ta biscuit • cookie • cracker

galletas ⓕ pl **saladas** ga·ye·tas sa·la·das crackers

gallina ⓕ ga·yee·na hen

ganso ⓜ gan·so goose

garbanzo ⓜ gar·ban·so chickpea

gelatina ⓕ khe·la·tee·na gelatin

germen ⓜ **de trigo** kher·men de tree·go wheat germ

germinado ⓜ **de soya** kher·mee·na·do de so·ya bean sprout

ginebra ⓕ khee·ne·bra gin

gorditas ⓕ pl gor·dee·tas thick corn **tortillas** fried then filled with beef, chicken or pork, then topped with cheese & lettuce

H

granada ⓕ gra·*na*·da grenadine • pomegranate

granola ⓕ gra·*no*·la muesli

grosella ⓕ gro·*se*·ya currant

guacamole ⓜ gwa·ka·*mo*·le mashed avocado mixed with lemon or lime juice, onion & chilli

guaraches ⓜ pl gwa·*ra*·ches **tortilla** shells piled high with **chorizo**, meat, potato, coriander & chilli salsa

guarnición ⓕ gwar·nee·*syon* garnish

guisado ⓜ gee·*sa*·do stew

guiso ⓜ *gee*·so stew

gusano ⓜ goo·*sa*·no worm

gusanos ⓜ pl **de maguey** goo·sa·nos de ma·*gay* worms that live in **maguey** – usually at the bottom of the bottle as a sign of true **mezcal**

— con salsa borracha kon *sal*·sa bo·*ra*·cha a dish of **maguey** worms fried in oil & accompanied by a sauce of roasted **chile pasilla**, garlic, onion, cheese & **pulque**

~ H ~

haba ⓕ *a*·ba broad bean

habanero ⓜ a·ba·*ne*·ro extremely spicy type of chilli

hamburguesa ⓕ am·boor·*ge*·sa hamburger

helado ⓜ e·*la*·do ice cream

hielo ⓜ *ye*·lo ice

hígado ⓜ *ee*·ga·do liver

— encebollado en·se·bo·*ya*·do liver with onions

higo ⓜ *ee*·go fig

hinojo ⓜ ee·*no*·kho fennel

hojas ⓕ pl o·khas leaves (banana, avocado, corn or **maguey**) used for flavouring, to wrap food for steaming or to line or cover earthenware pots

— de laurel de low·*rel* bay leaves

— de plátano de *pla*·ta·no banana leaves

— santas *san*·tas large anise-flavoured leaves

hojuelas ⓕ pl **de maíz** o·*khwe*·las de ma·*ees* corn flakes

huachinango ⓜ wa·chee·*nan*·go red snapper

— a la Veracruzana a la ve·ra·kroo·*sa*·na specialty of the port city of Veracruz where fresh red snapper is broiled in a lightly spiced sauce of tomato, onion & green olives

huarache ⓜ wa·*ra*·che flat & oval **tortilla** with beans and/or meat, topped with cream, cheese & various sauces (common street food)

huatape ⓜ **tamaulipeco** wa·*ta*·pe ta·mow·lee·*pe*·ko green prawn soup thickened with corn dough

huauzontle ⓜ wow·*son*·tle green vegetable whose buds are dipped in flour & fried

huevos ⓜ pl *hwe*·vos eggs

— entomatados en·to·ma·*ta*·dos eggs in a tomato sauce

— estrellados es·tre·*ya*·dos fried eggs

— fritos *free*·tos fried eggs

— revueltos re·*vwel*·tos scrambled eggs

— rancheros ran·*che*·ros eggs on **tortillas**, topped with chilli sauce

— tibios *tee*·byos soft-boiled eggs

huitlacoche ⓜ weet·la·*ko*·che black fungus that grows on young corn during the rainy season, used in crepes, **quesadillas** & soups

~ I ~

iguana ⓕ ee·*gwa*·na iguana – some species are protected and should not be eaten

~ J ~

jabalí ⓜ kha·ba·*lee* boar

jaiba ⓕ *khay*·ba crab

— de río de *ree*·o crayfish

jalapeño ⓜ kha·la·*pe*·nyo hot green chilli from Jalapa

jamón ⓜ kha·*mon* ham
jengibre ⓜ khen·*khee*·bre ginger
jerez ⓜ khe·*res* sherry
jícama ⓕ *khee*·ka·ma crunchy, sweet turnip • potato-like tuber often sold by street vendors, sliced & garnished with red chilli powder, salt & fresh lime juice
jitomates ⓜ pl khee·to·*ma*·tes red tomatoes, specifically plum or roma
— **cereza** se·re·sa cherry tomatoes
— **deshidratados** des·ee·dra·*ta*·dos sun-dried tomatoes
jugo ⓜ *khoo*·go juice
— **de fruta** de *froo*·ta fruit juice
— **de naranja** de na·*ran*·kha orange juice
— **fresco** *fres*·ko freshly squeezed juice

~ L ~

langosta ⓕ lan·*gos*·ta lobster
laurel ⓜ low·*rel* bay leaf
lavanda ⓕ la·*van*·da lavender
leche ⓕ *le*·che milk
— **de soya** de so·ya soy milk
— **descremada** des·kre·*ma*·da skimmed milk
— **entera** en·*te*·ra full cream milk
lechuga ⓕ le·*choo*·ga lettuce
lengua ⓕ *len*·gwa tongue
lenguado ⓜ len·*gwa*·do sole (fish)
lentejas ⓕ pl len·*te*·khas brown lentils
— **rojas** ro·khas red lentils
— **verdes** ver·des green lentils
levadura ⓕ le·va·*doo*·ra yeast
licor ⓜ lee·*kor* liqueur
licores ⓜ pl lee·*ko*·res spirits
lichi ⓜ *lee*·chee lychee
liebre ⓕ *lye*·bre hare
lima ⓕ *lee*·ma lime
limón ⓜ lee·*mon* lemon
— **agrio** a·*gryo* bitter lemon
— **sin semilla** seen se·*mee*·ya seedless lemon

limonada ⓕ lee·mo·*na*·da lemonade
lomo ⓜ *lo*·mo loin • rump • shoulder
longaniza ⓕ lon·ga·*nee*·sa dried speciality pork sausage
lonche ⓜ *lon*·che sandwich made with a long bun – in Guadalajara most of the bread is filled with meat, cheese, avocado & mayonnaise or cream
lucio ⓜ *loo*·syo pike (fish)

~ M ~

macadamia ⓕ ma·ka·*da*·mya macadamia
machaca ⓕ ma·*cha*·ka sheets of dried beef or beef jerky
machacado ⓜ ma·cha·*ka*·do dried meat
maguey ⓜ ma·*gay* any of the agave plants, used to make alcoholic drinks such as **pulque** and **tequila**
maíz ⓜ ma·ees corn • maize
— **molido** mo·*lee*·do de-husked dried maize kernels with the germ removed, usually softened in boiling water
malta ⓕ *mal*·ta malt
malteada ⓕ mal·te·*a*·da milkshake
mamey ⓜ ma·*may* rough brown fruit with bitter yellow inner skin & orangey flesh, used to make smoothies, gelatin, ice cream & mousses
mandarina ⓕ man·da·*ree*·na mandarin
mantequilla ⓕ man·te·*kee*·ya butter
manzana ⓕ man·*sa*·na apple
maracuyá ⓕ ma·ra·koo·*ya* passion fruit
margarina ⓕ mar·ga·*ree*·na margarine
Margarita ⓕ mar·ga·*ree*·ta cocktail made with **tequila**, lime juice, Cointreau & crushed ice, served in a chilled glass with salt on the rim
mariscos ⓜ pl ma·*rees*·kos seafood

L

masa ① *ma*·sa ground, cooked corn mixed with slaked lime and made into a dough or batter used for **tortillas**
— de harina de maíz de a·*ree*·na de ma·*ees* cornflour
— de harina de trigo de a·*ree*·na de *tree*·go wheat flour
maseca ① ma·*se*·ka type of cornflour used in **tortillas** & **tamales**
mayonesa ① ma·yo·*ne*·sa mayonnaise
mazapán ⓜ ma·sa·*pan* marzipan
medio *me*·dyo half • medium cooked
médula ① *me*·doo·la bone marrow, also called **tuétano**
mejillón ⓜ me·khee·*yon* mussel
mejorana ① me·kho·*ra*·na marjoram
melón ⓜ me·*lon* melon • cantaloupe
membrillo ⓜ mem·*bree*·yo quince
menta ① *men*·ta peppermint • mint
menudo ⓜ me·*noo*·do tripe stew – a hangover remedy (an acquired taste)
merienda ① me·*ryen*·da the equivalent of English afternoon tea
merluza ① mer·*loo*·sa hake
mermelada ① mer·me·*la*·da fruit jam • jelly • marmalade
mezcal ⓜ mes·*kal* distilled liquor made from **agave** – a worm is usually placed in the bottle
miel ① myel honey
migajas ① pl mee·*ga*·khas crumbs
mijo ⓜ *mee*·kho millet
milanesa ① mee·la·*ne*·sa pork, beef or chicken schnitzel – inferior cuts of beef are pounded to a thin slab, then fried in an egg & bread batter, served with mayonnaise & fresh limes & accompanied by rice, beans & salad
mixiotes ⓜ pl mee·*shyo*·tes lamb, chicken or rabbit meat wrapped in a thin layer of **maguey** leaves & steamed in a rich broth, then served with a mild green sauce, sliced avocado & **tortillas**
modongo ⓜ **jarocho** mon·*don*·go kha·*ro*·cho rich, stew-like dish with

ham, tripe, pork, chickpeas, coriander & **tortillas**
mojarra ① **a la veracruzana** mo·*kha*·ra a la ve·ra·kroo·*sa*·na spicy baked perch in a tomato, onion & green olive salsa
mole ⓜ *mo*·le the quintessential Mexican sauce, made using a variety of chillies, herbs, spices & chocolate
— almendrado al·men·*dra*·do a **mole** made mainly with almonds
— coloradito ko·lo·ra·*dee*·to Oaxacan **mole** made with chillies, sesame seeds, almonds, raisins, bananas & spices, ladled over chicken
— de olla de o·ya type of **mole** prepared with pork, lamb or smoked meat, cactus fruit & **epazote**
— de xico de *khee*·ko a slightly sweet mole
— naolinco na·o·*leen*·ko a spicy mole
— negro *ne*·gro a dark **mole**
— poblano po·*bla*·no type of **mole** made from deseeded & pureed chillies, onion, coriander, anise, cinnamon, garlic, toasted peanuts, almonds & sweetened chocolate
mollejas ① pl mo·*ye*·khas giblets
molletes ⓜ pl mo·*ye*·tes savoury, filled bread roll spread with refried beans & melted cheese & topped with fresh **salsa**
mondongo ⓜ mon·*don*·go a kind of stew with several regional variations
mora ① *mo*·ra mulberry
moronga ① mo·*ron*·ga black pudding
mostaza ① mos·*ta*·sa mustard

~ N ~

nabo ⓜ *na*·bo turnip
naranja ① na·*ran*·kha orange
— agria a·grya bitter orange used in marinades & sauces
— china ① *chee*·na kumquat

nieves ① pl *nye*·ves sherbets made with fruits or other ingredients such as **tequila**, avocado, shrimp, roseships or sweet corn

nixtamal ⓜ neek·sta·*mal* mixture of corn & lime used in tortilla dough (see **masa**)

nogada ① no·*ga*·da walnut or walnut sauce

nogal no·*gal* walnut tree

nopal ⓜ no·*pal* prickly pear cactus – the cactus pads (leaves) are cut into strips & boiled as a vegetable or added to scrambled eggs

nudillo ⓜ noo·*dee*·yo knuckle

nueva cocina ① **mexicana** *nwe*·va ko·*see*·na me·khee·*ka*·na 'new Mexican cuisine' – a movement among some chefs to combine traditional ingredients with contemporary preparations & presentations

nuez ① nwes nut

— cruda *kroo*·da raw nut

— de Castilla de kas·*tee*·ya walnut

— del Brasil del bra·*seel* brazil nut

— de la India de la *een*·dya cashew

— moscada mos·*ka*·da nutmeg

— pacana pa·*ka*·na pecan

— tostada tos·*ta*·da roasted nut

~ O ~

obleas ① pl o·*ble*·as coloured wafers filled with raw brown sugar syrup & decorated with toasted pumpkin seeds

octli ⓜ ok·tlee alcoholic drink made from a combination of juices from different agave plants

olivo ⓜ o·*lee*·vo olive tree

oporto ⓜ o·*por*·to port

ostión ⓜ os·*tyon* oyster

ostra ① os·tra oyster

oveja ① o·*ve*·kha sheep

~ P ~

palanquetas ① pl pa·lan·*ke*·tas traditional candy made with peanuts or pumpkin seeds conformed in rectangular or round shapes using caramelised sugar

paleta ① pa·*le*·ta lollipop • icy pole

— de agua de *a*·gwa icy pole made with water & fruit juice

— de leche de *le*·che icy pole made with milk & fruits or other ingredient such as vanilla, chocolate or nuts

palomitas ① pl **de maíz** pa·lo·*mee*·tas de ma·ees pop corn

pan ⓜ pan bread

— árabe *a*·ra·be pita bread

— de levadura fermentada de le·va·*doo*·ra fer·men·*ta*·da sourdough

— de muerto de *mwer*·to heavy bread used as an offering on the Day of the Dead

— de yema de *ye*·ma yellow, rich & heavy bread made with egg yolks

— dulce *dool*·se sweet bread

— duro *doo*·ro stale bread

— integral een·te·*gral* brown bread

— tostado tos·*ta*·do toasted bread

panuchos ⓜ pl pa·*noo*·chos finger food taken as an appetiser, these are bean-stuffed **tortillas**, fried crisp then topped with a tower of shredded turkey or chicken, tomato, lettuce & onions

papas ⓜ pl *pa*·pas potatoes

— a la francesa a la fran·*se*·sa chips • French fries

papadzules ⓜ pl pa·pad·*soo*·les fresh corn **tortillas** wrapped around a filling of chopped hard-boiled eggs then covered with sauce made from pumpkin seed & **epazote**

papitas ① pl **del monte** pa·*pee*·tas del *mon*·te wild potatoes

paprika ① pap·*ree*·ka paprika

P

parillada ⓕ pa·ree·ya·da flame-grilled meat platter

pasa ⓕ **(de uva)** pa·sa (de oo·va) raisin

pastel ⓜ pas·tel pastry • cake

— de tres leches de tres le·ches cake made with evaporated milk, condensed milk & evaporated cream

pastelería ⓕ pas·te·le·ree·a cake shop

pastelito ⓜ pas·te·lee·to pastry

patas ⓕ pl pa·tas hooves

pato ⓜ pa·to duck

pavo ⓜ pa·vo turkey

pechuga ⓕ pe·choo·ga breast

— de pollo de po·yo chicken breast

pepinillo ⓜ pe·pee·nee·yo gherkin

pepino ⓜ pe·pee·no cucumber

pepitoria ⓕ pe·pee·to·rya traditional candy made with coloured **obleas**

pera ⓕ pe·ra pear

perejil ⓜ pe·re·kheel parsley

pescadería ⓕ pes·ka·de·ree·a fishmonger

pescado ⓜ pes·ka·do fish

pibil ⓜ pee·beel sauce made from **achiote**, bitter orange juice, garlic, salt & pepper, used as a marinade for chicken or pork

picadillo ⓜ pee·ka·dee·yo mincemeat cooked with tomatoes, almonds, raisins & vegetables

pierna ⓕ pyer·na leg

piloncillo ⓜ pee·lon·see·yo raw brown sugar

pimentón ⓜ pee·men·ton cayenne • red pepper • paprika

pimienta ⓕ pee·myen·ta black pepper

— de cayena de ka·ye·na cayenne pepper

— entera en·te·ra ground pepper

— inglesa een·gle·sa allspice

— negra ne·gra black pepper

— recién molida re·syen mo·lee·da freshly ground black pepper

— verde ver·de green pepper

pimiento ⓜ pee·myen·to capsicum • pepper (bell)

pinole ⓜ pee·no·le flour made with a mixture of toasted corn & amaranth seeds

piña ⓕ pee·nya pineapple

piñatas ⓕ pl pee·nya·tas balloons or animal-shaped dolls made with clay or papier mache, filled with sweets, fruits, peanuts & toys

piñón ⓜ pee·nyon pine nut

pipián verde ⓜ pee·pyan ver·de a type of **mole** made with ground spices & pumpkin or squash seeds, green tomatoes, peanuts – served over pork or chicken

pistaches ⓜ pl pees·ta·ches pistachios

plátano ⓜ pla·ta·no banana • plantain

— dominico do·mee·nee·ko small & very sweet banana

— macho ma·cho large fried banana, served with sour cream & sugar

poc chuc ⓜ pok chook thin slice of pork, cooked on a grill & served on a sizzling plate with a bitter orange sauce & chopped onions

pollo ⓜ po·yo chicken

— a la pibil a la pee·beel chicken marinated in **pibil** sauce

— frito free·to fried chicken

— rostizado ros·tee·sa·do roast chicken

ponche ⓜ **de frutas** pon·che de froo·tas fruit punch prepared during Christmas made with guava, **tejocotes**, sugar cane, cinnamon, raisins, cloves & raw sugar

— con piquete kon pee·ke·te fruit punch with a shot of **tequila** or rum

poro ⓜ po·ro leek

postre ⓜ pos·tre dessert

pozole ⓜ po·so·le thick soup made of corn, chicken or pork, lettuce & slices of radish, traditionally eaten at Christmas

— **blanco** *blan*·ko corn soup prepared with stock but without chillies

— **rojo** *ro*·kho corn soup made with chilli

— **verde** *ver*·de corn soup made with green chillies & toasted pumpkin seeds

puchero ⓜ poo·*che*·ro stew made of chicken & vegetables

puerro ⓜ *pwe*·ro leek

pulpo ⓜ *pool*·po octopus

— **en su tinta** en soo *teen*·ta octopus in its own ink

pulque ⓜ *pool*·ke white, thick, sweet alcoholic drink made from the fermented sap of agave plants, especially the **maguey**

~ Q ~

queretanas ⓕ pl ke·re·*ta*·nas Queretaro-style **enchiladas** topped with shredded lettuce & other raw vegetables

quesadillas ⓕ pl ke·sa·dee·yas flour or corn **tortillas** with a savoury cheese filling • corn dough filled with different toppings such as mushrooms, mashed potatoes, **huitlacoche** & **rajas**

quesillo ⓜ ke·*see*·yo stringy goat's milk cheese from Oaxaca

queso ⓜ *ke*·so cheese

— **añejo** a·*nye*·kho hard, aged cheese with a sharp flavour similar to Parmesan

— **Chihuahua** chee·*wa*·wa creamy yellow cheese often used in **quesadillas**

— **crema** *kre*·ma cream cheese

— **de cabra** de *ka*·bra goat's cheese

— **fresco** *fres*·ko cheese made from cow's milk

— **fundido** foon·*dee*·do cheese fondue

— **manchego** man·*che*·go although this cheese is originally from La Mancha in Spain, it's a popular cheese in Mexico & used in many recipes

— **Oaxaca** wa·*ha*·ka Oaxacan cheese, made from goat's milk (see **quesillo**)

— **parmesano** par·me·*sa*·no Parmesan cheese

~ R ~

rábano ⓜ *ra*·ba·no radish

— **picante** pee·*kan*·te horseradish

rabo ⓜ *ra*·bo tail

rajas ⓕ pl *ra*·khas slices of chilli

— **con crema** kon *kre*·ma a dish made with **chile poblano** & sour cream

— **en escabeche** en es·ka·*be*·che pickled chillies

rana ⓕ *ra*·na frog

ranchera ⓕ ran·*che*·ra sauce made with chillies, tomatoes, onions, coriander – used for eggs or **enchiladas**

raspados ⓜ pl ras·*pa*·dos 'scrapings' – flavoured ice with fruit juice, sold by pushcart vendors as a refreshing treat

rebanada ⓕ re·ba·*na*·da a slice

regaliz ⓜ re·ga·*lees* liquorice

refresco ⓜ re·*fres*·ko soft drink

relleno ⓜ re·*ye*·no stuffing

— **negro** *ne*·gro green pepper, **chiles anchos** & **achiote**, served over shredded turkey & a hard-boiled egg

relleno/a ⓜ/ⓕ re·*ye*·no/a stuffed

reposado ⓜ re·po·*sa*·do an alcoholic drink such as **tequila** that has been aged two to 12 months

requesón ⓜ re·ke·*son* cottage cheese

res ⓕ res beef

riñón ⓜ ree·*nyon* kidney

robalo ⓜ ro·*ba*·lo sea bass

romero ⓜ ro·*me*·ro rosemary

ron Ⓜ ron rum

rosca Ⓕ **de reyes** *ros*·ka de re·*yes* eaten on Epiphany, this large, wreath-shaped pastry has a small china doll representing Christ, baked into it – whoever gets the piece with the doll in it throws a party on Candlemas Day

~ S ~

sal Ⓕ sal salt

salbutes Ⓜ pl sal·*boo*·tes fried crisp **tortillas** topped with a tower of shredded turkey or chicken, tomato, lettuce & onions

salchicha Ⓕ sal·*chee*·cha frankfurter

— de coctel de kok·*tel* small cocktail sausage

— de Viena de *vye*·na sausages used for hot dogs

salmón Ⓜ sal·*mon* salmon

salsa Ⓕ *sal*·sa a spicy, tomato-based sauce

— a la veracruzana a la ve·ra·kroo·*sa*·na sauce of tomato, onion & green olives

— bandera ban·*de*·ra 'flag sauce' – named for the red of the tomato, the white of the onion & the green of the chilli

— borracha bo·*ra*·cha 'drunken sauce' – made from roasted **chile pasilla**, garlic, onion, cheese & **pulque**

— de tomatillos sauce with green chillies, onion & coriander

— picante pee·*kan*·te hot sauce

— roja *ro*·kha red sauce made with plum tomatoes, onions, garlic & salt

— tártara *tar*·ta·ra tartare sauce

— verde *ver*·de green sauce made with **tomatillos**, green chillies, onion & coriander

sandía Ⓕ san·*dee*·a watermelon – a symbol of Mexico (the red, white & green correspond to the colours of the Mexican flag)

sangría Ⓕ san·*gree*·a refreshing cold drink of Spanish origin made with red wine, lemonade & sliced fresh fruit

sangrita Ⓕ san·*gree*·ta bright red, thickish mixture of crushed tomatoes (or tomato juice), orange juice, grenadine, chilli & salt – served chilled with a shot of **tequila**

sardina Ⓕ sar·*dee*·na sardine

semilla Ⓕ se·*mee*·ya seed

— de ajonjolí de a·khon·kho·*lee* sesame seed

— de amapola de a·ma·*po*·la poppy seed

— de apio de a·pyo celery seed

— de hinojo de ee·*no*·kho fennel seed

semita Ⓕ se·*mee*·ta round & flat sweet bread

semillas Ⓕ pl **de alcaravea** se·*mee*·yas de al·ka·ra·*ve*·a caraway seed

sémola Ⓕ se·*mo*·la semolina

sesos Ⓜ pl se·sos brains

sidra Ⓕ see·dra cider

sopa Ⓕ so·pa soup • chowder

— de coco de *ko*·ko coconut soup

— de lima de *lee*·ma lime soup

— de nopales de no·*pa*·les soup with cactus leaves

— de tortilla de tor·*tee*·ya chicken broth-based soup featuring strips of leftover corn **tortillas**

— seca *se*·ka 'dry soup' – a rice, pasta or tortilla-based dish

sope Ⓜ so·pe thick cornflour **tortilla** stuffed with refried beans, served with chicken or other meat with lettuce & cream on the top

~ T ~

tablillas Ⓕ pl **de chocolate** ta·*blee*·yas de cho·ko·*la*·te blocks of chocolate (for heating with water and drinking)

tacos ⓜ pl *ta*·kos folded corn **tortillas** filled with meat, beans & other ingredients

— al pastor al pas·*tor* **tacos** with meat cut from a roasting spit, served with fresh pineapple, onions, coriander & salsa

— árabe *a*·ra·be **tacos** made with slightly thicker wheat bread (pita bread)

— de carne asada de kar·ne a·sa·da **tacos** with minced beef

— de carnitas de kar·nee·tas **tacos** with finely chopped pork

— de pollo de po·yo chicken **tacos**

— dorados do·ra·dos deep fried **tacos**

tallo ⓜ *ta*·yo shank

tamales ⓜ pl ta·*ma*·les corn dough stuffed with meat, **mole**, green or red salsa, fruit or nothing at all, usually wrapped in banana leaves or sometimes in corn husks & steamed

tamarindo ⓜ ta·ma·*reen*·do tamarind, a fruit used for making **aguas**, **nieves** & desserts

taquería ⓕ ta·ke·*ree*·a place that specialises in serving **tacos**

taquito ⓜ ta·*kee*·to a small **tortilla** wrapped around meat or chicken

té ⓜ te tea

— de hierbabuena de yer·ba·*bwe*·na peppermint tea

— de limón de lee·*mon* lemongrass tea

— de manzanilla de man·sa·*nee*·ya chamomile tea

— de menta de *men*·ta mint tea

— descafeinado des·ka·fay·*na*·do decaffeinated tea

— negro *ne*·gro black tea

tejate ⓜ te·*kha*·te Oaxacan recipe for chocolate that includes **mamey** seeds, cacao flowers & corn dough

tejocote ⓜ te·kho·ko·te hawthorn

telera ⓕ te·*le*·ra French-style bread roll used to make **tortas**

tepache ⓜ te·*pa*·che alcoholic drink made from fermented pineapple

tequila ⓕ te·*kee*·la classic Mexican spirit distilled from the **maguey** plant

ternera ⓕ ter·*ne*·ra veal

tescalate ⓜ tes·ka·*la*·te type of chocolate popular in Chiapas, made by grinding the cacao beans with toasted corn & **achiote**

tlayuda ⓕ tla·*yoo*·da large, crisp **tortilla** topped with Oaxacan cheese, tomatoes & beans, also called **clayuda**

tocino ⓜ to·*see*·no bacon

— de lomo de *lo*·mo bacon (off the back)

tomate ⓜ **verde** to·*ma*·te *ver*·de see **tomatillo**

tomates ⓜ pl **deshidratados** to·*ma*·tes des·ee·dra·*ta*·dos sun-dried tomatoes

tomatillo ⓜ to·ma·*tee*·yo small green native tomato wrapped in a brownish papery husk – used for salsas (also known as **tomate verde**)

tomillo ⓜ to·*mee*·yo thyme

to'owloche ⓜ tow·*lo*·che 'wrapped in corn leaves' – Mayan **tamal** made by home chefs & served to people in the street on festival days

toro ⓜ *to*·ro bull

toronja ⓕ to·*ron*·kha grapefruit

torta ⓕ *tor*·ta sandwich made with crusty bread

tortillas ⓕ tor·*tee*·yas ubiquitous round flatbread made with corn or wheat flour, a staple in the Mexican diet for thousands of years – used in making **tacos**, **chalupas**, **huaraches**, **sopes** & **tostadas**

— de maíz de ma·ees corn **tortillas**

— de trigo de *tree*·go wheat **tortillas**

— yucatecas yoo·ka·*te*·kas see **papadzules**

tortillería ① tor·tee·ye·*ree*·a a bakery in which Mexicans buy their **tortillas** by the kilo

tostadas ① pl tos·*ta*·das fried corn tortillas

totopos ⓜ pl to·*to*·pos deep-fried wedges of stale corn **tortillas**

trigo ⓜ *tree*·go wheat

— integral een·te·*gral* whole-grain wheat

— sarraceno ⓜ sa·ra·se·no buckwheat

tripa ① *tree*·pa tripe

trucha ① *troo*·cha trout

tuna ① *too*·na prickly pear • cactus fruit

tuétano ⓜ *twe*·ta·no marrow

turrón ⓜ too·*ron* nougat

~ U ~

uchepos ⓜ pl oo·che·pos corn dough, wrapped in corn husks, steamed & served with fresh cream

uva ① **pasa** oo·va pa·sa raisin

uvas ① pl oo·vas grapes

~ V ~

vainilla ① vay·*nee*·ya vanilla

venado ⓜ ve·*na*·do venison • deer

verdulería ① ver·doo·le·*ree*·a greengrocer

verduras ① pl ver·*doo*·ras mixed greens

vinagre ⓜ vee·*na*·gre vinegar

— balsámico bal·*sa*·mee·ko balsamic vinegar

vino ⓜ *vee*·no wine

— afrutado a·froo·*ta*·do fruity wine

— blanco *blan*·ko white wine

— de la casa de la *ka*·sa house wine

— dulce *dool*·se sweet wine

— espumoso es·poo·*mo*·so sparkling wine

— ligeramente dulce lee·khe·ra·*men*·te *dool*·se lightly sweet wine

— muy seco mooy se·ko very dry wine

— nacional na·syo·*nal* Mexican wine

— seco se·ko dry wine

— semi-seco *se*·mee se·ko semi-dry wine

— tinto *teen*·to red wine

vuelve a la vida ⓜ *vwel*·ve a la vee·da 'go back to life' – seafood cocktail in a tomato salsa

~ W ~

whiskey ⓜ *wees*·kee whiskey

— canadiense ka·na·*dyen*·se rye whiskey

— de centeno de sen·*te*·no bourbon whiskey

~ X ~

xcatik ⓜ shka·*teek* kind of chilli found in Yucatán state

xtabentún ⓜ shta·ben·*toon* Mayan liqueur made from native flowers of the same name

~ Z ~

zanahoria ① sa·na·o·rya carrot

zapote ⓜ sa·*po*·te a fruit used for making desserts which comes in two varieties: **negro** (black) or **blanco** (white)

zarzamora ① sar·sa·*mo*·ra blackberry • dewberry

Dictionary
ENGLISH *to* SPANISH
inglés – español

Nouns in the dictionary have their gender indicated by ⓜ or ⓕ. If it's a plural noun, you'll also see pl. Where a word that could be either a noun or a verb has no gender indicated, it's a verb.

A

(to be) able poder po·*der*
aboard a bordo a *bor*·do
abortion aborto ⓜ a·*bor*·to
about sobre *so*·bre
above arriba a·*ree*·ba
abroad en el extranjero en el ek·stran·*khe*·ro
accept aceptar a·sep·*tar*
accident accidente ⓜ ak·see·*den*·te
accommodation alojamiento ⓜ a·lo·kha·*myen*·to
across a través a tra·*ves*
activist activista ⓜ&ⓕ ak·tee·*vees*·ta
acupuncture acupuntura ⓕ a·koo·poon·*too*·ra
adaptor adaptador ⓜ a·dap·ta·*dor*
address dirección ⓕ dee·rek·*syon*
administration administración ⓕ ad·mee·nees·tra·*syon*
admission price precio ⓜ de entrada *pre*·syo de en·*tra*·da
admit (acknowledge) reconocer re·ko·no·*ser*
admit (allow to enter) dejar entrar de·*khar* en·*trar*
admit (accept) admitir ad·mee·*teer*

adult adulto/a ⓜ/ⓕ a·*dool*·to/a
advertisement anuncio ⓜ a·*noon*·syo
advice consejo ⓜ kon·*se*·kho
advise aconsejar a·kon·se·*khar*
aerobics aeróbics ⓜ a·e·ro·beeks
Africa África *a*·free·ka
after después de des·*pwes* de
aftershave loción ⓕ para después del afeitado lo·*syon* pa·ra des·*pwes* del a·fay·*ta*·do
again otra vez o·tra ves
age edad ⓕ e·*dad*
aggressive agresivo/a ⓜ/ⓕ a·gre·*see*·vo/a
agree estar de acuerdo es·*tar* de a·*kwer*·do
agriculture agricultura ⓕ a·gree·kool·*too*·ra
AIDS SIDA ⓜ *see*·da
air aire ⓜ *ai*·re
airmail correo ⓜaéreo ko·re·o a·e·re·o
(by) airmail (por) vía ⓕ aérea (por) vee·a a·e·re·a
air-conditioning aire ⓜ acondicionado *ai*·re a·kon·dee·syo·*na*·do
airline aerolínea ⓕ a·e·ro·*lee*·ne·a

airport aeropuerto ⓜ a·e·ro·*pwer*·to

airport tax tasa ⓕ de aeropuerto
ta·sa de a·e·ro·*pwer*·to

alarm clock despertador ⓜ
des·per·ta·*dor*

alcohol alcohol ⓜ al·*kol*

all todo *to*·do

allergy alergia ⓕ a·*ler*·khya

allow permitir per·mee·*teer*

almond almendra ⓕ al·*men*·dra

almost casi *ka*·see

alone solo/a ⓜ/ⓕ *so*·lo/a

already ya ya

also también tam·*byen*

altar altar ⓜ al·*tar*

altitude altura ⓕ al·*too*·ra

always siempre *syem*·pre

amateur amateur ⓜ&ⓕ a·ma·*ter*

ambassador embajador/
embajadora ⓜ/ⓕ em·ba·kha·*dor*/
em·ba·kha·*do*·ra

among entre *en*·tre

anarchist anarquista ⓜ&ⓕ
a·nar·*kees*·ta

ancient antiguo/a ⓜ/ⓕ an·*tee*·gwo/a

and y ee

angry enojado/a ⓜ/ⓕ e·no·*kha*·do/a

animal animal ⓜ a·nee·*mal*

ankle tobillo ⓜ to·*bee*·yo

answer respuesta ⓕ res·*pwes*·ta

answering machine contestadora ⓕ
kon·tes·ta·*do*·ra

ant hormiga ⓕ or·*mee*·ga

anthology antología ⓕ
an·to·lo·*khee*·a

antibiotics antibióticos ⓜ pl
an·tee·*byo*·tee·kos

antimalarial tablets pastillas ⓕ pl
antipalúdicas pas·*tee*·yas
an·tee·pa·*loo*·dee·kas

antinuclear antinuclear
an·tee·noo·kle·*ar*

antique antigüedad ⓕ
an·tee·gwe·*dad*

antiseptic antiséptico ⓜ
an·tee·*sep*·tee·ko

any (singular) alguno/a ⓜ/ⓕ
al·*goo*·no/a

any (plural) algunos/as ⓜ/ⓕ
al·*goo*·nos/as

appendix apéndice ⓜ a·*pen*·dee·se

apple manzana ⓕ man·*sa*·na

appointment cita ⓕ *see*·ta

apricot chabacano ⓜ cha·ba·*ka*·no

archaeological arqueológico/a ⓜ/ⓕ
ar·ke·o·lo·*khee*·ko/a

archaeologist arqueólogo/a ⓜ/ⓕ
ar·ke·o·lo·go/a

architect arquitecto/a ⓜ/ⓕ
ar·kee·*tek*·to/a

architecture arquitectura ⓕ
ar·kee·tek·*too*·ra

argue discutir dees·koo·*teer*

arm brazo ⓜ *bra*·so

army ejército ⓜ e·*kher*·see·to

arrest arrestar a·res·*tar*

arrivals llegadas ⓕ pl ye·*ga*·das

arrive llegar ye·*gar*

art arte ⓜ *ar*·te

art gallery galería ⓕ de arte
ga·le·*ree*·a de *ar*·te

artichoke alcachofa ⓕ al·ka·*cho*·fa

artist artista ⓜ&ⓕ ar·*tees*·ta

ashtray cenicero ⓜ se·nee·*se*·ro

Asia Asia ⓕ *a*·sya

ask (a question) preguntar
pre·goon·*tar*

ask (for something) pedir pe·*deer*

aspirin aspirina ⓕ as·pee·*ree*·na

assault agresión ⓕ a·gre·*syon*

asthma asma ⓜ *as*·ma

at the back (behind) detrás de
de·*tras* de

athletics atletismo ⓜ at·le·*tees*·mo

atmosphere atmósfera ⓕ
at·*mos*·fe·ra

aubergine berenjena ⓕ
be·ren·*khe*·na

aunt tía ⓕ *tee*·a

Australia Australia ⓕ ow·*stra*·lya

Australian Rules football fútbol ⓜ
australiano *foot*·bol ows·tra·*lya*·no

automatic teller machine cajero ⓜ automático ka·khe·ro ow·to·ma·tee·ko

autumn otoño ⓜ o·to·nyo

avenue avenida ⓕ a·ve·nee·da

avocado aguacate ⓜ a·gwa·ka·te

Aztec azteca ⓜ&ⓕ as·te·ka

B

B&W (film) blanco y negro blan·ko ee ne·gro

baby bebé ⓜ be·be

baby food alimento ⓜ para bebé a·lee·men·to pa·ra be·be

baby powder talco ⓜ para bebé tal·ko pa·ra be·be

babysitter niñera ⓕ nee·nye·ra

back (of body) espalda ⓕ es·pal·da

back (of chair) respaldo ⓜ res·pal·do

backpack mochila ⓕ mo·chee·la

bacon tocino ⓜ to·see·no

bad malo/a ⓜ/ⓕ ma·lo/a

bag bolsa ⓕ bol·sa

baggage equipaje ⓜ e·kee·pa·khe

baggage allowance límite ⓜ de equipaje lee·mee·te de e·kee·pa·khe

baggage claim entrega ⓕ de equipaje en·tre·ga de e·kee·pa·khe

bakery panadería ⓕ pa·na·de·ree·a

balance (account) saldo ⓜ sal·do

balcony balcón ⓜ bal·kon

ball pelota ⓕ pe·lo·ta

ballet ballet ⓜ ba·le

banana plátano ⓜ pla·ta·no

band grupo ⓜ groo·po

bandage vendaje ⓜ ven·da·khe

Band-Aids curitas ⓕ pl koo·ree·tas

bank banco ⓜ ban·ko

bank account cuenta ⓕ bancaria kwen·ta ban·ka·rya

banknotes billetes ⓜ pl bee·ye·tes

baptism bautizo ⓜ bow·tee·so

bar bar ⓜ bar

bar (with live music) bar ⓜ con variedad bar kon va·rye·dad

barber peluquero ⓜ pe·loo·ke·ro

baseball béisbol ⓜ bays·bol

basket canasta ⓕ ka·nas·ta

basketball baloncesto ⓜ ba·lon·ses·to

bathtub tina ⓕ tee·na

bathing suit traje ⓜ de baño tra·khe de ba·nyo

bathroom baño ⓜ ba·nyo

battery (car) batería ⓕ ba·te·ree·a

battery (small) pila ⓕ pee·la

be (ongoing) ser ser

be (temporary) estar es·tar

beach playa ⓕ pla·ya

beans frijoles ⓜ pl free·kho·les

beautiful hermoso/a ⓜ/ⓕ er·mo·so/a

beauty salon salón ⓜ de belleza sa·lon de be·ye·sa

because porque por·ke

bed cama ⓕ ka·ma

bedding ropa ⓕ de cama ro·pa de ka·ma

bedroom habitación ⓕ a·bee·ta·syon

bee abeja ⓕ a·be·kha

beef carne ⓕ de res kar·ne de res

beer cerveza ⓕ ser·ve·sa

beetroot betabel ⓜ be·ta·bel

before antes an·tes

beggar limosnero/a ⓜ/ⓕ lee·mos·ne·ro/a

begin comenzar ko·men·sar

behind detrás de de·tras de

below abajo a·ba·kho

best mejor me·khor

bet apuesta ⓕ a·pwes·ta

better mejor me·khor

between entre en·tre

Bible Biblia ⓕ bee·blya

bicycle bicicleta ⓕ bee·see·kle·ta

big grande gran·de

bike bici ⓕ bee·see

bike chain cadena ⓕ de bici ka·de·na de bee·see

bike path carril ⓜ para bici ka·reel pa·ra bee·see

B

bill (account) cuenta ① *kwen*·ta
biodegradable biodegradable
bee·o·de·gra·*da*·ble
biography biografía ①
bee·o·gra·*fee*·a
bird pájaro ⓜ *pa*·kha·ro
birth certificate acta ① de
nacimiento *ak*·ta de na·*see*·*myen*·to
birthday cumpleaños ⓜ
koom·ple·a·*nyos*
birthday cake pastel ⓜ
de cumpleaños pas·*tel* de
koom·ple·a·*nyos*
biscuit galleta ① ga·*ye*·ta
bite (dog) mordedura ①
mor·de·*doo*·ra
bite (food) bocado ⓜ bo·*ka*·do
bite (insect) picadura ①
pee·ka·*doo*·ra
black negro/a ⓜ/① *ne*·gro/a
blanket cobija ① ko·*bee*·kha
bleed sangrar san·*grar*
blind ciego/a ⓜ/① *sye*·go/a
blister ampolla ① am·*po*·ya
blocked bloqueado/a ⓜ/①
blo·ke·*a*·do/a
blood sangre ① *san*·gre
blood group grupo ⓜ sanguíneo
groo·po san·*gee*·ne·o
blood pressure presión ① arterial
pre·*syon* ar·te·*ryal*
blood test análisis ⓜ de sangre
a·*na*·lee·sees de *san*·gre
blue azul a·*sool*
board (ship, etc) embarcar
em·bar·*kar*
boarding house pensión ①
pen·*syon*
boarding pass pase ⓜ de abordar
pa·se de a·bor·*dar*
boat barco ⓜ *bar*·ko
body cuerpo ⓜ *kwer*·po
bomb bomba ① *bom*·ba
bone hueso ⓜ *we*·so
book libro ⓜ *lee*·bro
book (reserve) reservar re·ser·*var*

booked out lleno/a ⓜ/① *ye*·no/a
bookshop librería ① lee·bre·*ree*·a
boots botas ① pl *bo*·tas
border frontera ① fron·*te*·ra
boring aburrido/a ⓜ/①
a·boo·*ree*·do/a
borrow pedir prestado pe·*deer*
pres·*ta*·do
botanic garden jardín ⓜ botánico
khar·*deen* bo·*ta*·nee·ko
both ambos/as ⓜ/① pl *am*·bos/as
bottle botella ① bo·*te*·ya
bottle opener destapador ⓜ
des·ta·pa·*dor*
bottle shop tienda ① de abarrotes
tyen·da de a·ba·*ro*·tes
bowl bol ⓜ bol
box caja ① *ka*·kha
boxer shorts boxers ⓜ pl *bok*·sers
boxing boxeo ⓜ bok·*se*·o
boy niño ⓜ *nee*·nyo
boyfriend novio ⓜ *no*·vyo
bra brassiere ⓜ bra·*syer*
Braille Braille ⓜ *brai*·le
brakes frenos ⓜ pl *fre*·nos
branch office sucursal ①
soo·koor·*sal*
brandy brandy ⓜ *bran*·dee
brave valiente va·*lyen*·te
bread pan ⓜ pan
bread roll bolillo ⓜ bo·*lee*·yo
brown bread pan ⓜ integral pan
een·te·*gral*
rye bread pan ⓜ de centeno pan de
sen·*te*·no
sourdough bread pan ⓜ de
levadura fermentada pan de
le·va·*doo*·ra fer·men·*ta*·da
white bread pan ⓜ blanco pan
blan·ko
break romper rom·*per*
break down descomponerse
des·kom·po·*ner*·se
breakfast desayuno ⓜ de·sa·*yoo*·no
breast (poultry) pechuga ①
pe·*choo*·ga

breasts senos ⓜ pl se·nos

breasts (colloquial) chichis ⓕ pl chee·chees

breathe respirar res·pee·rar

bribe soborno ⓜ so·bor·no

bribe sobornar so·bor·nar

bridge puente ⓜ pwen·te

briefcase portafolios ⓜ por·ta·fo·lyos

brilliant brillante bree·yan·te

bring traer tra·er

brochure folleto ⓜ fo·ye·to

broken roto/a ⓜ/ⓕ ro·to/a

bronchitis bronquitis ⓜ bron·kee·tees

brother hermano ⓜ er·ma·no

brown café ka·fe

bruise moretón ⓜ mo·re·ton

bucket cubeta ⓕ koo·be·ta

Buddhist budista ⓜ&ⓕ boo·dees·ta

budget presupuesto ⓜ pre·soo·pwes·to

buffet buffet ⓜ boo·fe

bug bicho ⓜ bee·cho

build construir kon·stroo·eer

building edificio ⓜ e·dee·fee·syo

bull toro ⓜ to·ro

bullfight corrida ⓕ (de toros) ko·ree·da (de to·ros)

bullring plaza ⓕ de toros pla·sa de to·ros

bum (body) nalga ⓕ nal·ga

burn quemadura ⓕ ke·ma·doo·ra

burn (something) quemar ke·mar

bus (city) autobús ⓜ ow·to·boos

bus (intercity) camión ⓜ ka·myon

bus station estación ⓕ de autobuses es·ta·syon de ow·to·boo·ses

bus stop parada ⓕ de autobuses pa·ra·da de ow·to·boo·ses

business negocios ⓜ pl ne·go·syos

business class clase ⓕ ejecutiva kla·se e·khe·koo·tee·va

business person comerciante ⓜ&ⓕ ko·mer·syan·te

busker artista callejero/a ⓜ/ⓕ ar·tees·ta ka·ye·khe·ro/a

busy ocupado/a ⓜ/ⓕ o·koo·pa·do/a

but pero pe·ro

butcher's shop carnicería ⓕ kar·nee·se·ree·a

butter mantequilla ⓕ man·te·kee·ya

butterfly mariposa ⓕ ma·ree·po·sa

buttons botones ⓜ pl bo·to·nes

buy comprar kom·prar

C

cabbage col ⓕ kol

cable cable ⓜ ka·ble

cable car teleférico ⓜ te·le·fe·ree·ko

cactus cactus ⓜ kak·toos

cactus worms gusanos ⓜ pl de maguey goo·sa·nos de ma·gay

cafe café ⓜ ka·fe

cake pastel ⓜ pas·tel

cake shop pastelería ⓕ pas·te·le·ree·a

calculator calculadora ⓕ kal·koo·la·do·ra

calendar calendario ⓜ ka·len·da·ryo

calf becerro ⓜ be·se·ro

camera cámara ⓕ fotográfica ka·ma·ra fo·to·gra·fee·ka

camera shop tienda ⓕ de fotografía tyen·da de fo·to·gra·fee·a

camp acampar a·kam·par

camping store tienda ⓕ de campismo tyen·da de kam·pees·mo

campsite área ⓕ para acampar a·re·a pa·ra a·kam·par

can (tin) lata ⓕ la·ta

can (be able) poder po·der

can opener abrelatas ⓜ a·bre·la·tas

Canada Canadá ka·na·da

cancel cancelar kan·se·lar

cancer cáncer ⓜ kan·ser

candle vela ⓕ ve·la

candy dulces ⓜ pl dool·ses

cantaloupe melón ⓜ cantaloupe me·lon kan·ta·loop

capsicum pimiento ⓜ pee·myen·to

car coche ⓜ ko·che

car hire renta ⓕ de coches ren·ta de ko·ches

C

car owner's title factura ⓕ del coche fak·*too*·ra del ko·*che*

car park estacionamiento ⓜ es·ta·syo·na·*myen*·to

car registration matrícula ⓕ ma·*tree*·koo·la

caravan caravana ⓕ ka·ra·*va*·na

cards cartas ⓕ pl *kar*·tas

care (about something) preocuparse por pre·o·koo·*par*·se por

care (for someone) cuidar de kwee·*dar* de

caring bondadoso/a ⓜ/ⓕ bon·da·*do*·so/a

carpenter carpintero ⓜ kar·peen·*te*·ro

carrot zanahoria ⓕ sa·na·o·rya

carry llevar ye·*var*

carton cartón ⓜ kar·*ton*

cash dinero ⓜ en efectivo dee·*ne*·ro en e·fek·*tee*·vo

cash (a cheque) cambiar (un cheque) kam·*byar* (oon *che*·ke)

cash register caja ⓕ registradora *ka*·kha re·khees·tra·*do*·ra

cashew nut nuez ⓕ de la India nwes de la *een*·dya

cashier cajero/a ⓜ/ⓕ ka·*khe*·ro/a

casino casino ⓜ ka·*see*·no

cassette cassette ⓕ ka·*set*

castle castillo ⓜ kas·*tee*·yo

casual work trabajo ⓜ eventual tra·*ba*·kho e·ven·*twal*

cat gato/a ⓜ/ⓕ *ga*·to/a

cathedral catedral ⓕ ka·te·*dral*

Catholic católico/a ⓜ/ⓕ ka·*to*·lee·ko/a

cauliflower coliflor ⓕ ko·lee·*flor*

caves cuevas ⓕ pl *kwe*·vas

CD cómpact ⓜ *kom*·pakt

celebrate (an event) celebrar se·le·*brar*

celebration celebración ⓕ se·le·bra·*syon*

cell phone celular ⓜ se·loo·*lar*

cemetery cementerio ⓜ se·men·*te*·ryo

cent centavo ⓜ sen·*ta*·vo

centimetre centímetro ⓜ sen·*tee*·me·tro

Central America Centroamérica ⓕ sen·tro·a·*me*·ree·ka

central heating calefacción ⓕ central ka·le·fak·*syon* sen·*tral*

centre centro ⓜ *sen*·tro

ceramic cerámica ⓕ se·*ra*·mee·ka

cereal cereal ⓜ se·re·*al*

certificate certificado ⓜ ser·tee·fee·*ka*·do

chair silla ⓕ *see*·ya

champagne champán ⓜ cham·*pan*

chance oportunidad ⓕ o·por·too·nee·*dad*

change (money) cambio ⓜ *kam*·byo

change cambiar kam·*byar*

changing rooms probadores ⓜ pl pro·ba·*do*·res

charming encantador/ encantadora ⓜ/ⓕ en·kan·ta·*dor*/ en·kan·ta·*do*·ra

chat up ligar lee·*gar*

cheap barato/a ⓜ/ⓕ ba·*ra*·to/a

cheat tramposo/a ⓜ/ⓕ tram·*po*·so/a

check revisar re·vee·*sar*

check (bank) cheque ⓜ *che*·ke

check (bill) cuenta ⓕ *kwen*·ta

check-in (flight) documentación ⓕ do·koo·men·ta·*syon*

check-in (hotel) registro ⓜ re·khees·*tro*

checkpoint control ⓜ kon·*trol*

cheese queso ⓜ *ke*·so

chef chef ⓜ&ⓕ chef

chemist (person) farmacéutico/a ⓜ/ⓕ far·ma·*sew*·tee·ko/a

chemist (shop) farmacia ⓕ far·*ma*·sya

cheque cheque ⓜ *che*·ke

chess ajedrez ⓜ a·khe·*dres*

chest pecho ⓜ *pe*·cho

chewing gum chicle ⓜ *chee*-kle
chicken pollo ⓜ *po*-yo
chicken breast pechuga ① de pollo pe-*choo*-ga de *po*-yo
chickpeas garbanzos ⓜ pl gar-*ban*-sos
child niño/a ⓜ/① *nee*-nyo/a
child's car seat asiento ⓜ de seguridad para bebés a-*syen*-to de se-goo-ree-*dad* pa-ra be-*bes*
childminding service guardería ① gwar-de-*ree*-a
children niños ⓜ&① pl *nee*-nyos
chilli chile ⓜ *chee*-le
chilli sauce salsa ① picante *sal*-sa pee-*kan*-te
chocolate chocolate ⓜ cho-ko-*la*-te
choose elegir e-le-*kheer*
Christian cristiano/a ⓜ/① krees-*tya*-no/a
Christmas Day Navidad ① na-vee-*dad*
Christmas Eve Nochebuena ① no-che-*bwe*-na
church iglesia ① ee-*gle*-sya
cider sidra ① *see*-dra
cigar puro ⓜ *poo*-ro
cigarette cigarro ⓜ see-*ga*-ro
cigarette lighter encendedor ⓜ en-sen-de-*dor*
cigarette machine máquina ① de tabaco *ma*-kee-na de ta-*ba*-ko
cigarette papers papel ⓜ para cigarros pa-*pel* pa-ra see-*ga*-ros
cinema cine ⓜ *see*-ne
cinnamon canela ① ka-*ne*-la
circus circo ⓜ *seer*-ko
citizenship ciudadanía ① syoo-da-da-*nee*-a
city ciudad ① syoo-*dad*
city centre centro ⓜ de la ciudad *sen*-tro de la syoo-*dad*
city walls murallas ① pl moo-*ra*-yas
civil rights derechos ⓜ pl civiles de-*re*-chos see-*vee*-les

classical clásico/a ⓜ/① *kla*-see-ko/a
clean limpio/a ⓜ/① *leem*-pyo/a
cleaning trabajo ⓜ de limpieza tra-*ba*-kho de leem-*pye*-sa
client cliente/a ⓜ/① klee-*en*-te/a
cliff acantilado ⓜ a-kan-tee-*la*-do
climb escalar es-ka-*lar*
cloak capa ⓜ *ka*-pa
cloakroom guardarropa ① gwar-da-*ro*-pa
clock reloj ⓜ re-*lokh*
close (nearby) cerca *ser*-ka
close (shut) cerrar se-*rar*
closed cerrado/a ⓜ/① se-*ra*-do/a
clothes line tendedero ⓜ ten-de-*de*-ro
clothing ropa ① *ro*-pa
clothing store tienda ① de ropa *tyen*-da de *ro*-pa
cloud nube ① *noo*-be
cloudy nublado noo-*bla*-do
clove (of garlic) diente (de ajo) *dyen*-te (de *a*-kho)
cloves clavos ⓜ pl de olor *kla*-vos de o-*lor*
clutch embrague ⓜ em-*bra*-ge
coach entrenador/entrenadora ⓜ/① en-tre-na-*dor*/en-tre-na-*do*-ra
coast costa ① *kos*-ta
cocaine cocaína ① ko-ka-*ee*-na
cockroach cucaracha ① koo-ka-*ra*-cha
cocoa cacao ⓜ ka-*kow*
coconut coco ⓜ *ko*-ko
codeine codeína ① ko-de-*ee*-na
coffee café ⓜ ka-*fe*
coins monedas ① pl mo-*ne*-das
cold frío/a ⓜ/① *free*-o/a
cold (illness) resfriado ⓜ res-free-*a*-do
colleague colega ⓜ&① ko-*le*-ga
collect call llamada ① por cobrar ya-*ma*-da por ko-*brar*
college universidad ① oo-nee-ver-see-*dad*
colour color ⓜ ko-*lor*

C

colour film película ⓕ en color
pe·*lee*·koo·la en ko·*lor*
comb peine ⓜ *pay*·ne
comb peinar pay·*nar*
come venir ve·*neer*
come (arrive) llegar ye·*gar*
comedy comedia ⓕ ko·*me*·dya
comfortable cómodo/a ⓜ/ⓕ
ko·mo·do/a
communion comunión ⓕ
ko·moo·*nyon*
communist comunista ⓜ&ⓕ
ko·moo·*nees*·ta
companion compañero/a ⓜ/ⓕ
kom·pa·*nye*·ro/a
company compañía ⓕ
kom·pa·*nyee*·a
compass brújula ⓕ *broo*·khoo·la
complain quejarse ke·*khar*·se
computer computadora ⓕ
kom·poo·ta·*do*·ra
computer game juego ⓜ
de computadora *khwe*·go de
kom·poo·ta·*do*·ra
concert concierto ⓜ kon·*syer*·to
conditioner acondicionador ⓜ
a·kon·dee·syo·na·*dor*
condoms condones ⓜ pl kon·*do*·nes
confession confesión ⓕ kon·fe·*syon*
confirm confirmar kon·feer·*mar*
connection conexión ⓕ ko·nek·*syon*
conservative conservador/
conservadora ⓜ/ⓕ kon·ser·va·*dor*/
kon·ser·va·*do*·ra
constipation estreñimiento ⓜ
es·tre·nyee·*myen*·to
consulate consulado ⓜ
kon·soo·la·do
contact lenses lentes ⓜ pl de
contacto *len*·tes de kon·*tak*·to
contraceptives anticonceptivos ⓜ pl
an·tee·kon·sep·*tee*·vos
contract contrato ⓜ kon·*tra*·to
convenience store tienda ⓕ *tyen*·da
convent convento ⓜ kon·*ven*·to
cook cocinero/a ⓜ/ⓕ ko·see·ne·ro/a

cook cocinar ko·see·*nar*
cookie galleta ⓕ ga·*ye*·ta
corn maíz ⓜ ma·*ees*
corn flakes hojuelas ⓕ pl de maíz
o·*khwe*·las de ma·ees
corner esquina ⓕ es·*kee*·na
corrupt corrupto/a ⓜ/ⓕ
ko·*roop*·to/a
cost costo ⓜ *kos*·to
cost costar kos·*tar*
cottage cheese queso ⓜ cottage
ke·so ko·*tash*
cotton algodón ⓜ al·go·*don*
cotton balls bolas ⓕ pl de algodón
bo·las de al·go·don
cough tos ⓕ tos
cough medicine jarabe ⓜ para la
tos kha·*ra*·be *pa*·ra la tos
count contar kon·*tar*
counter (in shop) mostrador ⓜ
mos·tra·*dor*
country país ⓜ pa·*ees*
countryside campo ⓜ *kam*·po
coupon cupón ⓜ koo·*pon*
courgette calabacita ⓕ
ka·la·ba·*see*·ta
court (tennis) cancha ⓕ de tenis
kan·cha de te·nees
cous cous cus cus ⓜ koos koos
cover charge cover ⓜ *ko*·ver
cow vaca ⓕ *va*·ka
crab cangrejo ⓜ kan·*gre*·kho
crackers galletas ⓕ pl saladas
ga·*ye*·tas sa·*la*·das
craft artesanía ⓕ pl ar·te·sa·*nee*·a
crash choque ⓜ *cho*·ke
crazy loco/a ⓜ/ⓕ *lo*·ko/a
cream crema ⓕ *kre*·ma
cream cheese queso ⓜ crema *ke*·so
kre·ma
creche guardería ⓕ gwar·de·*ree*·a
credit card tarjeta ⓕ de crédito
tar·*khe*·ta de *kre*·dee·to
cricket (sport) críquet ⓜ *kree*·ket
crop cosecha ⓕ ko·*se*·cha
crowded lleno/a ⓜ/ⓕ *ye*·no/a

cucumber pepino ⓜ pe·*pee*·no
cuddle abrazo ⓜ a·*bra*·so
cuddle abrazar a·bra·*sar*
cup taza ⓕ *ta*·sa
cupboard alacena ⓕ a·la·*se*·na
currency exchange cambio ⓜ (de moneda) *kam*·byo (de mo·*ne*·da)
current (electricity) corriente ⓕ ko·*ryen*·te
current affairs informativo ⓜ een·for·ma·*tee*·vo
curry curry ⓜ *koo*·ree
curry powder curry ⓜ en polvo *koo*·ree en *pol*·vo
custard flan ⓜ flan
customs aduana ⓕ a·*dwa*·na
cut cortar kor·*tar*
cutlery cubiertos ⓜ pl koo·*byer*·tos
CV currículum ⓜ koo·*ree*·koo·loom
cycle andar en bicicleta an·*dar* en bee·see·*kle*·ta
cycling ciclismo ⓜ see·*klees*·mo
cyclist ciclista ⓜ&ⓕ see·*klees*·ta
cystitis cistitis ⓕ sees·*tee*·tees

dad papá ⓜ pa·*pa*
daily diariamente dya·rya·*men*·te
dance bailar bai·*lar*
dancing baile ⓜ *bai*·le
dangerous peligroso/a ⓜ/ⓕ pe·lee·*gro*·so/a
dark oscuro/a ⓜ/ⓕ os·*koo*·ro/a
data projector cañon ⓜ proyector ka·*nyon* pro·yek·*tor*
date (appointment) cita ⓕ *see*·ta
date (day) fecha ⓕ *fe*·cha
date (a person) salir con sa·*leer* kon
date of birth fecha ⓕ de nacimiento *fe*·cha de na·see·*myen*·to
daughter hija ⓕ *ee*·kha
dawn amanecer ⓜ a·ma·ne·*ser*
day día ⓜ *dee*·a
day after tomorrow pasado mañana pa·*sa*·do ma·*nya*·na
day before yesterday antier an·*tyer*

D

dead muerto/a ⓜ/ⓕ *mwer*·to/a
deaf sordo/a ⓜ/ⓕ *sor*·do/a
deal (cards) repartir re·par·*teer*
decide decidir de·see·*deer*
deep profundo/a ⓜ/ⓕ pro·*foon*·do/a
deforestation deforestación ⓕ de·fo·res·ta·*syon*
degree título ⓜ *tee*·too·lo
delay demora ⓕ de·*mo*·ra
delirious delirante de·lee·*ran*·te
deliver entregar en·tre·*gar*
democracy democracia ⓕ de·mo·*kra*·sya
demonstration (protest) manifestación ⓕ ma·nee·fes·ta·*syon*
dental floss hilo ⓜ dental ee·lo den·*tal*
dentist dentista ⓕ den·*tees*·ta
deny negar ne·*gar*
deodorant desodorante ⓜ de·so·do·*ran*·te
depart salir de sa·*leer* de
department store tienda ⓕ departamental *tyen*·da de·par·ta·men·*tal*
departure salida ⓕ sa·*lee*·da
deposit (bank) depósito ⓜ de·po·see·to
descendant descendiente ⓜ de·sen·*dyen*·te
desert desierto ⓜ de·*syer*·to
design diseño ⓜ dee·*se*·nyo
destination destino ⓜ des·*tee*·no
destroy destruir des·troo·*eer*
detail detalle ⓜ de·*ta*·ye
diabetes diabetes ⓕ dee·a·be·tes
dial tone línea ⓕ *lee*·ne·a
diaper pañal ⓜ pa·*nyal*
diaphragm diafragma ⓜ dee·a·*frag*·ma
diarrhoea diarrea ⓕ dee·a·*re*·a
diary agenda ⓕ a·*khen*·da
dice dados ⓜ pl *da*·dos
dictionary diccionario ⓜ deek·syo·*na*·ryo
die morir mo·*reer*

E

diet dieta ① *dye*·ta
different diferente dee·fe·*ren*·te
difficult difícil dee·*fee*·seel
dining car vagón ⓜ restaurante va·*gon* res·tow·*ran*·te
dinner cena ① *se*·na
direct directo/a ⓜ/① dee·*rek*·to/a
direct-dial marcación ① directa mar·ka·*syon* dee·*rek*·ta
director director/directora ⓜ/① dee·*rek*·tor/dee·*rek*·to·ra
dirty sucio/a ⓜ/① *soo*·syo/a
disabled discapacitado/a ⓜ/① dees·ka·pa·see·*ta*·do/a
disco discoteca ① dees·ko·*te*·ka
discount descuento ⓜ des·*kwen*·to
discover descubrir des·koo·*breer*
discrimination discriminación ① dees·kree·mee·na·*syon*
disease enfermedad ① en·fer·me·*dad*
disk disco ⓜ *dees*·ko
disposable desechable de·se·*cha*·ble
diving submarinismo ⓜ soob·ma·ree·*nees*·mo
diving equipment equipo ⓜ para buceo e·*kee*·po pa·ra boo·*se*·o
divorced divorciado/a ⓜ/① dee·vor·*sya*·do/a
dizzy mareado/a ⓜ/① ma·re·a·do/a
do hacer a·*ser*
doctor doctor/doctora ⓜ/① dok·*tor*/dok·*to*·ra
documentary documental ⓜ do·koo·men·*tal*
dog perro/a ⓜ/① *pe*·ro/a
dole paro ⓜ *pa*·ro
doll muñeca ① moo·*nye*·ka
dollar dólar ⓜ *do*·lar
domestic flight vuelo ⓜ nacional vwe·lo na·syo·*nal*
donkey burro ⓜ *boo*·ro
door puerta ① *pwer*·ta
dope mota ① *mo*·ta
double doble *do*·ble
double bed cama ① matrimonial *ka*·ma ma·tree·mo·*nyal*

double room habitación ① doble a·bee·ta·*syon* *do*·ble
down hacia abajo a·sya a·*ba*·kho
downhill cuesta abajo *kwes*·ta a·*ba*·kho
dozen docena ① do·*se*·na
drama drama ⓜ *dra*·ma
draw dibujar dee·boo·*khar*
dream soñar so·*nyar*
dress vestido ⓜ ves·*tee*·do
dried fruit fruta ① seca *froo*·ta se·*ka*
drink bebida ① be·*bee*·da
drink tomar to·*mar*
drive conducir kon·doo·*seer*
drivers licence licencia ① de manejo lee·*sen*·sya de ma·*ne*·kho
drug (medicinal) medicina ① me·dee·see·na
drug addiction drogadicción ① dro·ga·deek·*syon*
drug dealer traficante ⓜ&① de drogas tra·fee·*kan*·te de *dro*·gas
drugs (illegal) drogas ① pl *dro*·gas
drums batería ① ba·te·*ree*·a
drumstick muslo ⓜ de pollo *moos*·lo de po·yo
drunk borracho/a ⓜ/① bo·*ra*·cho/a
dry seco/a ⓜ/① *se*·ko/a
dry secar se·*kar*
duck pato ⓜ *pa*·to
dummy (pacifier) chupón ⓜ choo·*pon*
during durante doo·*ran*·te
DVD DVD de ve de

E

each cada *ka*·da
ear oreja ① o·re·kha
early temprano tem·*pra*·no
earn ganar ga·*nar*
earplugs tapones ⓜ pl para los oídos ta·po·nes *pa*·ra los o·ee·dos
earrings aretes ⓜ pl a·re·tes
Earth Tierra ① *tye*·ra
earthquake terremoto ⓜ te·re·*mo*·to
east este *es*·te

Easter Pascua ① *pas*·kwa

easy fácil fa·*seel*

eat comer ko·*mer*

economy class clase ① turísta *kla*·se too·*rees*·ta

eczema eczema ① ek·*se*·ma

editor editor/editora ⑩/① e·dee·*tor*/e·dee·*to*·ra

education educación ① e·doo·ka·*syon*

eggplant berenjena ① be·ren·*khe*·na

egg huevo ⑩ *we*·vo

elections elecciones ① pl e·lek·*syo*·nes

electrical store ferretería ① fe·re·te·*ree*·a

electricity electricidad ① e·lek·tree·see·*dad*

elevator elevador ⑩ e·le·va·*dor*

embarrassed apenado/a ⑩/① a·pe·*na*·do/a

embassy embajada ① em·ba·*kha*·da

emergency emergencia ① e·mer·*khen*·sya

emotional emocional e·mo·syo·*nal*

employee empleado/a ⑩/① em·ple·*a*·do/a

employer jefe/jefa ⑩/① *khe*·fe/ *khe*·fa

empty vacío/a ⑩/① va·*see*·o/a

end fin ⑩ feen

end terminar ter·mee·*nar*

endangered species especies ① pl en peligro de extinción es·*pe*·syes en pe·*lee*·gro de ek·steen·*syon*

engine motor ⑩ mo·*tor*

engineer ingeniero/a ⑩/① een·khe·*nye*·ro/a

engineering ingeniería ① een·khe·nye·*ree*·a

England Inglaterra ① een·gla·*te*·ra

English (language) inglés ⑩ een·*gles*

enjoy (oneself) divertirse dee·ver·*teer*·se

enough suficiente soo·fee·*syen*·te

enter entrar en·*trar*

entertainment guide guía ① del ocio *gee*·a del o·*syo*

envelope sobre ⑩ *so*·bre

environment medio ⑩ ambiente *me*·dyo am·*byen*·te

epilepsy epilepsia ① e·pee·*lep*·sya

equal opportunity igualdad ① de oportunidades ee·gwal·*dad* de o·por·too·nee·*da*·des

equality igualdad ① ee·gwal·*dad*

equipment equipo ⑩ e·*kee*·po

escalator escaleras ① pl eléctricas es·ka·*le*·ras e·*lek*·tree·kas

Euro euro ⑩ e·oo·ro

Europe Europa ① e·oo·*ro*·pa

euthanasia eutanasia ① e·oo·ta·*na*·sya

evening noche ① *no*·che

everything todo *to*·do

example ejemplo ⑩ e·*khem*·plo

excellent excelente ek·se·*len*·te

excess baggage exceso ⑩ de equipaje ek·*se*·so de e·kee·*pa*·khe

exchange cambio ⑩ *kam*·byo

exchange (money) cambiar kam·*byar*

exchange rate tipo ⑩ de cambio *tee*·po de *kam*·byo

excluded excluído/a ⑩/① ek·skloo·ee·do/a

exhaust agotar a·go·*tar*

exhaust (car) escape ⑩ es·*ka*·pe

exhibit exponer ek·spo·*ner*

exhibition exposición ① ek·spo·see·*syon*

exit salida ① sa·*lee*·da

expensive caro/a ⑩/① *ka*·ro/a

experience experiencia ① ek·spe·*ryen*·sya

express expreso ⑩ ek·*spre*·so

express mail correo ⑩ expresso ko·*re*·o ek·*spre*·so

extension (visa) prórroga ① *pro*·ro·ga

eye ojo ⑩ o·kho

F

eyebrows cejas ① pl se·khas
eye drops gotas ① pl para los ojos
go·tas pa·ra los o·khos

F

fabric tela ① te·la
face cara ① ka·ra
face cloth toallita ① facial
to·a·yee·ta fa·syal
factory fábrica ① fa·bree·ka
factory worker obrero/a ⓜ/①
o·bre·ro/a
fall caída ① ka·ee·da
fall (season) otoño ⓜ o·to·nyo
family familia ① fa·mee·lya
family name apellido ⓜ a·pe·yee·do
famous famoso/a ⓜ/① fa·mo·so/a
fan (supporter) aficionado ⓜ
a·fee·syo·na·do
fan (machine) ventilador ⓜ
ven·tee·la·dor
far lejos le·khos
farewell despedida ① des·pe·dee·da
farm granja ① gran·kha
farmer granjero/a ⓜ/①
gran·khe·ro/a
fart pedo ⓜ pe·do
fast rápido/a ⓜ/① ra·pee·do/a
fat (person) gordo/a ⓜ/① gor·do/a
fat (grease) grasa ① gra·sa
father padre ⓜ pa·dre
father-in-law suegro ⓜ swe·gro
faucet llave ① (del agua) ya·ve (del
a·gwa)
fault falta ① fal·ta
faulty defectuoso/a ⓜ/①
de·fek·two·so/a
feed alimentar a·lee·men·tar
feel sentir sen·teer
feelings sentimientos ⓜ pl
sen·tee·myen·tos
fence cerca ① ser·ka
fencing (sport) esgrima ①
es·gree·ma
festival festival ⓜ fes·tee·val
fever fiebre ① fye·bre

few pocos/as ⓜ/① pl po·kos/as
fiance(e) prometido/a ⓜ/①
pro·me·tee·do/a
fiction ficción ① feek·syon
field campo ⓜ kam·po
fig higo ⓜ ee·go
fight pelea ① pe·le·a
fight luchar loo·char
fill llenar ye·nar
film película ① pe·lee·koo·la
film speed sensibilidad ①
sen·see·bee·lee·dad
filtered con ① filtro kon feel·tro
find encontrar en·kon·trar
fine multa ① mool·ta
finger dedo ⓜ de·do
finish terminar ter·mee·nar
fire (general) fuego ⓜ fwe·go
fire (building) incendio ⓜ
een·sen·dyo
fireplace chimenea ① chee·me·ne·a
firewood leña ① le·nya
first primero/a ⓜ/① pree·me·ro/a
first class primera clase ①
pree·me·ra kla·se
first name nombre ⓜ nom·bre
first-aid kit botiquín ⓜ bo·tee·keen
fish pez ⓜ pes
fish (as food) pescado ⓜ pes·ka·do
fish shop pescadería ①
pes·ka·de·ree·a
fishing pesca ① pes·ka
fizzy con gas kon gas
flag bandera ① ban·de·ra
flannel franela ① fra·ne·la
flashlight linterna ① leen·ter·na
flat plano/a ⓜ/① pla·no/a
flat (apartment) apartamento ⓜ
a·par·ta·men·to
flea pulga ① pool·ga
flippers aletas ① pl a·le·tas
flooding inundación ①
ee·noon·da·syon
floor (ground) suelo ⓜ swe·lo
floor (storey) piso ⓜ pee·so
florist florista ⓜ&① flo·rees·ta

flour harina ⓕ a·ree·na
flower flor ⓕ flor
flower seller vendedor/vendedora de flores ⓜ/ⓕ ven·de·dor/ven·de·do·ra de flo·res
flu gripe ⓕ gree·pe
fly volar vo·lar
foggy neblinoso/a ⓜ/ⓕ ne·blee·no·so/a
folk (music) folklórico/a ⓜ/ⓕ fol·klo·ree·ko/a
follow seguir se·geer
food comida ⓕ ko·mee·da
food supplies víveres ⓜ pl vee·ve·res
fool imbécil ⓜ&ⓕ eem·be·seel
foot pie ⓜ pye
football (soccer) fútbol ⓜ foot·bol
footpath banqueta ⓕ ban·ke·ta
for para pa·ra
foreign extranjero/a ⓜ/ⓕ ek·stran·khe·ro/a
foreign exchange office casa ⓕ de cambio ka·sa de kam·byo
forest bosque ⓜ bos·ke
forever para siempre pa·ra syem·pre
forget olvidar ol·vee·dar
forgive perdonar per·do·nar
fork tenedor ⓜ te·ne·dor
fortnight quincena ⓕ keen·se·na
foul asqueroso/a ⓜ/ⓕ as·ke·ro·so/a
foyer vestíbulo ⓜ ves·tee·boo·lo
fragile frágil fra·kheel
France Francia ⓕ fran·sya
free (not bound) libre lee·bre
free (of charge) gratis gra·tees
freeze congelar kon·khe·lar
friend amigo/a ⓜ/ⓕ a·mee·go/a
frost escarcha ⓕ es·kar·cha
frozen foods productos ⓜ pl congelados pro·dook·tos kon·khe·la·dos
fruit fruta ⓕ froo·ta
fruit picking recolección ⓕ de fruta re·ko·lek·syon de froo·ta
fry freír fre·eer

frying pan sartén ⓜ sar·ten
fuel combustible ⓜ kom·boos·tee·ble
full lleno/a ⓜ/ⓕ ye·no/a
full-time tiempo ⓜ completo tyem·po kom·ple·to
fun diversión ⓕ dee·ver·syon
funeral funeral ⓜ foo·ne·ral
funny divertido/a ⓜ/ⓕ dee·ver·tee·do/a
furniture muebles ⓜ pl mwe·bles
future futuro ⓜ foo·too·ro

G

garlic ajo ⓜ a·kho
gas (for cooking) gas ⓜ gas
gas (petrol) gasolina ⓕ ga·so·lee·na
gay gay gay
gelatin gelatina ⓕ khe·la·tee·na
general general khe·ne·ral
Germany Alemania ⓕ a·le·ma·nya
gift regalo ⓜ re·ga·lo
gin ginebra ⓕ khee·ne·bra
ginger jengibre ⓜ khen·khee·bre
girl chica ⓕ chee·ka
girl (child) niña ⓕ nee·nya
girlfriend novia ⓕ no·vya
give dar dar
give (a gift) regalar re·ga·lar
glandular fever enfermedad ⓕ del beso en·fer·me·dad del be·so
glass (drinking) vaso ⓜ va·so
glass (material) vidrio ⓜ vee·dryo
glass (of wine) copa ⓕ (de vino) ko·pa (de vee·no)
glasses lentes ⓜ pl len·tes
gloves guantes ⓜ pl gwan·tes
go ir eer
go out with salir con sa·leer kon
go shopping ir de compras eer de kom·pras
goal gol ⓜ gol
goalkeeper portero/a ⓜ/ⓕ por·te·ro/a
goat cabra ⓕ ka·bra
god dios ⓜ dyos

H

goddess diosa ⓕ *dyo*·sa

goggles goggles ⓜ pl *go*·gles

golf golf ⓜ golf

golf ball pelota ⓕ de golf pe·*lo*·ta de golf

golf course campo ⓜ de golf *kam*·po de golf

good bueno/a ⓜ/ⓕ *bwe*·no/a

goodbye adiós a·*dyos*

gorgeous guapo/a ⓜ/ⓕ *gwa*·po/a

government gobierno ⓜ go·*byer*·no

gram gramo ⓜ *gra*·mo

grandchild nieto/a ⓜ/ⓕ *nye*·to/a

grandfather abuelo ⓜ a·*bwe*·lo

grandmother abuela ⓕ a·*bwe*·la

grapefruit toronja ⓕ to·*ron*·kha

grapes uvas ⓕ pl *oo*·vas

grass pasto ⓜ *pas*·to

grasshoppers chapulines ⓜ pl cha·poo·*lee*·nes

grave tumba ⓕ *toom*·ba

gray gris grees

grease grasa ⓕ *gra*·sa

great padrísimo/a ⓜ/ⓕ pa·*dree*·see·mo/a

green verde *ver*·de

greengrocery verdulería ⓕ ver·doo·le·*ree*·a

grey gris grees

grocery tienda ⓕ de abarrotes *tyen*·da de a·ba·*ro*·tes

groundnut cacahuate ⓜ ka·ka·*wa*·te

grow crecer kre·*ser*

g-string tanga ⓕ *tan*·ga

guess adivinar a·dee·vee·*nar*

guide (audio) audioguía ⓕ ow·dyo·*gee*·a

guide (person) guía ⓜ&ⓕ *gee*·a

guide dog perro ⓜ guía *pe*·ro *gee*·a

guidebook guía ⓕ turística *gee*·a too·*rees*·tee·ka

guided tour recorrido ⓜ guiado re·ko·*ree*·do gee·*a*·do

guilty culpable kool·*pa*·ble

guitar guitarra ⓕ gee·*ta*·ra

gum goma ⓕ *go*·ma

gymnastics gimnasia ⓕ kheem·*na*·sya

gynaecologist ginecólogo/a ⓜ/ⓕ khee·ne·*ko*·lo·go/a

H

hair pelo ⓜ *pe*·lo

hairbrush cepillo ⓜ se·*pee*·yo

haircut corte ⓜ de pelo *kor*·te de *pe*·lo

hairdresser peluquero/a ⓜ/ⓕ pe·loo·*ke*·ro/a

halal halal kha·*lal*

half medio/a ⓜ/ⓕ *me*·dyo/a

half a litre medio litro ⓜ *me*·dyo *lee*·tro

hallucinate alucinar a·loo·see·*nar*

ham jamón ⓜ kha·*mon*

hammer martillo ⓜ mar·*tee*·yo

hammock hamaca ⓕ a·*ma*·ka

hand mano ⓕ *ma*·no

handbag bolsa ⓕ *bol*·sa

handicrafts artesanías ⓕ pl ar·te·sa·*nee*·as

handkerchief pañuelo ⓜ pa·*nywe*·lo

handlebar manubrio ⓜ ma·*noo*·bryo

handmade hecho/a ⓜ/ⓕ a mano *e*·cho/a a *ma*·no

handsome guapo/a ⓜ/ⓕ *gwa*·po/a

happy feliz fe·*lees*

harassment acoso ⓜ a·*ko*·so

harbour puerto ⓜ *pwer*·to

hard duro/a ⓜ/ⓕ *doo*·ro/a

hardware store tlapalería ⓕ tla·pa·le·*ree*·a

hash hachís ⓜ kha·*shees*

hat sombrero ⓜ som·*bre*·ro

have tener te·*ner*

have a cold tener gripa te·*ner* *gree*·pa

have fun divertirse dee·ver·*teer*·se

hay fever alergia ⓕ al polen a·*ler*·khya al *po*·len

he él el

head cabeza ⓕ ka·*be*·sa

headache dolor ⓜ de cabeza do·*lor* de ka·*be*·sa

headlights faros ⓜ pl *fa*·ros
health salud ⓕ sa·*lood*
hear oír o·*eer*
hearing aid audífono ⓜ
ow·*dee*·fo·no
heart corazón ⓜ ko·ra·*son*
heart condition cardiopatía ⓕ
kar·dyo·pa·*tee*·a
heat calor ⓜ ka·*lor*
heater calentador ⓜ ka·len·ta·*dor*
heating calefacción ⓕ ka·le·fak·*syon*
heavy pesado/a ⓜ/ⓕ pe·*sa*·do/a
helmet casco ⓜ *kas*·ko
help ayudar a·yoo·*dar*
hepatitis hepatitis ⓕ e·pa·*tee*·tees
her su soo
herbalist yerbero/a ⓜ/ⓕ
yer·*be*·ro/a
herbs hierbas ⓕ pl *yer*·bas
here aquí a·*kee*
heroin heroína ⓕ e·ro·ee·na
herring arenque ⓜ a·*ren*·ke
high alto/a ⓜ/ⓕ *al*·to/a
high school preparatoria ⓕ
pre·pa·ra·to·rya
hike ir de excursión eer de
ek·skoor·*syon*
hiking excursionismo ⓜ
ek·skoor·syo·*nees*·mo
hiking boots botas ⓕ pl de montaña
bo·tas de mon·*ta*·nya
hiking routes caminos ⓜ pl rurales
ka·*mee*·nos roo·*ra*·les
hill colina ⓕ ko·*lee*·na
Hindu hindú ⓜ&ⓕ een·*doo*
hire rentar ren·*tar*
his su soo
historical histórico/a ⓜ/ⓕ
ees·*to*·ree·ko/a
hitchhike pedir aventón pe·*deer*
a·ven·*ton*
HIV positive seropositivo/a ⓜ/ⓕ
se·ro·po·see·*tee*·vo/a
hockey hockey ⓜ *kho*·kee
holiday día ⓜ festivo *dee*·a
fes·*tee*·vo

holidays vacaciones ⓕ pl
va·ka·*syo*·nes
Holy Week Semana ⓕ Santa
se·*ma*·na san·ta
home casa ⓕ *ka*·sa
homeless sin hogar seen o·*gar*
homemaker ama ⓕ de casa *a*·ma
de *ka*·sa
homosexual homosexual ⓜ&ⓕ
o·mo·sek·*swal*
honey miel ⓕ myel
honeymoon luna ⓕ de miel *loo*·na
de myel
horoscope horóscopo ⓜ o·*ros*·ko·po
horse caballo ⓜ ka·*ba*·yo
horse riding equitación ⓕ
e·kee·ta·*syon*
hospital hospital ⓜ os·pee·*tal*
hospitality hotelería ⓕ o·te·le·*ree*·a
hot caliente ka·*lyen*·te
hot water agua ⓜ caliente *a*·gwa
ka·*lyen*·te
hotel hotel ⓜ o·*tel*
house casa ⓕ *ka*·sa
housework trabajo ⓜ de casa
tra·*ba*·kho de *ka*·sa
how cómo *ko*·mo
how much cuánto *kwan*·to
hug abrazo ⓜ a·*bra*·so
huge enorme e·*nor*·me
human rights derechos ⓜ pl
humanos de·*re*·chos oo·*ma*·nos
humanities humanidades ⓕ pl
oo·ma·nee·*da*·des
(be) hungry tener hambre te·*ner*
am·bre
hunting caza ⓕ *ka*·sa
(be in a) hurry tener prisa te·*ner*
pree·sa
hurt lastimar las·tee·*mar*
husband esposo ⓜ es·*po*·so

I

I yo yo
ice hielo ⓜ *ye*·lo
ice axe piolet ⓜ pyo·*let*

J

ice cream helado ⓜ e·*la*·do
ice-cream parlour heladería ⓕ
e·la·de·*ree*·a
ice hockey hockey ⓜ sobre hielo
kho·kee so·bre *ye*·lo
identification identificación ⓕ
ee·den·tee·fee·ka·*syon*
idiot idiota ⓜ&ⓕ ee·*dyo*·ta
if si see
ill enfermo/a ⓜ/ⓕ en·*fer*·mo/a
immigration inmigración ⓕ
een·mee·gra·*syon*
important importante
eem·por·*tan*·te
in a hurry de prisa *pree*·sa
in front of enfrente de en·*fren*·te de
included incluído/a ⓜ/ⓕ
een·kloo·*ee*·do/a
income tax impuesto ⓜ sobre la
renta eem·*pwes*·to so·bre la *ren*·ta
India India ⓕ *een*·dya
indicator indicador ⓜ
een·dee·ka·*dor*
indigestion indigestión ⓕ
een·dee·khes·*tyon*
industry industria ⓕ een·*doos*·trya
infection infección ⓕ een·fek·*syon*
inflammation inflamación ⓕ
een·fla·ma·*syon*
influenza gripe ⓕ *gree*·pe
ingredient ingrediente ⓜ
een·gre·*dyen*·te
inject inyectar een·yek·*tar*
injection inyección ⓕ een·yek·*syon*
injury herida ⓕ e·*ree*·da
innocent inocente ee·no·*sen*·te
inside adentro a·*den*·tro
instructor instructor/
instructora ⓜ/ⓕ een·strook·*tor*/
eens·trook·*to*·ra
insurance seguro ⓜ se·*goo*·ro
interesting interesante
een·te·re·*san*·te
intermission descanso ⓜ des·*kan*·so
international internacional
een·ter·na·syo·*nal*

internet internet ⓕ een·ter·*net*
— cafe cibercafé ⓜ see·ber·ka·*fe*
interpreter intérprete ⓜ&ⓕ
een·*ter*·pre·te
intersection intersección ⓕ
een·ter·sek·*syon*
interview entrevista ⓕ
en·tre·*vees*·ta
invite invitar een·vee·*tar*
Ireland Irlanda ⓕ eer·*lan*·da
iron (for clothes) plancha ⓕ
plan·cha
island isla ⓕ *ees*·la
IT informática ⓕ een·for·*ma*·tee·ka
itch comezón ⓜ ko·me·*son*
itemised detallado/a ⓜ/ⓕ
de·ta·*ya*·do/a
itinerary itinerario ⓜ
ee·tee·ne·*ra*·ryo
IUD DIU ⓜ dee·oo

J

jacket chamarra ⓕ cha·*ma*·ra
jail cárcel ⓕ *kar*·sel
jam mermelada ⓕ mer·me·*la*·da
Japan Japón ⓜ kha·*pon*
jar jarra ⓕ *kha*·ra
jaw mandíbula ⓕ man·*dee*·boo·la
jealous celoso/a ⓜ/ⓕ se·*lo*·so/a
jeans jeans ⓜ pl yeens
jeep jeep ⓜ yeep
Jehova's witness testigo ⓜ de
Jehová tes·*tee*·go de khe·o·*va*
jet lag jet lag ⓜ yet lag
jewellery joyería ⓕ kho·ye·*ree*·a
Jewish judío/a ⓜ/ⓕ khoo·*dee*·o/a
job trabajo ⓜ tra·*ba*·kho
jockey jockey ⓜ *yo*·kee
jogging correr ko·*rer*
joke broma ⓕ *bro*·ma
joke bromear bro·me·*ar*
journalist periodista ⓜ&ⓕ
pe·ryo·*dees*·ta
judge juez ⓜ&ⓕ khwes
juice jugo ⓜ *khoo*·go
jump saltar sal·*tar*

jumper (sweater) sweater ⓜ
swe·ter

jumper leads cables ⓜ pl
pasacorrientes *ka*·bles
pa·sa·ko·*ryen*·tes

ketchup cátsup ⓜ *kat*·soop
key llave ⓕ *ya*·ve
keyboard teclado ⓜ te·*kla*·do
kick patear pa·te·*ar*
kick (a goal) meter (un gol) me·*ter*
(oon gol)
kill matar ma·*tar*
kilogram kilo ⓜ *kee*·lo
kilometre kilómetro ⓜ kee·*lo*·me·tro
kind amable a·*ma*·ble
kindergarten jardín ⓜ de niños
khar·*deen* de *nee*·nyos
king rey ⓜ ray
kiss beso ⓜ *be*·so
kiss besar be·*sar*
kitchen cocina ⓕ ko·*see*·na
kitten gatito/a ⓜ/ⓕ ga·*tee*·to/a
kiwifruit kiwi ⓜ *kee*·wee
knapsack mochila ⓕ mo·*chee*·la
knee rodilla ⓕ ro·*dee*·ya
knife cuchillo ⓜ koo·*chee*·yo
know (someone) conocer ko·no·*ser*
know (something) saber sa·*ber*
kosher kosher *ko*·sher

labourer obrero/a ⓜ/ⓕ o·*bre*·ro/a
lace encaje ⓜ en·*ka*·khe
lager cerveza ⓕ clara ser·*ve*·sa
kla·ra
lake lago ⓜ *la*·go
lamb borrego ⓜ bo·*rre*·go
land tierra ⓕ *tye*·ra
landlady propietaria ⓕ
pro·pye·*ta*·rya
landlord propietario ⓜ
pro·pye·*ta*·ryo
languages idiomas ⓜ pl ee·*dyo*·mas

laptop laptop ⓜ *lap*·top
lard manteca ⓕ man·*te*·ka
large grande *gran*·de
laser pointer señalador ⓜ láser
se·nya·la·*dor* *la*·ser
late tarde *tar*·de
laugh reír re·*eer*
laundrette lavandería ⓕ
la·van·de·*ree*·a
laundry lavandería ⓕ la·van·de·*ree*·a
law ley ⓕ lay
law (field of study) derecho ⓜ
de·*re*·cho
lawyer abogado/a ⓜ/ⓕ a·bo·*ga*·do/a
leader líder ⓜ&ⓕ *lee*·der
leaf hoja ⓕ o·kha
learn aprender a·pren·*der*
leather cuero ⓜ *kwe*·ro
lecturer profesor/profesora ⓜ/ⓕ
pro·fe·*sor*/pro·fe·*so*·ra
ledge saliente ⓜ sa·*lyen*·te
leek poro ⓜ *po*·ro
left izquierda ⓕ ees·*kyer*·da
left luggage consigna ⓕ kon·*seeg*·na
left-wing de izquierda de ees·*kyer*·da
leg pierna ⓕ *pyer*·na
legal legal le·*gal*
legislation legislación ⓕ
le·khees·la·*syon*
lemon limón ⓜ lee·*mon*
lemonade limonada ⓕ lee·mo·*na*·da
Lent Cuaresma ⓕ kwa·*res*·ma
lens objetivo ⓜ ob·khe·*tee*·vo
lentils lentejas ⓕ pl len·*te*·khas
lesbian lesbiana ⓕ les·bee·*a*·na
less menos *me*·nos
letter carta ⓕ *kar*·ta
lettuce lechuga ⓕ le·*choo*·ga
liar mentiroso/a ⓜ/ⓕ
men·tee·*ro*·so/a
library biblioteca ⓕ bee·blyo·*te*·ka
lice piojos ⓜ pl *pyo*·khos
license plate number número ⓜ de
placa *noo*·me·ro de *pla*·ka
lie (not stand) recostarse
re·kos·*tar*·se

M

life vida ⓕ *vee*·da
life jacket chaleco ⓜ salvavidas cha·*le*·ko sal·va·vee·das
lift elevador ⓜ e·le·va·*dor*
light (of weight) ligero/a ⓜ/ⓕ lee·*khe*·ro/a
light luz ⓕ loos
light bulb foco ⓜ *fo*·ko
light meter fotómetro ⓜ fo·*to*·me·tro
lighter encendedor ⓜ en·sen·de·*dor*
lights luces ⓕ pl *loo*·ses
like gustar goos·*tar*
lime lima ⓕ *lee*·ma
line línea ⓕ *lee*·ne·a
lip balm bálsamo ⓜ para labios *bal*·sa·mo pa·ra *la*·byos
lips labios ⓜ pl *la*·byos
lipstick lápiz ⓜ labial *la*·pees la·*byal*
liquor store tienda ⓕ de abarrotes *tyen*·da de a·ba·*ro*·tes
listen escuchar es·koo·*char*
live vivir vee·*veer*
liver hígado ⓜ *ee*·ga·do
lizard lagartija ⓕ la·gar·*tee*·kha
local local lo·*kal*
lock cerradura ⓕ se·ra·*doo*·ra
lock cerrar se·*rar*
locked cerrado/a con llave ⓜ/ⓕ se·*ra*·do/a kon *ya*·ve
lollies dulces ⓜ pl *dool*·ses
long largo/a ⓜ/ⓕ *lar*·go/a
long-distance larga distancia ⓕ *lar*·ga dees·*tan*·sya
look mirar mee·*rar*
look after cuidar kwee·*dar*
look for buscar boos·*kar*
lookout mirador ⓜ mee·ra·*dor*
loose suelto/a ⓜ/ⓕ *swel*·to/a
loose change cambio ⓜ en monedas *kam*·byo en mo·*ne*·das
lose perder per·*der*
lost perdido/a ⓜ/ⓕ per·*dee*·do/a
lost property office oficina ⓕ de objetos perdidos o·fee·*see*·na de ob·*khe*·tos per·*dee*·dos
loud ruidoso/a ⓜ/ⓕ rwee·*do*·so/a

love amar a·*mar*
lover amante ⓜ&ⓕ a·*man*·te
low bajo/a ⓜ/ⓕ *ba*·kho/a
lubricant lubricante ⓜ loo·bree·*kan*·te
luck suerte ⓕ *swer*·te
lucky afortunado/a ⓜ/ⓕ a·for·too·*na*·do/a
luggage equipaje ⓜ e·kee·*pa*·khe
luggage lockers casilleros ⓜ pl ka·see·*ye*·ros
luggage tag etiqueta ⓕ para equipaje e·tee·*ke*·ta pa·ra e·kee·*pa*·khe
lump bulto ⓜ *bool*·to
lunch almuerzo ⓜ al·*mwer*·so
lungs pulmones ⓜ pl pool·*mo*·nes
luxury lujo ⓜ *loo*·kho

M

machine máquina ⓕ *ma*·kee·na
made of (cotton) hecho/a ⓜ/ⓕ de (algodón) *e*·cho/a de (al·go·*don*)
magazine revista ⓕ re·*vees*·ta
magician mago/a ⓜ/ⓕ *ma*·go/a
mail correo ⓜ ko·*re*·o
mailbox buzón ⓜ boo·*son*
main principal preen·see·*pal*
make hacer a·*ser*
make fun of burlarse de boor·*lar*·se de
make-up maquillaje ⓜ ma·kee·*ya*·khe
mammogram mamograma ⓜ ma·mo·*gra*·ma
man hombre ⓜ *om*·bre
manager director/directora ⓜ/ⓕ dee·rek·*tor*/dee·rek·*to*·ra
mandarin mandarina ⓕ man·da·*ree*·na
mango mango ⓜ *man*·go
manual worker obrero/a ⓜ/ⓕ o·*bre*·ro/a
many muchos/as ⓜ/ⓕ pl *moo*·chos/as
map mapa ⓜ *ma*·pa
margarine margarina ⓕ mar·ga·*ree*·na

M

marijuana marihuana ⓕ
ma·ree·*wa*·na

marital status estado ⓜ civil
es·*ta*·do see·*veel*

market mercado ⓜ mer·*ka*·do

marmalade mermelada ⓕ
mer·me·*la*·da

marriage matrimonio ⓜ
ma·tree·*mo*·nyo

married casado/a ⓜ/ⓕ ka·*sa*·do/a

marry casarse ka·*sar*·se

martial arts artes ⓕ pl marciales
ar·tes mar·*sya*·les

mass misa ⓕ *mee*·sa

massage masaje ⓜ ma·*sa*·khe

masseur/masseuse masajista ⓜ&ⓕ
ma·sa·*khees*·ta

mat petate ⓜ pe·*ta*·te

match (game) partido ⓜ
par·*tee*·do

matches cerillos ⓜ pl se·*ree*·yos

mattress colchón ⓜ kol·*chon*

maybe tal vez tal ves

mayonnaise mayonesa ⓕ
ma·yo·*ne*·sa

mayor alcalde ⓜ&ⓕ al·*kal*·de

measles sarampión ⓜ sa·ram·*pyon*

meat carne ⓕ *kar*·ne

mechanic mecánico/a ⓜ/ⓕ
me·*ka*·nee·ko/a

media medios ⓜ pl de comunicación
me·dyos de ko·moo·nee·ka·*syon*

medicine medicina ⓕ me·dee·*see*·na

meet encontrar en·kon·*trar*

melon melón ⓜ me·*lon*

member miembro ⓜ *myem*·bro

menstruation menstruación ⓕ
men·strwa·*syon*

menu carta ⓕ *kar*·ta

message mensaje ⓜ men·*sa*·khe

metal metal ⓜ me·*tal*

metre metro ⓜ *me*·tro

metro station estación ⓕ del metro
es·ta·*syon* del *me*·tro

microwave horno ⓜ de microondas
or·no de mee·kro·*on*·das

midnight medianoche ⓕ
me·dya·*no*·che

migraine migraña ⓕ mee·*gra*·nya

military militar mee·lee·*tar*

military service servicio ⓜ militar
ser·*vee*·syo mee·lee·*tar*

milk leche ⓕ *le*·che

millimetre milímetro ⓜ
mee·*lee*·me·tro

million millón ⓜ mee·*yon*

mince meat carne ⓕ molida *kar*·ne
mo·*lee*·da

mind cuidar kwee·*dar*

mineral water agua ⓜ mineral
a·gwa mee·ne·*ral*

mints pastillas ⓕ pl de menta
pas·*tee*·yas de *men*·ta

minute minuto ⓜ mee·*noo*·to

mirror espejo ⓜ es·*pe*·kho

miscarriage aborto ⓜ natural
a·*bor*·to na·too·*ral*

miss (feel absence of) extrañar
ek·stra·*nyar*

mistake error ⓜ e·*ror*

mix mezclar mes·*klar*

mobile phone celular ⓜ se·loo·*lar*

modem módem ⓜ *mo*·dem

moisturiser crema ⓕ hidratante
kre·ma ee·dra·*tan*·te

monastery monasterio ⓜ
mo·nas·*te*·ryo

money dinero ⓜ dee·*ne*·ro

month mes ⓜ mes

monument monumento ⓜ
mo·noo·*men*·to

moon luna ⓕ *loo*·na

morning mañana ⓕ ma·*nya*·na

morning sickness náuseas ⓕ pl
del embarazo *now*·se·as del
em·ba·*ra*·so

mosque mezquita ⓕ mes·*kee*·ta

mosquito mosquito ⓜ
mos·*kee*·to

mosquito coil repelente ⓜ contra
mosquitos re·pe·*len*·te kon·tra
mos·*kee*·tos

N

mosquito net mosquitero ⓜ
mos·kee·*te*·ro
mother madre ⓕ *ma*·dre
mother-in-law suegra ⓕ *swe*·gra
motorboat lancha ⓕ de motor
lan·cha de mo·*tor*
motorcycle motocicleta ⓕ
mo·to·see·*kle*·ta
motorway carretera ⓕ ka·re·*te*·ra
mountain montaña ⓕ mon·*ta*·nya
mountain bike bicicleta ⓕ de
montaña bee·see·*kle*·ta de
mon·*ta*·nya
mountain path brecha ⓕ *bre*·cha
mountain range cordillera ⓕ
kor·dee·*ye*·ra
mountaineering alpinismo ⓜ
al·pee·*nees*·mo
mouse ratón ⓜ ra·*ton*
mouse (computer) mouse ⓜ mows
mouth boca ⓕ *bo*·ka
movie película ⓕ pe·*lee*·koo·la
mp3 player reproductor ⓜ de mp3
re·pro·dook·*tor* de e·me pe tres
mud lodo ⓜ *lo*·do
muesli granola ⓕ gra·*no*·la
mum mamá ⓕ ma·*ma*
muscle músculo ⓜ *moos*·koo·lo
museum museo ⓜ moo·*se*·o
mushroom champiñón ⓜ
cham·pee·*nyon*
music música ⓕ *moo*·see·ka
musician músico/a ⓜ/ⓕ
moo·see·ko/a
Muslim musulmán/musulmana ⓜ/ⓕ
moo·sool·*man*/moo·sool·*ma*·na
mussels mejillones ⓜ pl
me·khee·*yo*·nes
mustard mostaza ⓕ mos·*ta*·sa
mute mudo/a ⓜ/ⓕ *moo*·do/a
my mi/mis sg/pl mee/mees

N

nail clippers cortauñas ⓜ
kor·ta·oo·nyas
name nombre ⓜ *nom*·bre

napkin servilleta ⓕ ser·vee·*ye*·ta
nappy pañal ⓜ pa·*nyal*
nappy rash rosadura ⓕ ro·sa·*doo*·ra
national park parque ⓜ nacional
par·ke na·syo·*nal*
nationality nacionalidad ⓕ
na·syo·na·lee·*dad*
nature naturaleza ⓕ na·too·ra·*le*·sa
naturopathy naturopatía ⓕ
na·too·ro·pa·*tee*·a
nausea náusea ⓕ *now*·se·a
near cerca *ser*·ka
nearby cerca *ser*·ka
nearest más cercano/a ⓜ/ⓕ mas
ser·*ka*·no/a
necessary necesario/a ⓜ/ⓕ
ne·se·*sa*·ryo/a
neck cuello ⓜ *kwe*·yo
necklace collar ⓜ ko·*yar*
need necesitar ne·se·see·*tar*
needle (sewing) aguja ⓕ a·*goo*·kha
needle (syringe) jeringa ⓕ
khe·*reen*·ga
negatives negativos ⓜ pl
ne·ga·*tee*·vos
neither tampoco tam·*po*·ko
net red ⓕ red
network red ⓕ red
Netherlands Holanda ⓕ o·*lan*·da
never nunca *noon*·ka
new nuevo/a ⓜ/ⓕ *nwe*·vo/a
New Year Año Nuevo ⓜ a·nyo
nwe·vo
New Year's Day día ⓜ de Año Nuevo
dee·a de a·nyo *nwe*·vo
New Year's Eve fin ⓜ de año feen
de a·nyo
New Zealand Nueva ⓕ Zelandia
nwe·va se·*lan*·dya
news noticias ⓕ pl no·*tee*·syas
news stand puesto ⓜ de periódicos
pwes·to de pe·*ryo*·dee·kos
newsagency agencia ⓕ de noticias
a·*khen*·sya de no·*tee*·syas
newspaper periódico ⓜ
pe·*ryo*·dee·ko

next próximo/a ⓜ/ⓕ *prok·see·mo/a*

next (month) (el mes) que viene (el mes) ke *vye·*ne

next to al lado de al *la·*do de

nice simpático/a ⓜ/ⓕ *seem·pa·tee·ko/a*

nickname apodo ⓜ *a·po·*do

night noche ⓕ *no·*che

no no no

noisy ruidoso/a ⓜ/ⓕ *rwee·do·so/a*

none nada *na·*da

non-smoking no fumar no foo·*mar*

noodles fideos ⓜ pl fee·*de·*os

noon mediodía ⓜ me·dyo·*dee·*a

north norte ⓜ *nor·*te

nose nariz ⓕ na·*rees*

notebook cuaderno ⓜ kwa·*der·*no

nothing nada *na·*da

now ahora a·*o·*ra

nuclear energy energía ⓕ nuclear e·ner·*khee·*a noo·kle·*ar*

nuclear testing pruebas ⓕ pl nucleares *prwe·*bas noo·kle·*a·*res

nuclear waste desperdicios ⓜ pl nucleares des·per·*dee·*syos noo·kle·*a·*res

number número ⓜ *noo·*me·ro

nun monja ⓕ *mon·*kha

nurse enfermero/a ⓜ/ⓕ en·fer·*me·*ro/a

nuts nueces ⓕ pl *nwe·*ses

O

oats avena ⓕ a·*ve·*na

ocean océano ⓜ o·*se·*a·no

off (spoiled) echado/a ⓜ/ⓕ a perder e·*cha·*do/a a per·*der*

office oficina ⓕ o·fee·*see·*na

office worker empleado/a ⓜ/ⓕ em·ple·*a·*do/a

offside fuera de lugar *fwe·*ra de loo·*gar*

often seguido se·*gee·*do

oil aceite ⓜ a·*say·*te

old viejo/a ⓜ/ⓕ *vye·*kho/a

olive oil aceite ⓜ de oliva a·*say·*te de o·*lee·*va

Olympic Games Juegos ⓜ pl Olímpicos *khwe·*gos o·*leem·*pee·kos

on en en

once una vez oo·na ves

one-way ticket boleto ⓜ sencillo bo·*le·*to sen·*see·*yo

onion cebolla ⓕ se·*bo·*ya

only sólo *so·*lo

open abierto/a ⓜ/ⓕ a·*byer·*to/a

open abrir a·*breer*

opening hours horario ⓜ de servicio o·*ra·*ryo de ser·*vee·*syo

opera ópera ⓕ o·*pe·*ra

operation operación ⓕ o·pe·ra·*syon*

operator operador/operadora ⓜ/ⓕ o·pe·ra·*dor*/o·pe·ra·*do·*ra

opinion opinión ⓕ o·pee·*nyon*

opposite frente a *fren·*te a

or o o

orange naranja ⓕ na·*ran·*kha

orange juice jugo ⓜ de naranja *khoo·*go de na·*ran·*kha

orchestra orquesta ⓕ or·*kes·*ta

order (command) orden ⓕ *or·*den

order (placement) orden ⓜ *or·*den

order ordenar or·de·*nar*

ordinary corriente ko·*ryen·*te

orgasm orgasmo ⓜ or·*gas·*mo

original original o·ree·khee·*nal*

other otro/a ⓜ/ⓕ o·*tro/a*

our nuestro/a ⓜ/ⓕ *nwes·*tro/a

outside exterior ⓜ ek·ste·*ryor*

ovarian cyst quiste ⓜ ovárico *kees·*te o·*va·*ree·ko

oven horno ⓜ *or·*no

overcoat abrigo ⓜ a·*bree·*go

overdose sobredosis ⓕ so·bre·*do·*sees

overhead projector proyector ⓜ de acetatos pro·yek·*tor* de a·se·*ta·*tos

owe deber de·*ber*

owner dueño/a ⓜ/ⓕ *dwe·*nyo/a

oxygen oxígeno ⓜ ok·*see·*khe·no

oyster ostión ⓜ os·*tyon*

ozone layer capa ⓕ de ozono *ka·*pa de o·*so·*no

P

P

pacemaker marcapasos ⓜ
mar·ka·pa·sos

pacifier chupón ⓜ choo·*pon*

package paquete ⓜ pa·*ke*·te

packet paquete ⓜ pa·*ke*·te

padlock candado ⓜ kan·*da*·do

page página ⓕ *pa*·khee·na

pain dolor ⓜ do·*lor*

painful doloroso/a ⓜ/ⓕ
do·lo·*ro*·so/a

painkillers analgésicos ⓜ pl
a·nal·*khe*·see·kos

paint pintar peen·*tar*

painter pintor/pintora ⓜ/ⓕ
peen·*tor*/peen·*to*·ra

painting pintura ⓕ peen·*too*·ra

pair (couple) par ⓜ par

palace palacio ⓜ pa·*la*·syo

palm pilot palm ⓜ palm

pan sartén ⓕ sar·*ten*

pants pantalones ⓜ pl pan·ta·*lo*·nes

panty liners pantiprotectores ⓜ pl
pan·tee·pro·tek·*to*·res

pantyhose pantimedias ⓕ pl
pan·tee·*me*·dyas

pap smear papanicolaou ⓜ
pa·pa·nee·ko·*low*

paper papel ⓜ pa·*pel*

paperwork trámites ⓜ *tra*·mee·tes

paraplegic parapléjico/a ⓜ/ⓕ
pa·ra·*ple*·khee·ko/a

parcel paquete ⓜ pa·*ke*·te

parents padres ⓜ pl *pa*·dres

park parque ⓜ *par*·ke

park (car) estacionar es·ta·syo·*nar*

parliament parlamento ⓜ
par·la·*men*·to

parsley perejil ⓜ pe·re·*kheel*

part parte ⓕ *par*·te

partner (intimate) pareja ⓕ
pa·*re*·kha

part-time medio tiempo *me*·dyo
tyem·po

party fiesta ⓕ *fyes*·ta

party (political) partido ⓜ
par·*tee*·do

pass pase ⓜ *pa*·se

passenger pasajero/a ⓜ/ⓕ
pa·sa·*khe*·ro/a

passport pasaporte ⓜ pa·sa·*por*·te

passport number número ⓜ de
pasaporte *noo*·me·ro de pa·sa·*por*·te

past pasado ⓜ pa·*sa*·do

pasta pasta ⓕ *pas*·ta

pate (food) paté ⓜ pa·*te*

path sendero ⓜ sen·*de*·ro

pay pagar pa·*gar*

payment pago ⓜ *pa*·go

peace paz ⓕ pas

peach durazno ⓜ doo·*ras*·no

peak cumbre ⓕ *koom*·bre

peanuts cacahuates ⓜ ka·ka·*wa*·tes

pear pera ⓕ *pe*·ra

peas chícharos ⓜ pl *chee*·cha·ros

pedal pedal ⓜ pe·*dal*

pedestrian peatón ⓜ pe·a·*ton*

pedestrian crossing cruce ⓜ
peatonal *kroo*·se pe·a·to·*nal*

pen pluma ⓕ *ploo*·ma

pencil lápiz ⓜ *la*·pees

penis pene ⓜ *pe*·ne

penknife navaja ⓕ na·*va*·kha

pensioner jubilado/a ⓜ/ⓕ
khoo·bee·*la*·do/a

people gente ⓕ *khen*·te

pepper (bell) pimiento ⓜ
pee·*myen*·to

pepper (spice) pimienta ⓕ
pee·*myen*·ta

per (day) por (día) por (*dee*·a)

percent por ciento por *syen*·to

performance desempeño ⓜ
des·em·*pe*·nyo

perfume perfume ⓜ per·*foo*·me

period pain cólico ⓜ menstrual
ko·lee·ko men·*strwal*

permission permiso ⓜ per·*mee*·so

permit permiso ⓜ per·*mee*·so

permit permitir per·mee·*teer*

person persona ⓕ per·*so*·na

perspire sudar soo·*dar*
petition petición ⓕ pe·tee·*syon*
petrol gasolina ⓕ ga·so·lee·na
pharmacy farmacia ⓕ far·*ma*·sya
phone book directorio ⓜ telefónico
dee·rek·*to*·ryo te·le·*fo*·nee·ko
phone box teléfono ⓜ público
te·*le*·fo·no *poo*·blee·ko
phone card tarjeta ⓕ de teléfono
tar·*khe*·ta de te·*le*·fo·no
photo fotografía ⓕ fo·to·gra·*fee*·a
photocopier fotocopiadora ⓕ
fo·to·ko·pya·*do*·ra
photographer fotógrafo/a ⓜ/ⓕ
fo·*to*·gra·fo/a
photography fotografía ⓕ
fo·to·gra·*fee*·a
phrasebook libro ⓜ de frases
lee·bro de *fra*·ses
pick-up (truck) pickup pee·*kop* ·
camioneta ka·myo·*ne*·ta
pick up (lift) levantar le·*van*·tar
pick up (seduce) ligar lee·*gar*
pickaxe pico ⓜ *pee*·ko
picnic día ⓜ de campo *dee*·a de
kam·po
pie pay ⓜ pay
piece pedazo ⓜ pe·*da*·so
pig cerdo ⓜ *ser*·do
pill pastilla ⓕ pas·*tee*·ya
the Pill la píldora ⓕ la *peel*·do·ra
pillow almohada ⓕ al·*mwa*·da
pillowcase funda ⓕ de almohada
foon·da de al·*mwa*·da
pineapple piña ⓕ *pee*·nya
pink rosa *ro*·sa
pistachio pistache ⓜ pees·*ta*·che
place lugar ⓜ loo·*gar*
place of birth lugar ⓜ de
nacimiento loo·*gar* de na·see·*myen*·to
plane avión ⓜ a·*vyon*
planet planeta ⓕ pla·*ne*·ta
plant planta ⓕ *plan*·ta
plant sembrar sem·*brar*
plastic plástico ⓜ *plas*·tee·ko
plate plato ⓜ *pla*·to

plateau meseta ⓕ me·*se*·ta
platform plataforma ⓕ pla·ta·*for*·ma
play obra ⓕ *o*·bra
play (an instrument) tocar to·*kar*
play (game/sport) jugar khoo·*gar*
plug (bath) tapón ⓜ ta·*pon*
plug (electrical) chavija ⓕ
cha·*vee*·kha
plum ciruela ⓕ seer·*we*·la
pocket bolsillo ⓜ bol·*see*·yo
poetry poesía ⓕ po·e·*see*·a
point apuntar a·poon·*tar*
point (tip) punto ⓜ *poon*·to
poisonous venenoso/a ⓜ/ⓕ
ve·ne·*no*·so/a
poker póquer ⓜ *po*·ker
police policía ⓕ po·lee·*see*·a
police officer oficial ⓜ de policía
o·fee·*syal* de po·lee·*see*·a
police station estación ⓕ de policía
es·ta·*syon* de po·lee·*see*·a
policy política ⓕ po·*lee*·tee·ka
policy (insurance) póliza ⓕ *po*·lee·sa
politician político/a ⓜ/ⓕ
po·*lee*·tee·ko/a
politics política ⓕ po·*lee*·tee·ka
pollen polen ⓜ *po*·len
polls encuestas ⓕ pl en·*kwes*·tas
pollution contaminación ⓕ
kon·ta·mee·na·*syon*
pony pony ⓜ *po*·nee
pool (game) billar ⓜ bee·*yar*
pool (swimming) alberca ⓕ al·*ber*·ka
poor pobre *po*·bre
pope Papa ⓜ *pa*·pa
popular popular po·poo·*lar*
pork cerdo ⓜ *ser*·do
pork sausage chorizo ⓜ cho·*ree*·so
port puerto ⓜ *pwer*·to
port (wine) oporto ⓜ o·*por*·to
portable CD player reproductor ⓜ
de cómpacts portátil re·pro·*dook*·tor
de *kom*·paks por·ta·teel
possible posible po·*see*·ble
post code código ⓜ postal
ko·dee·go pos·*tal*

post office oficina ⓕ de correos
o·fee·see·na de ko·re·os

postage timbre ⓜ teem·bre

postcard postal ⓕ pos·tal

poste restante lista ⓕ de correos
lees·ta de ko·re·os

poster póster ⓜ pos·ter

pot (kitchen) cazuela ⓕ kas·we·la

pot (for plant) maceta ⓕ ma·se·ta

pot (marijuana) mota ⓕ mo·ta

potato papa ⓕ pa·pa

pottery alfarería ⓕ al·fa·re·ree·a

pound (money) libra ⓕ lee·bra

poverty pobreza ⓕ po·bre·sa

power poder ⓜ po·der

prawn camarón ⓜ ka·ma·ron

prayer oración ⓕ o·ra·syon

prayer book libro ⓜ de oraciones
lee·bro de o·ra·syo·nes

prefer preferir pre·fe·reer

pregnancy test kit prueba ⓕ de
embarazo prwe·ba de em·ba·ra·so

pregnant embarazada
em·ba·ra·sa·da

premenstrual tension síndrome ⓜ
premenstrual seen·dro·me
pre·men·strwal

prepare preparar pre·pa·rar

president presidente/a ⓜ/ⓕ
pre·see·den·te/a

pressure presión ⓕ pre·syon

pretty bonito/a ⓜ/ⓕ bo·nee·to/a

prevent prevenir pre·ve·neer

price precio ⓜ pre·syo

priest sacerdote ⓜ sa·ser·do·te

primary school primaria ⓜ
pree·ma·rya

prime minister (man) primer
ministro ⓜ pree·mer mee·nees·tro

prime minister (woman) primera
ministra ⓕ pree·me·ra mee·nees·tra

printer impresora ⓕ eem·pre·so·ra

prison cárcel ⓕ kar·sel

prisoner prisionero/a ⓜ/ⓕ
pree·syo·ne·ro/a

private privado/a ⓜ/ⓕ pree·va·do/a

private hospital hospital ⓜ privado
os·pee·tal pree·va·do

produce producir pro·doo·seer

profit ganancia ⓜ ga·nan·sya

programme programa ⓜ pro·gra·ma

projector proyector ⓜ pro·yek·tor

promise promesa ⓕ pro·me·sa

protect proteger pro·te·kher

protected protegido/a ⓜ/ⓕ
pro·te·khee·do/a

protest protesta ⓕ pro·tes·ta

protest protestar pro·tes·tar

provisions provisiones ⓕ pl
pro·vee·syo·nes

prune ciruela ⓕ pasa seer·we·la
pa·sa

pub bar ⓜ bar

public telephone teléfono ⓜ
público te·le·fo·no poo·blee·ko

public toilets baños ⓜ pl públicos
ba·nyos poo·blee·kos

pull jalar kha·lar

pump bomba ⓕ bom·ba

pumpkin calabaza ⓕ ka·la·ba·sa

puncture ponchar pon·char

punish castigar kas·tee·gar

puppy cachorro ⓜ ka·cho·ro

pure puro/a ⓜ/ⓕ poo·ro/a

purple morado/a ⓜ/ⓕ mo·ra·do/a

push empujar em·poo·khar

put poner po·ner

Q

qualifications aptitudes ⓕ pl
ap·tee·too·des

quality calidad ⓕ ka·lee·dad

quarantine cuarentena ⓕ
kwa·ren·te·na

quarrel pelea ⓕ pe·le·a

quarter cuarto ⓜ kwar·to

queen reina ⓕ ray·na

question pregunta ⓕ pre·goon·ta

question preguntar pre·goon·tar

queue fila ⓕ fee·la

quick rápido/a ⓜ/ⓕ ra·pee·do/a

quiet tranquilo/a ⓜ/ⓕ tran·kee·lo/a

quiet tranquilidad ⓕ
tran·kee·lee·*dad*
quit renunciar re·noon·*syar*

R

rabbit conejo ⓜ ko·*ne*·kho
race (sport) carrera ⓕ ka·*re*·ra
racetrack pista ⓕ *pees*·ta
racing bike bicicleta ⓕ de carreras
bee·see·*kle*·ta de ka·*re*·ras
racquet raqueta ⓕ ra·*ke*·ta
radiator radiador ⓜ ra·dya·*dor*
railway station estación ⓕ de tren
es·ta·*syon* de tren
rain lluvia ⓕ *yoo*·vya
raincoat impermeable ⓜ
eem·per·me·*a*·ble
rainbow arcoiris ⓜ ar·ko·ee·rees
raisin uva ⓕ pasa oo·va *pa*·sa
rally rally ⓜ *ra*·lee
rape violar vyo·*lar*
rare raro/a ⓜ/ⓕ *ra*·ro/a
rash irritación ⓕ ee·ree·ta·*syon*
raspberry frambuesa ⓕ fram·*bwe*·sa
rat rata ⓕ *ra*·ta
rate of pay salario ⓜ sa·*la*·ryo
raw crudo/a ⓜ/ⓕ *kroo*·do/a
razor rastrillo ⓜ ras·*tree*·yo
razor blades navajas ⓕ pl de
razurar na·va·khas de ra·soo·*rar*
read leer le·*er*
ready listo/a ⓜ/ⓕ *lees*·to/a
real estate agent agente ⓜ
inmobiliario a·*khen*·te
een·mo·bee·*lya*·ryo
realise darse cuenta de *dar*·se
kwen·ta de
realistic realista re·a·*lees*·ta
reason razón ⓕ ra·*son*
receipt recibo ⓜ re·*see*·bo
receive recibir re·see·*beer*
recently recientemente
re·syen·te·*men*·te
recognise reconocer re·ko·no·*ser*
recommend recomendar
re·ko·men·*dar*

recording grabación ⓕ gra·ba·*syon*
recyclable reciclable re·see·*kla*·ble
recycle reciclar re·see·*klar*
red rojo/a ⓜ/ⓕ *ro*·kho/a
referee árbitro ⓜ *ar*·bee·tro
reference referencia ⓕ re·fe·*ren*·sya
refrigerator refrigerador ⓜ
re·free·khe·ra·*dor*
refugee refugiado/a ⓜ/ⓕ
re·foo·*khya*·do/a
refund reembolso ⓜ re·em·*bol*·so
refund reembolsar re·em·bol·*sar*
refuse negar(se) ne·*gar*·(se)
registered mail correo ⓜ
certificado ko·re·o ser·tee·fee·*ka*·do
regret lamentar la·men·*tar*
relationship relación ⓕ re·la·*syon*
relax relajarse re·la·*khar*·se
relic reliquia ⓕ re·*lee*·kya
religion religión ⓕ re·lee·*khyon*
religious religioso/a ⓜ/ⓕ
re·lee·*khyo*·so/a
remember recordar re·kor·*dar*
remote remoto/a ⓜ/ⓕ re·*mo*·to/a
remote control control ⓜ remoto
kon·*trol* re·*mo*·to
rent renta ⓕ *ren*·ta
rent rentar ren·*tar*
repair reparar re·pa·*rar*
repeat repetir re·pe·*teer*
republic república ⓕ
re·*poo*·blee·ka
reservation reservación ⓕ
re·ser·va·*syon*
reserve reservar re·ser·*var*
rest descansar des·kan·*sar*
restaurant restaurante ⓜ
res·tow·*ran*·te
resumé currículum ⓜ
koo·*ree*·koo·loom
retired jubilado/a ⓜ/ⓕ
khoo·bee·*la*·do/a
return volver vol·*ver*
return ticket boleto ⓜ de viaje
redondo bo·*le*·to de *vya*·khe
re·*don*·do

S

review crítica ⓕ *kree·tee·ka*
rhythm ritmo ⓜ *reet·mo*
rice arroz ⓜ *a·ros*
rich rico/a ⓜ/ⓕ *ree·ko/a*
ride paseo ⓜ *pa·se·o*
ride montar *mon·tar*
right (correct) correcto/a ⓜ/ⓕ *ko·rek·to/a*
right (not left) derecha *de·re·cha*
right-wing de derecha *de de·re·cha*
ring anillo ⓕ *a·nee·yo*
ring llamar por teléfono *ya·mar por te·le·fo·no*
rip-off estafa ⓕ *es·ta·fa*
risk riesgo ⓜ *ryes·go*
river río ⓜ *ree·o*
road camino ⓜ *ka·mee·no*
rob robar *ro·bar*
rock roca ⓕ *ro·ka*
rock (music) rock ⓜ *rok*
rock climbing escalada ⓕ en roca *es·ka·la·da en ro·ka*
rock group grupo ⓜ de rock *groo·po de rok*
rollerblading patinar *pa·tee·nar*
romantic romántico/a ⓜ/ⓕ *ro·man·tee·ko/a*
room habitación ⓕ *a·bee·ta·syon*
room number número ⓜ de habitación *noo·me·ro de a·bee·ta·syon*
rope cuerda ⓕ *kwer·da*
round redondo/a ⓜ/ⓕ *re·don·do/a*
roundabout glorieta ⓕ *glo·rye·ta*
route ruta ⓕ *roo·ta*
rowing remo ⓜ *re·mo*
rubbish basura ⓕ *ba·soo·ra*
rug alfombra ⓕ *al·fom·bra*
rugby rugby ⓜ *roog·bee*
ruins ruinas ⓕ pl *rwee·nas*
rules reglas ⓕ pl *re·glas*
rum ron ⓜ *ron*
run correr *ko·rer*
run out of quedarse sin *ke·dar·se seen*

S

sad triste *trees·te*
saddle silla ⓕ de montar *see·ya de mon·tar*
safe caja ⓕ fuerte *ka·kha fwer·te*
safe seguro/a ⓜ/ⓕ *se·goo·ro/a*
safe sex sexo ⓜ seguro *sek·so se·goo·ro*
saint santo/a ⓜ/ⓕ *san·to/a*
salad ensalada ⓕ *en·sa·la·da*
salami salami ⓜ *sa·la·mee*
salary salario ⓜ *sa·la·ryo*
sales tax IVA ⓜ *ee·va*
salmon salmón ⓜ *sal·mon*
salt sal ⓕ *sal*
same igual *ee·gwal*
sand arena ⓕ *a·re·na*
sandals sandalias ⓕ pl *san·da·lyas*
sanitary napkins toallas ⓕ pl femeninas *to·a·yas fe·me·nee·nas*
sauna sauna ⓕ *sow·na*
sausage salchicha ⓕ *sal·chee·cha*
save salvar *sal·var*
save (money) ahorrar *a·o·rar*
say decir *de·seer*
scale (climb) escalar *es·ka·lar*
scarf bufanda ⓕ *boo·fan·da*
school escuela ⓕ *es·kwe·la*
science ciencias ⓕ pl *syen·syas*
scientist científico/a ⓜ/ⓕ *syen·tee·fee·ko/a*
scissors tijeras ⓕ pl *tee·khe·ras*
score anotar *a·no·tar*
scoreboard marcador ⓜ *mar·ka·dor*
Scotland Escocia ⓕ *es·ko·sya*
screen pantalla ⓕ *pan·ta·ya*
script guión ⓜ *gee·on*
sculpture escultura ⓕ *es·kool·too·ra*
sea mar ⓜ *mar*
seasick mareado/a ⓜ/ⓕ *ma·re·a·do/a*
seaside costa ⓕ *kos·ta*
season estación ⓕ *es·ta·syon*

season (in sport) temporada ⓕ tem·po·ra·da

seat asiento ⓜ a·syen·to

seatbelt cinturón ⓜ de seguridad seen·too·ron de se·goo·ree·dad

second segundo ⓜ se·goon·do

second segundo/a ⓜ/ⓕ se·goon·do/a

secondary school secundaria ⓕ se·goon·da·rya

second-hand de segunda mano de se·goon·da ma·no

secretary secretario/a ⓜ/ⓕ se·kre·ta·ryo/a

see ver ver

selfish egoísta e·go·ees·ta

self-service autoservicio ⓜ ow·to·ser·vee·syo

sell vender ven·der

send enviar en·vyar

sensible sensible sen·see·ble

sensual sensual sen·swal

separate separado/a ⓜ/ⓕ se·pa·ra·do/a

separate separar se·pa·rar

series serie ⓕ se·rye

serious serio/a ⓜ/ⓕ se·ryo/a

service station gasolinera ⓕ ga·so·lee·ne·ra

service charge cubierto ⓜ koo·byer·to

set menu menú ⓜ me·noo

several varios/as ⓜ/ⓕ va·ryos/as

sew coser ko·ser

sex sexo ⓜ sek·so

sexism sexismo ⓜ sek·sees·mo

sexy sexy sek·see

shadow sombra ⓕ som·bra

shampoo champú ⓜ cham·poo

shape forma ⓕ for·ma

share (with) compartir kom·par·teer

shave rasurar ra·soo·rar

shaving cream espuma ⓕ de rasurar es·poo·ma de ra·soo·rar

she élla e·ya

sheep oveja ⓕ o·ve·kha

sheet (bed) sábana ⓕ sa·ba·na

sheet (of paper) hoja ⓕ o·kha

shelf repisa ⓕ re·pee·sa

ship barco ⓜ bar·ko

ship enviar en·vee·ar

shirt camisa ⓕ ka·mee·sa

shoe shop zapatería ⓕ sa·pa·te·ree·a

shoes zapatos ⓜ pl sa·pa·tos

shoot disparar dees·pa·rar

shop tienda ⓕ tyen·da

shopping centre centro ⓜ comercial sen·tro ko·mer·syal

short (height) bajo/a ⓜ/ⓕ ba·kho/a

short (length) corto/a ⓜ/ⓕ kor·to/a

shortage escasez ⓕ es·ka·ses

shorts shorts ⓜ pl shorts

shoulder hombro ⓜ om·bro

shout gritar gree·tar

show espectáculo ⓜ es·pek·ta·koo·lo

show mostrar mos·trar

shower regadera ⓕ re·ga·de·ra

shrine capilla ⓕ ka·pee·ya

shut cerrado/a ⓜ/ⓕ se·ra·do/a

shut cerrar se·rar

shy tímido/a ⓜ/ⓕ tee·mee·do/a

sick enfermo/a ⓜ/ⓕ en·fer·mo/a

side lado ⓜ la·do

sign señal ⓕ se·nyal

sign firmar feer·mar

signature firma ⓕ feer·ma

silk seda ⓕ se·da

silver plateado/a ⓜ/ⓕ pla·te·a·do/a

silver plata ⓕ pla·ta

SIM card tarjeta ⓕ SIM tar·khe·ta seem

similar similar see·mee·lar

simple sencillo/a ⓜ/ⓕ sen·see·yo/a

since (time) desde des·de

sing cantar kan·tar

singer cantante ⓜ&ⓕ kan·tan·te

single soltero/a ⓜ/ⓕ sol·te·ro/a

single room habitación ⓕ individual a·bee·ta·syon een·dee·vee·dwal

S

singlet camiseta ⓕ ka·mee·se·ta
sister hermana ⓕ er·*ma*·na
sit sentarse sen·*tar*·se
size (clothes) talla ⓕ *ta*·ya
size (general) tamaño ⓜ ta·*ma*·nyo
skateboarding andar en patineta an·*dar* en pa·tee·*ne*·ta
skateboard patineta ⓕ pa·tee·*ne*·ta
ski esquiar es·kee·*ar*
skiing esquí ⓜ es·*kee*
skimmed milk leche ⓕ descremada *le*·che des·kre·*ma*·da
skin piel ⓕ pyel
skirt falda ⓕ *fal*·da
sky cielo ⓜ *sye*·lo
sleep dormir dor·*meer*
sleeping bag bolsa ⓕ de dormir *bol*·sa de dor·*meer*
sleeping car coche ⓜ cama *ko*·che *ka*·ma
sleeping pills pastillas ⓕ pl para dormir pas·*tee*·yas *pa*·ra dor·*meer*
(be) sleepy tener sueño te·*ner* *swe*·nyo
slide transparencia ⓕ trans·pa·*ren*·sya
slow lento/a ⓜ/ⓕ *len*·to/a
slowly despacio des·*pa*·syo
small pequeño/a ⓜ/ⓕ pe·*ke*·nyo/a
smell olor ⓜ o·*lor*
smell oler o·*ler*
smile sonreír son·re·*eer*
smoke fumar foo·*mar*
SMS capability capacidad ⓕ de SMS ka·pa·see·*dad* de e·se e·me e·se
snack botana ⓕ bo·*ta*·na
snail caracol ⓜ ka·ra·*kol*
snake serpiente ⓕ ser·*pyen*·te
snorkelling esnorkelear es·nor·ke·le·*ar*
snow nieve ⓕ *nye*·ve
snowboarding snowboarding es·now·bor·deen
soap jabón ⓜ kha·*bon*
soap opera telenovela ⓕ te·le·no·*ve*·la

soccer fútbol ⓜ *foot*·bol
social welfare seguridad ⓕ social se·goo·ree·*dad* so·*syal*
socialist socialista ⓜ&ⓕ so·sya·*lees*·ta
socks calcetines ⓜ pl kal·se·*tee*·nes
soft drink refresco ⓜ re·*fres*·ko
soldier soldado ⓜ sol·*da*·do
some algún al·*goon*
someone alguien al·gyen
something algo *al*·go
sometimes de vez en cuando de ves en *kwan*·do
son hijo ⓜ ee·kho
song canción ⓕ kan·*syon*
soon pronto *pron*·to
sore adolorido/a ⓜ/ⓕ a·do·lo·ree·do/a
soup sopa ⓕ *so*·pa
sour cream crema ⓕ agria *kre*·ma *a*·grya
south sur ⓜ soor
souvenir suvenir ⓜ soo·ve·*neer*
souvenir shop tienda ⓕ de suvenirs *tyen*·da de soo·ve·*neers*
soy milk leche ⓕ de soya *le*·che de *so*·ya
soy sauce salsa ⓕ de soya *sal*·sa de *so*·ya
space espacio ⓜ es·*pa*·syo
Spain España ⓕ es·*pa*·nya
sparkling espumoso/a ⓜ/ⓕ es·poo·*mo*·so/a
speak hablar a·*blar*
special especial es·pe·*syal*
specialist especialista ⓜ&ⓕ es·pe·sya·*lees*·ta
speed velocidad ⓕ ve·lo·see·*dad*
speedometer velocímetro ⓜ ve·lo·*see*·me·tro
spermicide espermecida ⓕ es·per·me·*see*·da
spider araña ⓕ a·*ra*·nya
spinach espinaca ⓕ es·pee·*na*·ka
spoon cuchara ⓕ koo·*cha*·ra
sport deportes ⓜ pl de·*por*·tes

sports store tienda ⓕ de deportes *tyen*·da de de·*por*·tes

sportsperson deportista ⓜ&ⓕ de·por·*tees*·ta

sprain torcedura ⓕ tor·se·*doo*·ra

spring (wire) resorte ⓜ re·*sor*·te

spring (season) primavera ⓕ pree·ma·*ve*·ra

square cuadrado ⓜ kwa·*dra*·do

square (town) zócalo ⓜ *so*·ka·lo

stadium estadio ⓜ es·*ta*·dyo

stage escenario ⓜ e·se·*na*·ryo

stairway escalera ⓕ es·ka·*le*·ra

stamp sello ⓜ *se*·yo

stand-by ticket boleto ⓜ en lista de espera bo·*le*·to en *lees*·ta de es·*pe*·ra

stars estrellas ⓕ pl es·*tre*·yas

start comenzar ko·men·*sar*

station estación ⓕ es·ta·*syon*

statue estatua ⓕ es·*ta*·twa

stay (at a hotel) alojarse a·lo·*khar*·se

stay (remain) permanecer per·*ma*·ne·ser

stay (somewhere) quedarse ke·*dar*·se

steak (beef) bistec ⓜ bees·*tek*

steal robar ro·*bar*

steep empinado/a ⓜ/ⓕ em·pee·*na*·do/a

step paso ⓜ *pa*·so

stereo equipo ⓜ estereofónico e·*kee*·po es·te·re·o·*fo*·nee·ko

stingy tacaño/a ⓜ/ⓕ ta·*ka*·nyo/a

stock (broth) caldo ⓜ *kal*·do

stockings calcetas ⓕ pl *kal*·se·tas

stomach estómago ⓜ es·*to*·ma·go

stomachache dolor ⓜ de estómago do·*lor* de es·*to*·ma·go

stone piedra ⓕ *pye*·dra

stoned ciego/a ⓜ/ⓕ *sye*·go/a

stop parada ⓕ pa·*ra*·da

stop parar pa·*rar*

store tienda ⓕ *tyen*·da

storm tormenta ⓕ tor·*men*·ta

story cuento ⓜ *kwen*·to

stove estufa ⓕ es·*too*·fa

straight derecho/a ⓜ/ⓕ de·*re*·cho/a

strange extraño/a ⓜ/ⓕ ek·*stra*·nyo/a

stranger desconocido/a ⓜ/ⓕ des·ko·no·*see*·do/a

strawberry fresa ⓕ *fre*·sa

stream arroyo ⓜ a·*ro*·yo

street calle ⓕ *ka*·ye

string cuerda ⓕ *kwer*·da

strong fuerte *fwer*·te

stubborn terco/a ⓜ/ⓕ *ter*·ko/a

student estudiante ⓜ&ⓕ es·too·*dyan*·te

studio estudio ⓜ es·*too*·dyo

stupid estúpido/a ⓜ/ⓕ es·*too*·pee·do/a

style estilo ⓜ es·*tee*·lo

subtitles subtítulos ⓜ pl soob·*tee*·too·los

suburb colonia ⓜ ko·*lo*·nya

subway metro ⓜ *me*·tro

suffer sufrir soo·*freer*

sugar azúcar ⓜ a·*soo*·kar

suitcase maleta ⓕ ma·*le*·ta

summer verano ⓜ ve·*ra*·no

sun sol ⓜ sol

sunblock bloqueador ⓜ solar blo·ke·a·*dor* so·*lar*

sunburn quemadura ⓕ de sol ke·ma·*doo*·ra de sol

sun-dried tomatoes tomates ⓜ pl deshidratados to·*ma*·tes des·ee·dra·*ta*·dos

sunflower oil aceite ⓜ de girasol a·*say*·te de khee·ra·*sol*

sunglasses lentes ⓕ pl de sol *len*·tes de sol

sunny soleado so·le·a·do

sunrise amanecer ⓜ a·ma·ne·*ser*

sunset puesta ⓕ de sol *pwes*·ta de sol

supermarket supermercado ⓜ soo·per·mer·*ka*·do

superstition superstición ⓕ soo·per·stee·*syon*

T

supporters aficionados ⓜ&ⓕ pl
a·fee·syo·na·dos
surf surfear soor·fe·ar
surface mail correo ⓜ terrestre
ko·re·o te·res·tre
surfboard tabla ⓕ de surf ta·bla
de soorf
surname apellido ⓜ a·pe·yee·do
surprise sorpresa ⓕ sor·pre·sa
survive sobrevivir so·bre·vee·veer
sweater sueter ⓜ swe·ter
sweet dulce dool·se
sweets (candy) dulces ⓜ pl
dool·ses
swim nadar na·dar
swimming pool alberca ⓕ al·ber·ka
swimsuit traje ⓜ de baño tra·khe
de ba·nyo
synagogue sinagoga ⓕ see·na·go·ga
synthetic sintético/a ⓜ/ⓕ
seen·te·tee·ko/a
syringe jeringa ⓕ khe·reen·ga

T

table mesa ⓕ me·sa
table tennis ping pong ⓜ peen·pon
tablecloth mantel ⓜ man·tel
tail cola ⓕ ko·la
tailor sastre ⓜ sas·tre
take (away) llevar lye·var
take (the train) tomar (el tren)
to·mar (el tren)
take (photos) tomar (fotos) to·mar
fo·tos
talk hablar a·blar
tall alto/a ⓜ/ⓕ al·to/a
tampons tampones ⓜ pl tam·po·nes
tanning lotion bronceador ⓜ
bron·se·a·dor
tap grifo ⓜ gree·fo
tasty sabroso/a ⓜ/ⓕ sa·bro·so/a
tax impuesto ⓜ eem·pwes·to
taxi taxi ⓜ tak·see
taxi driver taxista ⓜ&ⓕ tak·sees·ta
taxi stand sitio ⓜ de taxis see·tyo
de tak·sees

tea té ⓜ te
teacher maestro/maestra ⓜ/ⓕ
ma·es·tro/ma·es·tra
team equipo ⓜ e·kee·po
teaspoon cucharita ⓕ
koo·cha·ree·ta
technique técnica ⓕ tek·nee·ka
teeth dientes ⓜ pl dyen·tes
telegram telegrama ⓕ te·le·gra·ma
telephone teléfono ⓜ te·le·fo·no
telephone llamar (por teléfono)
ya·mar (por te·le·fo·no)
telephone centre central ⓕ
telefónica sen·tral te·le·fo·nee·ka
telephoto lens teleobjetivo ⓜ
te·le·ob·khe·tee·vo
telescope telescopio ⓜ te·les·ko·pyo
television televisión ⓕ
te·le·vee·syon
tell decir de·seer
temperature (fever) fiebre ⓕ
fye·bre
temperature (weather)
temperatura ⓕ tem·pe·ra·too·ra
temple templo ⓜ tem·plo
tennis tenis ⓜ te·nees
tennis court cancha ⓕ de tenis
kan·cha de te·nees
tent tienda ⓕ (de campaña) tyen·da
(de kam·pa·nya)
tent pegs estacas ⓕ pl es·ta·kas
terrible terrible te·ree·ble
test prueba ⓕ prwe·ba
thank dar gracias dar gra·syas
theatre teatro ⓜ te·a·tro
their su soo
they ellos/ellas ⓜ/ⓕ e·yos/e·yas
thief ladrón/ladrona ⓜ/ⓕ la·dron/
la·dro·na
thin delgado/a ⓜ/ⓕ del·ga·do/a
think pensar pen·sar
third tercero ter·se·ro
(be) thirsty tener sed te·ner sed
this éste/ésta ⓜ/ⓕ es·te/es·ta
this (month) este (mes) es·te (mes)
throat garganta ⓕ gar·gan·ta

thrush infección ⓕ de garganta
een·fek·*syon* de gar·*gan*·ta
ticket boleto ⓜ bo·*le*·to
ticket collector inspector/
inspectora ⓜ/ⓕ een·spek·*tor*/
een·spek·*to*·ra
ticket machine venta ⓕ automática
de boletos *ven*·ta ow·to·ma·*tee*·ka de
bo·*le*·tos
ticket office taquilla ⓕ ta·*kee*·ya
tide marea ⓕ ma·*re*·a
tight apretado/a ⓜ/ⓕ a·pre·*ta*·do/a
time tiempo ⓜ *tyem*·po
time difference diferencia ⓕ de
horas dee·fe·*ren*·sya de o·ras
timetable horario ⓜ o·ra·ryo
tin lata ⓕ *la*·ta
tin opener abrelatas ⓜ a·bre·*la*·tas
tiny pequeño/a ⓜ/ⓕ pe·*ke*·nyo/a
tip (gratuity) propina ⓕ
pro·*pee*·na
tired cansado/a ⓜ/ⓕ kan·*sa*·do/a
tissues kleenex ⓜ pl *klee*·neks
toast pan tostado ⓜ pan tos·*ta*·do
toaster tostador ⓜ tos·ta·*dor*
tobacco tabaco ⓜ ta·*ba*·ko
tobacconist tabaquería ⓕ
ta·ba·ke·*ree*·a
today hoy oy
toe dedo ⓜ del pie *de*·do del pye
tofu tofú ⓜ to·*foo*
together juntos/as ⓜ/ⓕ
khoon·tos/as
toilet baño ⓜ *ba*·nyo
toilet paper papel ⓜ higiénico
pa·*pel* ee·*khye*·nee·ko
tomato jitomate ⓜ khee·to·*ma*·te
tomato sauce catsup ⓜ *kat*·soop
tomorrow mañana ma·*nya*·na
tomorrow afternoon mañana en la
tarde ma·*nya*·na en la *tar*·de
tomorrow evening mañana en la
noche ma·*nya*·na en la *no*·che
tomorrow morning mañana en
la mañana ma·*nya*·na en la ma·*nya*·na
tonight esta noche es·ta *no*·che

too (expensive) muy (caro/a) ⓜ/ⓕ
mooy (*ka*·ro/a)
too much demasiado de·ma·*sya*·do
tooth (back) muela ⓕ *mwe*·la
toothache dolor ⓜ de muelas do·*lor*
de *mwe*·las
toothbrush cepillo ⓜ de dientes
se·*pee*·yo de *dyen*·tes
toothpaste pasta ⓕ de dientes
pas·ta de *dyen*·tes
toothpick palillo ⓜ pa·*lee*·yo
torch linterna ⓕ leen·*ter*·na
touch tocar to·*kar*
tour excursión ⓕ ek·skoor·*syon*
tourist turista ⓜ&ⓕ too·*rees*·ta
tourist office oficina ⓕ de turismo
o·fee·*see*·na de too·*rees*·mo
towards hacia a·sya
towel toalla ⓕ to·a·ya
tower torre ⓕ *to*·re
toxic waste residuos ⓜ pl tóxicos
re·*see*·dwos *tok*·see·kos
toyshop juguetería ⓕ
khoo·ge·te·*ree*·a
track (footprints) rastro ⓜ *ras*·tro
track (path) sendero ⓜ sen·*de*·ro
track (sport) pista ⓕ *pees*·ta
trade comercio ⓜ ko·*mer*·syo
traffic tráfico ⓜ *tra*·fee·ko
traffic lights semáforos ⓜ pl
se·*ma*·fo·ros
trail camino ⓜ ka·*mee*·no
train tren ⓜ tren
train station estación ⓕ de tren
es·ta·*syon* de tren
tram tranvía ⓜ tran·*vee*·a
transit lounge sala ⓕ de tránsito
sa·la de *tran*·see·to
translate traducir tra·doo·*seer*
transport transporte ⓜ trans·*por*·te
travel viajar vya·*khar*
travel agency agencia ⓕ de viajes
a·*khen*·sya de *vya*·khes
travel books guías ⓕ pl turísticas
gee·as too·*rees*·tee·kas
travel sickness mareo ⓜ ma·*re*·o

U

travellers cheques cheques ⓜ pl de viajero che·kes de vya·khe·ro
tree árbol ⓜ ar·bol
trip viaje ⓜ vya·khe
trousers pantalones ⓜ pl pan·ta·lo·nes
truck camión ⓜ ka·myon
trust confianza ⓕ kon·fee·an·sa
trust confiar kon·fee·ar
try probar pro·bar
try (attempt) intentar een·ten·tar
T-shirt camiseta ⓕ ka·mee·se·ta
tube (tyre) cámara ⓕ de llanta ka·ma·ra de yan·ta
tuna atún ⓜ a·toon
tune melodía ⓕ me·lo·dee·a
turkey pavo ⓜ pa·vo
turn dar vuelta dar vwel·ta
TV televisión ⓕ te·le·vee·syon
TV series serie ⓕ se·rye
tweezers pinzas ⓕ pl peen·sas
twice dos veces dos ve·ses
twin beds dos camas dos ka·mas
twins gemelos/as ⓜ/ⓕ pl khe·me·los/as
type tipo ⓜ tee·po
type escribir a máquina es·kree·beer a ma·kee·na
typical típico/a ⓜ/ⓕ tee·pee·ko/a
tyre llanta ⓕ yan·ta

U

ultrasound ultrasonido ⓜ ool·tra·so·nee·do
umbrella paraguas ⓜ pa·ra·gwas
umpire árbitro ⓜ ar·bee·tro
uncomfortable incómodo/a ⓜ/ⓕ een·ko·mo·do/a
underpants (men) truzas ⓕ pl troo·sas
underpants (women) pantaletas ⓕ pl pan·ta·le·tas
understand comprender kom·pren·der
underwear ropa ⓕ interior ro·pa een·te·ryor

unemployed desempleado/a ⓜ/ⓕ des·em·ple·a·do/a
unfair injusto/a ⓜ/ⓕ een·khoos·to/a
uniform uniforme ⓜ oo·nee·for·me
universe universo ⓜ oo·nee·ver·so
university universidad ⓕ oo·nee·ver·see·dad
unleaded sin plomo seen plo·mo
unsafe inseguro/a ⓜ/ⓕ een·se·goo·ro/a
until (June) hasta (junio) as·ta (khoo·nyo)
unusual raro/a ⓜ/ⓕ ra·ro/a
up arriba a·ree·ba
uphill cuesta arriba kwes·ta a·ree·ba
urgent urgente oor·khen·te
USA Estados ⓜ pl Unidos (de América) es·ta·dos oo·nee·dos (de a·me·ree·ka)
useful útil oo·teel

V

vacant vacante va·kan·te
vacation vacaciones ⓕ pl va·ka·syo·nes
vaccination vacuna ⓕ va·koo·na
vagina vagina ⓕ va·khee·na
validate validar va·lee·dar
valley valle ⓜ va·ye
valuable valioso/a ⓜ/ⓕ va·lyo·so/a
value valor ⓜ va·lor
van vagoneta ⓕ va·go·ne·ta
veal ternera ⓕ ter·ne·ra
vegan vegetariano/a estricto/a ⓜ/ⓕ ve·khe·ta·rya·no/a es·treek·to/a
vegetable legumbre ⓕ le·goom·bre
vegetables verduras ⓕ pl ver·doo·ras
vegetarian vegetariano/a ⓜ/ⓕ ve·khe·ta·rya·no/a
vein vena ⓕ ve·na
venereal disease enfermedad ⓕ venérea en·fer·me·dad ve·ne·re·a
venue jurisdicción ⓕ khoo·rees·deek·syon

very muy mooy
video tape videocassette ① vee·de·o·ka·*set*
view vista ① *vees*·ta
village pueblo ⓜ *pwe*·blo
vine vid ① veed
vinegar vinagre ⓜ vee·*na*·gre
vineyard viñedo ⓜ vee·*nye*·do
virus virus ⓜ *vee*·roos
visa visa ① *vee*·sa
visit visitar vee·see·*tar*
vitamins vitaminas ① pl vee·ta·*mee*·nas
vodka vodka ① *vod*·ka
voice voz ① vos
volume volumen ⓜ vo·*loo*·men
vote votar vo·*tar*

wage sueldo ⓜ *swel*·do
wait esperar es·pe·*rar*
waiter mesero/a ⓜ/① me·*se*·ro/a
waiting room sala ① de espera *sa*·la de es·*pe*·ra
walk caminar ka·mee·*nar*
wall (inside) pared ① pa·*red*
wallet cartera ① kar·*te*·ra
want querer ke·*rer*
war guerra ① *ge*·ra
wardrobe closet ⓜ *klo*·set
warm templado/a ⓜ/① tem·*pla*·do/a
warn advertir ad·ver·*teer*
wash (oneself) lavarse la·*var*·se
wash (something) lavar la·*var*
wash cloth jerga ① *kher*·ga
washing machine lavadora ① la·va·*do*·ra
watch reloj ⓜ de pulsera re·*lokh* de pool·*se*·ra
watch mirar mee·*rar*
water agua ① *a*·gwa
boiled water agua ① hervida *a*·gwa er·*vee*·da
still water agua ① sin gas *a*·gwa seen gas

tap water agua ① de la llave *a*·gwa de la *ya*·ve
waterfall cascada ① kas·*ka*·da
watermelon sandía ① san·*dee*·a
waterproof impermeable eem·per·me·*a*·ble
waterskiing esquí ⓜ acuático es·*kee* a·*kwa*·tee·ko
wave ola ① *o*·la
way camino ⓜ ka·*mee*·no
we nosotros/as ⓜ/① pl no·*so*·tros/as
weak débil *de*·beel
wealthy rico/a ⓜ/① *ree*·ko/a
wear llevar ye·*var*
weather tiempo ⓜ *tyem*·po
wedding boda ① *bo*·da
wedding cake pastel ⓜ de bodas pas·*tel* de *bo*·das
wedding present regalo ⓜ de bodas re·*ga*·lo de *bo*·das
weekend fin ⓜ de semana feen de se·*ma*·na
weigh pesar pe·*sar*
weight peso ⓜ *pe*·so
weights pesas ① pl *pe*·sas
welcome bienvenida ① byen·ve·*nee*·da
welcome dar la bienvenida dar la byen·ve·*nee*·da
welfare bienestar ⓜ byen·es·*tar*
well bien byen
well pozo ⓜ *po*·so
west oeste ⓜ o·*es*·te
wet mojado/a ⓜ/① mo·*kha*·do/a
wetsuit wetsuit ⓜ wet·*soot*
what qué ke
wheel rueda ① *rwe*·da
wheelchair silla ① de ruedas *see*·ya de *rwe*·das
when cuándo *kwan*·do
where dónde *don*·de
white blanco/a ⓜ/① *blan*·ko/a
whiteboard pizzarón ⓜ blanco pee·sa·*ron blan*·ko
who quién kyen

Y

why por qué por *ke*
wide ancho/a ⓜ/ⓕ *an*·cho/a
wife esposa ⓕ es·*po*·sa
win ganar ga·*nar*
wind viento ⓜ *vyen*·to
window ventana ⓕ ven·*ta*·na
window-shopping mirar los aparadores mee·*rar* los a·pa·ra·do·res
windscreen parabrisas ⓜ pa·ra·*bree*·sas
windsurfing hacer windsurf a·*ser weend*·soorf
wine vino ⓜ *vee*·no
winery bodega ⓕ de vinos bo·*de*·ga de *vee*·nos
wings alas ⓕ pl *a*·las
winner ganador/ganadora ⓜ/ⓕ ga·na·*dor*/ga·na·*do*·ra
winter invierno ⓜ een·*vyer*·no
wire alambre ⓜ a·*lam*·bre
wish desear de·se·*ar*
with con kon
within (an hour) dentro de (una hora) *den*·tro de (oo·na o·ra)
without sin seen
woman mujer ⓕ moo·*kher*
wonderful maravilloso/a ⓜ/ⓕ ma·ra·vee·*yo*·so/a
wood madera ⓕ ma·*de*·ra
wool lana ⓕ *la*·na
word palabra ⓕ pa·*la*·bra
work trabajo ⓜ tra·*ba*·kho
work trabajar tra·ba·*khar*
work experience experiencia ⓕ laboral ek·spe·*ryen*·sya la·bo·*ral*
work permit permiso ⓜ de trabajo per·*mee*·so de tra·*ba*·kho
workout entrenamiento ⓜ en·tre·na·*myen*·to
workshop taller ⓜ ta·*yer*
world mundo ⓜ *moon*·do
World Cup Copa ⓕ Mundial *ko*·pa moon·*dyal*
worms lombrices ⓕ pl lom·*bree*·ses
worried preocupado/a ⓜ/ⓕ pre·o·koo·*pa*·do/a

worship rezar re·*sar*
wrist muñeca ⓕ moo·*nye*·ka
write escribir es·kree·*beer*
writer escritor/escritora ⓜ/ⓕ es·kree·*tor*/es·kree·*to*·ra
wrong equivocado/a ⓜ/ⓕ e·kee·vo·*ka*·do/a

Y

year año ⓜ *a*·nyo
yellow amarillo/a ⓜ/ⓕ a·ma·*ree*·yo/a
yes sí see
(not) yet todavía (no) to·da·*vee*·a (no)
yesterday ayer a·*yer*
yoga yoga ⓜ *yo*·ga
yogurt yogurt ⓜ yo·*goort*
you sg inf tú too
you sg pol Usted oos·*ted*
you pl inf&pol Ustedes oos·*te*·des
young joven *kho*·ven
your inf sg/pl tu/tus too/toos
your pol sg/pl su/sus soo/soos
youth hostel albergue ⓜ juvenil al·*ber*·ge khoo·ve·*neel*

Z

zodiac zodíaco ⓜ so·*dee*·a·ko
zoo zoológico ⓜ so·o·*lo*·khee·ko
zoom lens telefoto ⓜ te·le·*fo*·to

Dictionary
SPANISH to ENGLISH
español – inglés

A

Nouns in the dictionary have their gender indicated by ⓜ or ⓕ. If it's a plural noun, you'll also see pl. Where a word that could be either a noun or a verb has no gender indicated, it's a verb. For all words relating to local food, see the **menu decoder** (p189).

A

a bordo a bor·do aboard

abajo a·ba·kho below • down

abeja ⓕ a·be·kha bee

abierto/a ⓜ/ⓕ a·byer·to/a open

abogado/a ⓜ/ⓕ a·bo·ga·do/a lawyer

aborto ⓜ a·bor·to abortion

— natural na·too·ral miscarriage

abrazar a·bra·sar cuddle • hug

abrazo ⓜ a·bra·so hug

abrelatas ⓜ a·bre·la·tas can opener • tin opener

abrigo ⓜ a·bree·go overcoat

abrir a·breer open

abuela ⓕ a·bwe·la grandmother

abuelo ⓜ a·bwe·lo grandfather

aburrido/a ⓜ/ⓕ a·boo·ree·do/a bored • boring

acabar a·ka·bar end

acampar a·kam·par camp

acantilado ⓜ a·kan·tee·la·do cliff

accidente ⓜ ak·see·den·te accident

aceptar a·sep·tar accept

acondicionador ⓜ a·kon·dee·syo·na·dor conditioner

acoso ⓜ a·ko·so harassment

acta ⓕ **de nacimiento** ak·ta de na·see·myen·to birth certificate

acupuntura ⓕ a·koo·poon·too·ra acupuncture

adaptador ⓜ a·dap·ta·dor adaptor

adentro a·den·tro inside

adiós a·dyos goodbye

adivinar a·dee·vee·nar guess

administración ⓕ ad·mee·nees·tra·syon administration

admitir ad·mee·teer admit • allow

adolorido/a ⓜ/ⓕ ado·lo·ree·do/a sore

aduana ⓕ a·dwa·na customs

adulto/a ⓜ/ⓕ a·dool·to/a adult

advertir ad·ver·teer warn

aerolínea ⓕ a·e·ro·lee·ne·a airline

aeropuerto ⓜ a·e·ro·pwer·to airport

aficionados ⓜ&ⓕ pl a·fee·syo·na·dos supporters

afortunado/a ⓜ/ⓕ a·for·too·na·do/a lucky

agencia ⓕ **de noticias** a·khen·sya de no·tee·syas newsagency

agencia ⓕ **de viajes** a·khen·sya de vya·khes travel agency

A

agenda ⓕ a·*khen*·da diary
agente ⓜ **inmobiliario** a·*khen*·te een·mo·bee·*lya*·ryo real estate agent
agotar a·go·*tar* exhaust
agresivo/a ⓜ/ⓕ a·gre·*see*·vo/a aggressive
agricultura ⓕ a·gree·kool·*too*·ra agriculture
agua ⓕ a·gwa water
aguja ⓕ a·*goo*·kha needle (sewing)
ahora a·o·ra now
ahorrar a·o·*rar* save (money)
aire ⓜ *ai*·re air
— acondicionado a·kon·dee·syo·*na*·do air-conditioning
ajedrez ⓜ a·khe·*dres* chess
ajo ⓜ a·kho garlic
al lado de al *la*·do de next to
alacena ⓕ a·la·*se*·na cupboard
alambre ⓜ a·*lam*·bre wire
alas ⓕ pl *a*·las wings
alba ⓕ *al*·ba dawn
alberca ⓕ al·*ber*·ka swimming pool
albergue ⓜ **juvenil** al·*ber*·ge khoo·ve·*neel* youth hostel
alcalde ⓜ&ⓕ al·*kal*·de mayor
Alemania ⓕ a·le·*ma*·nya Germany
alergia ⓕ a·*ler*·khya allergy
— al polen al *po*·len hay fever
aletas pl ⓕ a·*le*·tas flippers
alfarería ⓕ al·fa·re·*ree*·a pottery
alfombra ⓕ al·*fom*·bra rug
algo *al*·go something
algodón ⓜ al·go·*don* cotton
alguien *al*·gyen someone
algún al·*goon* some
alguno/a ⓜ/ⓕ sg al·*goo*·no/a any
algunos/as ⓜ/ⓕ pl al·*goo*·nos/as some
alimentar a·lee·men·*tar* feed
alimento ⓜ **para bebé** a·lee·*men*·to *pa*·ra be·*be* baby food
almohada ⓕ al·*mwa*·da pillow
almuerzo ⓜ al·*mwer*·so lunch
alojamiento ⓜ a·lo·kha·*myen*·to accommodation

alojarse a·lo·*khar*·se stay (somewhere)
alpinismo ⓜ al·pee·*nees*·mo mountaineering
altar ⓜ al·*tar* altar
alto/a ⓜ/ⓕ *al*·to/a high • tall
altura ⓕ al·*too*·ra altitude
alucinar a·loo·see·*nar* hallucinate
ama ⓕ **de casa** a·ma de *ka*·sa homemaker
amable a·*ma*·ble kind
amanecer ⓜ a·ma·ne·*ser* dawn • sunrise
amante ⓜ&ⓕ a·*man*·te lover
amar a·*mar* love
amarillo/a ⓜ/ⓕ a·ma·*ree*·yo/a yellow
amigo/a ⓜ/ⓕ a·*mee*·go/a friend
ampolla ⓕ am·*po*·ya blister
analgésicos ⓜ pl a·nal·*khe*·see·kos painkillers
análisis ⓜ **de sangre** a·*na*·lee·sees de *san*·gre blood test
anarquista ⓜ&ⓕ a·nar·*kees*·ta anarchist
ancho/a ⓜ/ⓕ *an*·cho/a wide
andar an·*dar* go • walk
— en bicicleta en be·see·*kle*·ta cycle
— en patineta en pa·tee·*ne*·ta skateboarding
anillo ⓕ a·*nee*·yo ring
animal ⓜ a·nee·*mal* animal
anotar a·no·*tar* score
antier an·*tyer* day before yesterday
anteojos ⓜ pl an·te·o·khos glasses
antibióticos ⓜ pl an·tee·*byo*·tee·kos antibiotics
anticonceptivos ⓜ pl an·tee·kon·sep·*tee*·vos contraceptives
antigüedad ⓕ an·tee·gwe·*dad* antique
antiguo/a ⓜ/ⓕ an·*tee*·gwo/a ancient
antiséptico ⓜ an·tee·*sep*·tee·ko antiseptic
antología ⓕ an·to·lo·*khee*·a anthology

anuncio ⓜ a·*noon*·syo advertisement
año ⓜ a·nyo year
apellido ⓜ a·pe·*yee*·do family name
apenado/a ⓜ/ⓕ a·pe·*na*·do/a embarrassed
apéndice ⓜ a·*pen*·dee·se appendix
apodo ⓜ a·po·do nickname
aprender a·pren·*der* learn
apretado/a ⓜ/ⓕ a·pre·*ta*·do/a tight
aptitudes ⓕ pl ap·tee·*too*·des qualifications
apuesta ⓕ a·*pwes*·ta bet
apuntar a·poon·*tar* point
aquí a·*kee* here
araña ⓕ a·ra·nya spider
árbitro ⓜ ar·bee·tro umpire • referee
árbol ⓜ ar·bol tree
arcoiris ⓜ ar·co·ee·rees rainbow
área ⓕ **para acampar** a·re·a pa·ra a·kam·*par* campsite
arena ⓕ a·re·na sand
aretes ⓜ pl a·re·tes earrings
arqueológico/a ⓜ/ⓕ ar·ke·o·lo·khee·ko/a archaeological
archeólogo/a ⓜ/ⓕ ar·ke·o·lo·go/a archeologist
arquitecto/a ⓜ/ⓕ ar·kee·tek·to/a architect
arquitectura ⓕ ar·kee·tek·*too*·ra architecture
arriba a·ree·ba above • up
arroyo ⓜ a·ro·yo stream
arte ⓜ ar·te art
artes ⓜ pl **marciales** ar·tes mar·*sya*·les martial arts
artesanía ⓕ ar·te·sa·*nee*·a handicraft
artista ⓜ&ⓕ ar·*tees*·ta artist
— callejero/a ⓜ/ⓕ ka·ye·*khe*·ro/a busker
asiento ⓜ a·*syen*·to seat
— de seguridad para bebés de se·goo·ree·*dad* pa·ra be·*bes* child seat
asma ⓜ as·ma asthma
aspirina ⓕ as·pee·ree·na aspirin

asqueroso/a ⓜ/ⓕ as·ke·ro·so/a foul
atletismo ⓜ at·le·*tees*·mo athletics
atmósfera ⓕ at·*mos*·fe·ra atmosphere
audífono ⓜ ow·dee·fo·no hearing aid
audioguía ⓕ ow·dyo·*gee*·a guide (audio)
autobús ⓜ ow·to·*boos* bus (city)
autoservicio ⓜ ow·to·ser·*vee*·syo self-service
avenida ⓕ a·ve·nee·da avenue
avión ⓜ a·*vyon* plane
ayer a·*yer* yesterday
ayudar a·yoo·*dar* help
azteca as·te·ka Aztec
azul a·*sool* blue

B

bailar bai·*lar* dance
baile ⓜ *bai*·le dancing
bajo/a ⓜ/ⓕ ba·kho/a low • short (height)
balcón ⓜ bal·*kon* balcony
baloncesto ⓜ ba·lon·*ses*·to basketball
bálsamo ⓜ **para labios** *bal*·sa·mo pa·ra la·byos lip balm
banco ⓜ ban·ko bank
bandera ⓕ ban·*de*·ra flag
baño ⓜ ba·nyo toilet • bathroom
baños ⓜ pl **públicos** ba·nyos *poo*·blee·kos public toilet
banqueta ⓕ ban·*ke*·ta footpath
bar ⓜ bar bar • pub
— con variedad kon va·rye·*dad* bar (with live music)
barato/a ⓜ/ⓕ ba·ra·to/a cheap
barco ⓜ bar·ko ship
barrio ⓜ *bar*·yo suburb
basura ⓕ ba·*soo*·ra rubbish
batería ⓕ ba·te·*ree*·a drums • battery (car)
bautizo ⓜ bow·*tee*·so baptism
bebé ⓜ be·*be* baby
bebida ⓕ be·*bee*·da drink
becerro ⓜ be·se·ro calf

C

besar be·*sar* kiss
beso ⓜ *be*·so kiss
biblioteca ⓕ bee·blyo·*te*·ka library
bicho ⓜ *bee*·cho bug
bici ⓕ *bee*·see bike
bicicleta ⓕ bee·see·*kle*·ta bicycle
— de carreras de ka·*re*·ras racing bike
— de montaña de mon·*ta*·nya mountain bike
bien byen well
bienestar ⓜ byen·es·*tar* welfare
bienvenida ⓕ byen·ve·*nee*·da welcome
billetes ⓜ pl bee·*ye*·tes banknotes
biodegradable byo·de·gra·*da*·ble biodegradable
biografía ⓕ byo·gra·*fee*·a biography
blanco *blan*·ko white
blanco/a ⓜ/ⓕ *blan*·ko/a white
bloqueado/a ⓜ/ⓕ blo·ke·*a*·do/a blocked
bloqueador ⓜ **solar** blo·ke·a·*dor* so·*lar* sunblock
boca ⓕ *bo*·ka mouth
bocado ⓜ bo·*ka*·do bite (food)
boda ⓕ *bo*·da wedding
bodega ⓕ **de vinos** bo·*de*·ga de *vee*·nos winery
bol ⓜ bol bowl
bolas ⓕ pl **de algodón** *bo*·las de al·go·*don* cotton balls
boleto ⓜ bo·*le*·to ticket
— de viaje redondo de *vya*·khe re·*don*·do return ticket
— en lista de espera en *lees*·ta de es·*pe*·ra standby ticket
— sencillo sen·*see*·yo one-way ticket
bolsa ⓕ *bol*·sa bag • handbag
— de dormir de dor·*meer* sleeping bag
bolsillo ⓜ bol·*see*·yo pocket
bomba ⓕ *bom*·ba pump • bomb
bondadoso/a ⓜ/ⓕ bon·da·*do*·so/a caring
bonito/a ⓜ/ⓕ bo·*nee*·to/a pretty
borracho/a ⓜ/ⓕ bo·*ra*·cho/a drunk

bosque ⓜ *bos*·ke forest
botana ⓕ bo·*ta*·na snack
botas ⓕ pl *bo*·tas boots
— de montaña de mon·*ta*·nya hiking boots
bote ⓜ *bo*·te boat
botella ⓕ bo·*te*·ya bottle
botiquín ⓜ bo·tee·*keen* first-aid kit
botones ⓜ pl bo·*to*·nes buttons
boxeo ⓜ bok·*se*·o boxing
brazo ⓜ *bra*·so arm
brecha ⓕ *bre*·cha mountain path
brillante bree·*yan*·te brilliant
broma ⓕ *bro*·ma joke
bromear bro·me·*ar* joke
bronceador ⓜ bron·se·a·*dor* tanning lotion
bronquitis ⓕ bron·*kee*·tees bronchitis
brújula ⓕ *broo*·khoo·la compass
budista ⓜ&ⓕ boo·*dees*·ta Buddhist
bueno/a ⓜ/ⓕ *bwe*·no/a good
bufanda ⓕ boo·*fan*·da scarf
bulto ⓜ *bool*·to lump
burlarse de boor·*lar*·se de make fun of
burro ⓜ *boo*·ro donkey
buscar boos·*kar* look for
buzón ⓜ boo·*son* mailbox

C

caballo ⓜ ka·*ba*·yo horse
cabeza ⓕ ka·*be*·sa head
cable ⓜ *ka*·ble cable
cables ⓜ pl **pasacorriente** *ka*·bles pa·sa·ko·*ryen*·tes jumper leads
cabra ⓕ *ka*·bra goat
cachorro ⓜ ka·*cho*·ro puppy
cada *ka*·da each
cadena ⓕ **de bici** ka·*de*·na de *bee*·see bike chain
café ⓜ ka·*fe* coffee • cafe
caída ⓕ ka·*ee*·da fall (tumble)
caja ⓕ *ka*·kha box
— fuerte *fwer*·te safe
— registradora re·khees·tra·*do*·ra cash register

cajero/a ⓜ/ⓕ ka·*khe*·ro/a cashier
cajero ⓜ **automático** ka·*khe*·ro ow·to·ma·*tee*·ko ATM
calcetines ⓜ pl kal·se·*tee*·nes socks
calculadora ⓕ kal·koo·la·*do*·ra calculator
caldo ⓜ *kal*·do stock (soup)
calefacción central ka·le·fak·*syon* sen·*tral* central heating
calendario ⓜ ka·len·*da*·ryo calendar
calentador ⓜ ka·len·ta·*dor* heater
calidad ⓕ ka·lee·*dad* quality
caliente ka·*lyen*·te hot
calle ⓕ *ka*·ye street
calor ⓜ ka·*lor* heat
cama ⓕ *ka*·ma bed
— **matrimonial** ma·tree·mo·*nyal* double bed
cámara de llanta *ka*·ma·ra de *yan*·ta tube (tyre)
cámara fotográfica *ka*·ma·ra fo·to·*gra*·fee·ka camera
cambiar kam·*byar* change • exchange (money)
— **un cheque** oon *che*·ke cash a cheque
cambio ⓜ *kam*·byo exchange • change (money)
— **de moneda** de mo·*ne*·da currency exchange
— **en monedas** en mo·*ne*·das loose change
caminar ka·mee·*nar* walk
camino ⓜ ka·*mee*·no road • trail • way
caminos rurales ⓜ pl ka·*mee*·nos roo·*ra*·les hiking route
camión ⓜ ka·*myon* intercity bus • truck
camioneta ⓕ ka·myo·*ne*·ta pickup • ute
camisa ⓕ ka·*mee*·sa shirt
camiseta ⓕ ka·mee·*se*·ta singlet • T-shirt
campo ⓜ *kam*·po field • countryside
— **de golf** de golf golf course
canasta ⓕ ka·*nas*·ta basket

cancelar kan·se·*lar* cancel
cancha de tenis ⓕ *kan*·cha de *te*·nees tennis court
canción ⓕ kan·*syon* song
candado ⓜ kan·*da*·do padlock
cansado/a ⓜ/ⓕ kan·*sa*·do/a tired
cantante ⓜ&ⓕ kan·*tan*·te singer
cantar kan·*tar* sing
cantimplora ⓕ kan·teem·*plo*·ra water bottle
capa ⓕ *ka*·pa cloak
— **de ozono** de o·*so*·no ozone layer
capilla ⓕ ka·*pee*·ya shrine
cara ⓕ *ka*·ra face
caracol ⓜ ka·ra·*kol* snail
caravana ⓕ ka·ra·*va*·na caravan
cárcel ⓕ *kar*·sel prison • jail
cardiopatía ⓕ kar·dyo·pa·*tee*·a heart condition
carne ⓕ *kar*·ne meat
carnicería ⓕ kar·nee·se·*ree*·a butcher's shop
caro/a ⓜ/ⓕ *ka*·ro/a expensive
carpintero ⓜ kar·peen·*te*·ro carpenter
carrera ⓕ ka·*re*·ra race (sport) • university studies
carretera ⓕ ka·re·*te*·ra motorway
carril para bici ka·*reel* pa·ra *bee*·see bike path
carta ⓕ *kar*·ta letter • menu
cartas ⓕ pl *kar*·tas playing cards
cartón ⓜ kar·*ton* cardboard • carton
casa ⓕ *ka*·sa house
— **de cambio** de *kam*·byo foreign exchange office
casarse ka·*sar*·se marry
cascada ⓕ kas·*ka*·da waterfall
casco ⓜ *kas*·ko helmet
casi *ka*·see almost
casilleros ⓜ pl ka·see·*ye*·ros luggage lockers
castigar kas·tee·*gar* punish
castillo ⓜ kas·*tee*·yo castle
catedral ⓕ ka·te·*dral* cathedral

católico/a ⓜ/ⓕ ka·to·lee·ko/a Catholic

caza ⓕ ka·sa hunting

cazuela ⓕ ka·swe·la pot (kitchen)

cejas ⓕ pl se·khas eyebrows

celebración ⓕ se·le·bra·syon celebration

celebrar se·le·brar celebrate (an event)

celoso/a ⓜ/ⓕ se·lo·so/a jealous

cementerio ⓜ se·men·te·ryo cemetery

cena ⓕ se·na dinner

cenicero ⓜ se·nee·se·ro ashtray

centavo ⓜ sen·ta·vo cent

centímetro ⓜ sen·tee·me·tro centimetre

central ⓕ **telefónica** sen·tral te·le·fo·nee·ka telephone centre

centro ⓜ sen·tro centre

— comercial ko·mer·syal shopping centre

— de la ciudad de la syoo·dad city centre

Centroamérica ⓕ sen·tro·a·me·ree·ka Central America

cepillo ⓜ se·pee·yo hairbrush

— de dientes de dyen·tes toothbrush

cerámica ⓕ se·ra·mee·ka ceramic

cerca ⓕ ser·ka fence

cerca ser·ka near • nearby

cerillos ⓜ pl se·ree·yos matches

cerrado/a ⓜ/ⓕ se·ra·do/a closed • shut

— con llave kon ya·ve locked

cerradura ⓕ se·ra·doo·ra lock

cerrar se·rar close • lock • shut

certificado ⓜ ser·tee·fee·ka·do certificate • registered (mail)

cerveza ⓕ ser·ve·sa beer

chaleco ⓜ **salvavidas** cha·le·ko sal·va·vee·das life jacket

chamarra ⓕ cha·ma·ra jacket

champán ⓜ cham·pan champagne

chapulines ⓜ pl cha·poo·lee·nes grasshoppers

chavija ⓕ cha·vee·kha plug (electrical)

cheque ⓜ che·ke cheque • check (bank)

cheques ⓜ pl **de viajero** che·kes de vya·khe·ro travellers cheques

chichis ⓕ pl inf chee·chees breasts

chicle ⓜ chee·kle chewing gum

chica ⓕ chee·ka girl

chico ⓜ chee·ko boy

chico/a ⓜ/ⓕ chee·ko/a small

chimenea ⓕ chee·me·ne·a fireplace

chip ⓜ cheep SIM card

choque ⓜ cho·ke crash

chupón ⓜ choo·pon dummy • pacifier

cibercafé ⓜ see·ber·ka·fe internet cafe

ciclismo ⓜ see·klees·mo cycling

ciclista ⓜ&ⓕ see·klees·ta cyclist

ciego/a ⓜ/ⓕ sye·go/a blind • stoned

cielo ⓜ sye·lo sky

ciencias ⓕ pl syen·syas science

científico/a ⓜ/ⓕ syen·tee·fee·ko/a scientist

cigarro ⓜ see·ga·ro cigarette

cine ⓜ see·ne cinema

cinturón ⓜ **de seguridad** seen·too·ron de se·goo·ree·dad seatbelt

circo ⓜ seer·ko circus

cita ⓕ see·ta appointment • date

ciudad ⓕ syoo·dad city

ciudadanía ⓕ syoo·da·da·nee·a citizenship

clase ⓕ **ejecutiva** kla·se e·khe·koo·tee·va business class

clase ⓕ **turística** kla·se too·rees·tee·ka economy class

clásico/a ⓜ/ⓕ kla·see·ko/a classical

clavos ⓜ pl **de olor** kla·vos de o·lor cloves

cliente/a ⓜ/ⓕ klee·en·te/a client

cobija ⓕ ko·*bee*·kha blanket

cocaína ⓕ ko·ka·ee·na cocaine

coche ⓜ *ko*·che car

— **cama** *ka*·ma sleeping car

cocina ⓕ ko·*see*·na kitchen

cocinar ko·see·*nar* cook

cocinero ⓜ ko·see·*ne*·ro cook

codeína ⓕ ko·de·ee·na codeine

código ⓜ **postal** ko·dee·go pos·*tal* post code

cola ⓕ *ko*·la bottom • queue • tail

colchón ⓜ kol·*chon* mattress

colega ⓜ&ⓕ ko·*le*·ga colleague

cólico ⓜ **menstrual** *ko*·lee·ko men·*strwal* period pain

colina ⓕ ko·*lee*·na hill

collar ⓜ ko·*yar* necklace

colonia ⓜ ko·*lo*·nya suburb

color ⓜ ko·*lor* colour

combustible ⓜ kom·boos·*tee*·ble fuel

comedia ⓕ ko·*me* dya comedy

comenzar ko·men·*sar* begin • start

comer ko·*mer* eat

comerciante ⓜ&ⓕ ko·mer·*syan*·te business person

comercio ⓜ ko·*mer*·syo trade

comezón ⓜ ko·me·*son* itch

comida ⓕ ko·*mee*·da food

cómo *ko*·mo how

cómodo/a ⓜ/ⓕ *ko*·mo·do/a comfortable

compañero/a ⓜ/ⓕ kom·pa·*nye*·ro/a companion

compañía ⓕ kom·pa·*nyee*·a company

compartir kom·par·*teer* share (with)

comprar kom·*prar* buy

comprender kom·pren·*der* understand

compromiso ⓜ kom·pro·*mee*·so commitment

computadora ⓕ kom·poo·ta·*do*·ra computer

— **portátil** por·*ta*·teel laptop

comunión ⓕ ko·moo·*nyon* communion

comunista ⓜ&ⓕ ko·moo·*nees*·ta communist

con kon with

concierto ⓜ kon·*syer*·to concert

condones ⓜ pl kon·*do*·nes condoms

conducir kon·doo·*seer* drive

conectar ko·nek·*tar* plug

conejo ⓜ ko·*ne*·kho rabbit

conexión ⓕ ko·nek·*syon* connection

confesión ⓕ kon·fe·*syon* confession

confianza ⓕ kon·fee·*an*·sa trust

confiar kon·fee·*ar* trust

confirmar kon·feer·*mar* confirm

conocer ko·no·*ser* know (someone)

consejo ⓜ kon·*se*·kho advice

conservador(a) ⓜ/ⓕ kon·ser·va·*dor*/kon·ser·va·*do*·ra conservative

consigna ⓕ kon·*seeg*·na left luggage

construir kon·stroo·*eer* build

consulado ⓜ kon·soo·*la*·do consulate

contaminación ⓕ kon·ta·mee·na·*syon* pollution

contar kon·*tar* count

contestadora ⓕ kon·tes·ta·*do*·ra answering machine

contrato ⓜ kon·*tra*·to contract

control ⓜ kon·*trol* checkpoint

— **remoto** re·*mo*·to remote control

convento ⓜ kon·*ven*·to convent

copa ⓕ *ko*·pa glass

corazón ⓜ ko·ra·*son* heart

cordillera ⓕ kor·dee·*ye*·ra mountain range

correcto/a ⓜ/ⓕ ko·*rek*·to/a right (correct)

correo ⓜ ko·*re*·o mail

— **aéreo** a·e·re·o airmail

— **certificado** ser·tee·fee·*ka*·do registered mail

C

— **expresso** ek·*spre*·so express mail
— **terrestre** te·*res*·tre surface mail
correr ko·*rer* run
corrida (de toros) ⓕ ko·*ree*·da (de *to*·ros) bullfight
corriente ⓕ ko·*ryen*·te current (electricity)
corriente ko·*ryen*·te ordinary
corrupto/a ⓜ/ⓕ ko·*roop*·to/a corrupt
cortar kor·*tar* cut
cortauñas ⓜ kor·ta·*oo*·nyas nail clippers
corte ⓜ **de pelo** *kor*·te de *pe*·lo haircut
corto/a ⓜ/ⓕ *kor*·to/a short (length)
cosecha ⓕ ko·*se*·cha crop
coser ko·*ser* sew
costa ⓕ *kos*·ta coast • seaside
costar kos·*tar* cost
costo ⓜ *kos*·to cost
cover ⓜ *ko*·ver cover charge
crecer kre·*ser* grow
crema ⓕ *kre*·ma cream
— **hidratante** ee·dra·*tan*·te moisturiser
cristiano/a ⓜ/ⓕ krees·*tya*·no/a Christian
crítica ⓕ *kree*·tee·ka review
crudo/a ⓜ/ⓕ *kroo*·do/a raw
cuaderno ⓜ kwa·*der*·no notebook
cuadrado ⓜ kwa·*dra*·do square (shape)
cuando *kwan*·do when
cuanto *kwan*·to how much
cuarentena ⓕ kwa·ren·*te*·na quarantine
cuarto ⓜ *kwar*·to quarter • room
cubeta ⓕ koo·*be*·ta bucket
cubiertos ⓜ pl koo·*byer*·tos cutlery
cucaracha ⓕ koo·ka·*ra*·cha cockroach
cuchara ⓕ koo·*cha*·ra spoon

cucharita ⓕ koo·cha·*ree*·ta teaspoon
cuchillo ⓜ koo·*chee*·yo knife
cuenta ⓕ *kwen*·ta bill (account)
— **bancaria** ban·*ka*·rya bank account
cuento ⓜ *kwen*·to story
cuerda ⓕ *kwer*·da rope • string
cuero ⓜ *kwe*·ro leather
cuerpo ⓜ *kwer*·po body
cuesta abajo *kwes*·ta a·*ba*·kho downhill
cuesta arriba *kwes*·ta a·*ree*·ba uphill
cuevas ⓕ pl *kwe*·vas caves
cuidar kwee·*dar* look after • mind
cuidar de kwee·*dar* de care for
culo ⓜ *koo*·lo bum (ass)
culpable kool·*pa*·ble guilty
cumbre ⓕ *koom*·bre peak
cumpleaños ⓜ koom·ple·*a*·nyos birthday
cupón ⓜ koo·*pon* coupon
curitas ⓕ pl koo·*ree*·tas Band-Aids
currículum ⓜ koo·*ree*·koo·loom CV • resumé

D

dados ⓜ pl *da*·dos dice
dar dar give
— **gracias** *gra*·syas thank
— **la bienvenida** la byen·ve·*nee*·da welcome
— **vuelta** *vwel*·ta turn
darse cuenta de *dar*·se *kwen*·ta de realise
de de of • from
— **(cuatro) estrellas** (*kwa*·tro) es·*tre*·yas (four-)star
— **derecha** de·*re*·cha right-wing
— **izquierda** ees·*kyer*·da left-wing
— **segunda mano** se·*goon*·da *ma*·no second-hand
— **vez en cuando** ves en *kwan*·do sometimes

deber de·*ber* owe

débil *de*·beel weak

decidir de·see·*deer* decide

decir de·*seer* say • tell

dedo ⓜ *de*·do finger

— del pie del pye toe

defectuoso/a ⓜ/ⓕ de·fek·*two*·so/a faulty

deforestación ⓕ de·fo·res·ta·*syon* deforestation

dejar de·*khar* quit

delgado/a ⓜ/ⓕ del·*ga*·do/a thin

delirante de·lee·*ran*·te delirious

demasiado de·ma·*sya*·do too (much)

democracia ⓕ de·mo·*kra*·sya democracy

demora ⓕ de·*mo*·ra delay

dentista ⓜ den·*tees*·ta dentist

dentro de (una hora) den·tro de (*oo*·na o·ra) within (an hour)

deportes ⓜ pl de·*por*·tes sport

deportista ⓜ&ⓕ de·por·*tees*·ta sportsperson

depósito ⓜ de·*po*·see·to deposit (bank)

derecha de·*re*·cha right (not left)

derecho de·*re*·cho straight

derechos ⓜ pl rights

— civiles see·*vee*·les civil rights

— humanos oo·*ma*·nos human rights

desayuno de·sa·*yoo*·no breakfast

descansar des·kan·*sar* rest

descanso ⓜ des·*kan*·so intermission

descendiente ⓜ de·sen·*dyen*·te descendant

descomponerse des·kom·po·*ner*·se break down

desconocido/a ⓜ/ⓕ des·ko·no·*see*·do/a stranger

descubrir des·koo·*breer* discover

descuento ⓜ des·*kwen*·to discount

desde *des*·de since (time)

desear de·se·*ar* wish

desechable de·se·*cha*·ble disposable

desempeño ⓜ des·em·*pe*·nyo performance

desempleado/a ⓜ/ⓕ des·em·ple·a·do/a unemployed

desierto ⓜ de·*syer*·to desert

desodorante ⓜ de·so·do·*ran*·te deodorant

despacio des·*pa*·syo slowly

despedida ⓕ des·pe·*dee*·da farewell

desperdicios ⓜ pl **nucleares** des·per·*dee*·syos noo·kle·*a*·res nuclear waste

despertador ⓜ des·per·ta·*dor* alarm clock

después de des·*pwes* de after

destapador ⓜ des·ta·pa·*dor* bottle opener

destino ⓜ des·*tee*·no destination

destruir des·troo·*eer* destroy

detallado/a ⓜ/ⓕ de·ta·*ya*·do/a itemised

detalle ⓜ de·*ta*·ye detail

detener de·te·*ner* arrest

detrás de de·*tras* de behind • at the back

día ⓜ *dee*·a day

— de campo de *kam*·po picnic

— festivo fes·*tee*·vo holiday

diafragma ⓜ dee·a·*frag*·ma diaphragm

diariamente dya·rya·*men*·te daily

diarrea ⓕ dee·a·*re*·a diarrhoea

dibujar dee·boo·*khar* draw

diccionario ⓜ deek·syo·*na*·ryo dictionary

dientes ⓜ pl *dyen*·tes teeth

dieta ⓕ *dye*·ta diet

diferencia ⓕ **de horas** dee·fe·*ren*·sya de o·ras time difference

diferente dee·fe·*ren*·te different

difícil dee·*fee*·seel difficult

dinero ⓜ dee·*ne*·ro money

— en efectivo en e·fek·*tee*·vo cash

dios ⓜ dyos god

diosa ⓕ *dyo*·sa goddess

E

dirección ⓕ dee·rek·*syon* address

directo/a ⓜ/ⓕ dee·*rek*·to/a direct

director(a) ⓜ/ⓕ dee·rek·*tor*/
dee·rek·*to*·ra director • manager

directorio ⓜ **telefónico**
dee·rek·*to*·ryo te·le·*fo*·nee·ko phone
book

discapacitado/a ⓜ/ⓕ
dees·ka·pa·see·*ta*·do/a disabled

disco ⓜ *dees*·ko disk

discriminación ⓕ
dees·kree·mee·na·*syon*
discrimination

discutir dees·koo·*teer* argue

diseño ⓜ dee·*se*·nyo design

disparar dees·pa·*rar* shoot

DIU ⓜ dee·*oo* IUD

diversión ⓕ dee·ver·*syon* fun

divertido/a ⓜ/ⓕ dee·ver·*tee*·do/a
funny

divertirse dee·ver·*teer*·se enjoy
oneself • have fun

divorciado/a ⓜ/ⓕ dee·vor·*sya*·do/a
divorced

doble *do*·ble double

docena ⓕ do·*se*·na dozen

doctor(a) ⓜ/ⓕ dok·*tor*/dok·*to*·ra
doctor

documentación ⓕ
do·koo·men·ta·*syon* check·in •
paperwork

documental ⓜ do·koo·men·*tal*
documentary

dolor ⓜ do·*lor* pain

— **de cabeza** de ka·*be*·sa headache

— **de estómago** de es·*to*·ma·go
stomachache

— **de muelas** de *mwe*·las toothache

doloroso/a ⓜ/ⓕ do·lo·*ro*·so/a
painful

donde *don*·de where

dormir dor·*meer* sleep

dos camas dos *ka*·mas twin beds

dos veces dos *ve*·ses twice

droga ⓕ *dro*·ga drug

drogadicción ⓕ dro·ga·deek·*syon*
drug addiction

drogas ⓕ pl *dro*·gas drugs (illegal)

dueño/a ⓜ/ⓕ *dwe*·nyo/a owner

duro/a ⓜ/ⓕ *doo*·ro/a hard

E

edad ⓕ e·*dad* age

edificio ⓜ e·dee·*fee*·syo building

educación ⓕ e·doo·ka·*syon*
education

egoísta e·go·*ees*·ta selfish

ejemplo ⓜ e·*khem*·plo example

él el he

elecciones ⓕ pl e·lek·*syo*·nes
elections

electricidad ⓕ e·lek·tree·see·*dad*
electricity

elegir e·le·*kheer* choose

elevador ⓜ e·le·va·*dor* lift • elevator

ella *e*·ya she

ellos/ellas ⓜ/ⓕ e·yos/e·yas they

embajada ⓕ em·ba·*kha*·da
embassy

embajador(a) ⓜ/ⓕ em·ba·kha·*dor*/
em·ba·kha·*do*·ra ambassador

embarazada em·ba·ra·*sa*·da
pregnant

embarcar em·bar·*kar* board (ship,
etc)

embrague ⓜ em·*bra*·ge clutch

emergencia ⓕ e·mer·*khen*·sya
emergency

emocional e·mo·syo·*nal* emotional

empinado/a ⓜ/ⓕ em·pee·*na*·do/a
steep

empleado/a ⓜ&ⓕ em·ple·*a*·do/a
office worker • employee

empujar em·poo·*khar* push

en en on

— **casa** *ka*·sa (at) home

— **el extranjero** el ek·stran·*khe*·ro
abroad

encaje ⓜ en·*ka*·khe lace

encantador(a) ⓜ/ⓕ en·kan·ta·*dor*/
en·kan·ta·*do*·ra charming

encendedor m en·sen·de·*dor* cigarette lighter

encontrar en·kon·*trar* find • meet

encuestas f pl en·*kwes*·tas polls • surveys

energía f **nuclear** e·ner·*khee*·a noo·*kle*·ar nuclear energy

enfermedad f en·fer·me·*dad* disease

— del beso del *be*·so glandular fever

— venérea ve·ne·*re*·a venereal disease

enfermero/a m/f en·fer·*me*·ro/a nurse

enfermo/a m/f en·*fer*·mo/a sick • ill

enfrente de en·*fren*·te de in front of

enojado/a m/f e·no·*kha*·do/a angry

enorme e·*nor*·me huge

enseñar en·se·*nyar* teach • show

entrar en·*trar* enter

entre en·tre between • among

entrega f **de equipaje** en·*tre*·ga de e·kee·*pa*·khe baggage claim

entregar en·tre·*gar* deliver

entrenador(a) m/f en·tre·na·*dor*/ en·tre·na·*do*·ra coach

entrenamiento m en·tre·na·*myen*·to workout

entrevista f en·tre·*vees*·ta interview

enviar en·*vyar* send

epilepsia f e·pee·*lep*·sya epilepsy

equipaje m e·kee·*pa*·khe luggage • baggage

equipo m e·*kee*·po team • equipment

— estereofónico es·te·re·o·*fo*·nee·ko stereo

— para buceo *pa*·ra boo·*se*·o diving equipment

equitación f e·kee·ta·*syon* horse riding

equivocado/a m/f e·kee·vo·*ka*·do/a wrong (mistaken)

error m e·*ror* mistake

escalada f **en roca** es·ka·*la*·da en *ro*·ka rock climbing

escalar es·ka·*lar* climb

escalera f es·ka·*le*·ra stairway

escaleras f pl **eléctricas** es·ka·*le*·ras e·*lek*·tree·kas escalator

escape m es·*ka*·pe exhaust pipe

escarcha f es·*kar*·cha frost

escasez f es·ka·*ses* shortage

escenario m e·se·*na*·ryo stage

escribir es·kree·*beer* write

— a máquina a *ma*·kee·na type

escritor(a) m/f es·kree·*tor*/ es·kree·*to*·ra writer

escuchar es·koo·*char* listen

escuela f es·*kwe*·la school

escultura f es·kool·*too*·ra sculpture

esa f e·sa that

ese m e·se that

esgrima f es·*gree*·ma fencing (sport)

esnorkelear es·nor·ke·le·*ar* snorkelling

espacio m es·*pa*·syo space

espalda f es·*pal*·da back (body)

España f es·*pa*·nya Spain

especial es·pe·*syal* special

especialista m&f es·pe·sya·*lees*·ta specialist

especies f pl **en peligro de extinción** es·*pe*·syes en pe·*lee*·gro de ek·steen·*syon* endangered species

espectáculo m es·pek·*ta*·koo·lo show

espejo m es·*pe*·kho mirror

esperar es·pe·*rar* wait

esposa f es·*po*·sa wife

esposo m es·*po*·so husband

espuma f **de rasurar** es·*poo*·ma de ra·soo·*rar* shaving cream

espumoso/a m/f es·poo·*mo*·so/a sparkling

esquí m es·*kee* skiing

— acuático a·*kwa*·tee·ko waterskiing

F

esquiar es·kee·*ar* ski

esquina ① es·*kee*·na corner

estacas ① pl es·*ta*·kas tent pegs

estación ① es·ta·*syon* station •
season

— de autobuses de ow·to·*boo*·ses
bus station

— del metro es·ta·*syon* del *me*·tro
metro station

— de policía de po·lee·*see*·a police
station

— de tren de tren railway station •
train station

estacionamiento ⓜ
es·ta·syo·na·*myen*·to car park

estacionar es·ta·syo·*nar* park (car)

estadio ⓜ es·*ta*·dyo stadium

estado ⓜ **civil** es·*ta*·do see·*veel*
marital status

Estados ⓜ pl **Unidos (de América)**
es·*ta*·dos oo·*nee*·dos (de a·*me*·ree·ka)
USA

estafa ① es·*ta*·fa rip-off

estar es·*tar* be

— de acuerdo de a·*kwer*·do agree

estatua ① es·*ta*·twa statue

este es·te east

éste/ésta ⓜ/① es·te/es·ta this

estilo ⓜ es·*tee*·lo style

ésto es·to this one

estómago ⓜ es·*to*·ma·go stomach

estrella ① es·*tre*·ya star

estreñimiento ⓜ
es·tre·nyee·*myen*·to constipation

estudiante ⓜ&① es·too·*dyan*·te
student

estudio ⓜ es·*too*·dyo studio

estufa ① es·*too*·fa stove

estúpido/a ⓜ/① es·*too*·pee·do/a
stupid

etiqueta ① **para equipaje** e·tee·*ke*·ta
pa·ra e·kee·*pa*·khe luggage tag

eutanasia ① e·oo·ta·*na*·sya
euthanasia

eventual e·ven·*twal* casual

excelente ek·se·*len*·te excellent

excluído/a ⓜ/① ek·skloo·ee·*do*/a
excluded

excursión ① ek·skoor·*syon* tour

excursionismo ⓜ
ek·skoor·syo·*nees*·mo hiking

experiencia ① ek·spe·*ryen*·sya
experience

— laboral la·bo·*ral* work experience

exponer ek·spo·*ner* exhibit

exposición ① ek·spo·see·*syon*
exhibition

expreso ek·*spre*·so express

exterior ⓜ ek·ste·*ryor* outside

extrañar ek·stra·*nyar* miss (feel
absence)

extranjero/a ⓜ/① ek·stran·*khe*·ro/a
foreign

extraño/a ⓜ/① ek·*stra*·nyo/a strange

F

fábrica ① *fa*·bree·ka factory

fácil *fa*·seel easy

factura ① **del coche** fak·*too*·ra del
ko·che car owner's title

falda ① *fal*·da skirt

falta ① *fal*·ta fault

familia ① fa·*mee*·lya family

famoso/a ⓜ/① fa·*mo*·so/a famous

farmacéutico/a ⓜ/①
far·ma·*sew*·tee·ko chemist (person)

farmacia ① far·*ma*·sya pharmacy •
chemist (shop)

faros ⓜ pl *fa*·ros headlights

fecha ① *fe*·cha date (time)

— de nacimiento de na·see·*myen*·to
date of birth

feliz fe·*lees* happy

ferretería ① fe·re·te·*ree*·a electrical
store

ficción ① feek·*syon* fiction

fiebre ① *fye*·bre fever

fiesta ① *fyes*·ta party

fin ⓜ feen end

— de semana de se·*ma*·na weekend

firma ① *feer*·ma signature

firmar feer·*mar* sign

flor ① flor flower

florista ⓜ&① flo·*rees*·ta florist

foco ⓜ *fo*·ko light bulb

folklórico/a ⓜ/① fol·*klo*·ree·ko/a folk

folleto ⓜ fo·*ye*·to brochure

forma ① *for*·ma shape

fotografía ① fo·to·gra·*fee*·a photo • photography

fotógrafo/a ⓜ/① fo·*to*·gra·fo/a photographer

fotómetro ⓜ fo·*to*·me·tro light meter

frágil *fra*·kheel fragile

Francia ① *fran*·sya France

franela ① fra·*ne*·la flannel

freír fre·*eer* fry

frenos ⓜ pl *fre*·nos brakes

frente a *fren*·te a opposite

frío/a ⓜ/① *free*·o/a cold

frontera ① fron·*te*·ra border

fruta ① *froo*·ta fruit

fuego ⓜ *fwe*·go fire

fuera de lugar *fwe*·ra de loo·*gar* offside

fuerte *fwer*·te strong

fumar foo·*mar* smoke

funda ① **de almohada** *foon*·da de al·*mwa*·da pillowcase

funeral ⓜ foo·ne·*ral* funeral

fútbol ⓜ *foot*·bol football • soccer

futuro ⓜ foo·*too*·ro future

G

galería ① **de arte** ga·le·*ree*·a de *ar*·te art gallery

ganador(a) ⓜ/① ga·na·*dor*/ ga·na·*do*·ra winner

ganancia ⓜ ga·*nan*·sya profit

ganar ga·*nar* win • earn

garganta ① gar·*gan*·ta throat

gasolina ① ga·so·*lee*·na petrol

gasolinera ① ga·so·lee·*ne*·ra service station

gatito/a ⓜ/① ga·*tee*·to/a kitten

gato/a ⓜ/① *ga*·to/a cat

gelatina ① khe·la·*tee*·na gelatin

gemelos/as ⓜ/① pl khe·*me*·los/as twins

general khe·ne·*ral* general

gente ① *khen*·te people

gimnasia ① kheem·*na*·sya gymnastics

ginebra ① khee·*ne*·bra gin

ginecólogo/a ⓜ/① khe·ne·*ko*·lo·go/a gynaecologist

glorieta ① glo·*rye*·ta roundabout

gobierno ⓜ go·*byer*·no government

goggles ⓜ pl go·gles goggles

goma ① *go*·ma gum

gordo/a ⓜ/① *gor*·do/a fat

gotas ① pl **para los ojos** *go*·tas *pa*·ra los o·*khos* eye drops

grabación ① gra·ba·*syon* recording

gramo ⓜ *gra*·mo gram

grande *gran*·de big • large

granja ① *gran*·kha farm

granjero/a ⓜ/① gran·*khe*·ro/a farmer

grasa *gra*·sa fat (meat) • grease

gripe ① *gree*·pe influenza

gris grees grey

gritar gree·*tar* shout

grupo ⓜ *groo*·po band

— sanguíneo san·*gee*·ne·o blood group

guantes ⓜ pl *gwan*·tes gloves

guapo/a ⓜ/① *gwa*·po/a gorgeous

guardarropa ⓜ gwar·da·*ro*·pa cloakroom

guardería ① gwar·de·*ree*·a childminding service • creche

guerra ① *ge*·ra war

güey ⓜ gway mate • pal

guía ⓜ&① *gee*·a guide (person)

guía ① *gee*·a guidebook

— del ocio del o·*syo* entertainment guide

— turística too·*rees*·tee·ka guidebook

H

guión m gee·*on* script
guitarra f gee·*ta*·ra guitar
gusanos m pl **de maguey**
goo·*sa*·nos de ma·*gay* cactus worms
gustar goos·*tar* like

H

habitación f a·bee·ta·*syon* room •
bedroom
— doble *do*·ble double room
— individual een·dee·vee·*dwal* single
room
hablar a·*blar* speak • talk
hacer a·*ser* do • make
hachís m kha·*shees* hash
hacia a·sya towards
hamaca f a·*ma*·ka hammock
hambre f *am*·bre hunger
harina f a·*ree*·na flour
hasta (junio) *as*·ta (*khoo*·nyo) until
(June)
hecho/a m/f e·cho/a made
— a mano a *ma*·no handmade
— de (algodón) de (al·go·*don*) made
of (cotton)
heladería f e·la·de·*ree*·a ice-cream
parlour
helado m e·*la*·do ice cream
herida f e·*ree*·da injury
hermana f er·*ma*·na sister
hermano m er·*ma*·no brother
hermoso/a m/f er·*mo*·so/a
beautiful
heroína f e·ro·ee·na heroin
hielo m *ye*·lo ice
hierbas f pl *yer*·bas herbs
hígado m *ee*·ga·do liver
hija f *ee*·kha daughter
hijo m *ee*·kho son
hijos m pl *ee*·khos children
hilo m **dental** *ee*·lo den·*tal* dental
floss
hindú een·*doo* Hindu
hipódromo m ee·*po*·dro·mo
racetrack (horses)

histórico/a m/f ees·*to*·ree·ko/a
historical
hoja f *o*·kha leaf • sheet (of paper)
Holanda f o·*lan*·da Netherlands
hombre m *om*·bre man
hombro m *om*·bro shoulder
hora f *o*·ra time • hour
horario m o·*ra*·ryo timetable
— de servicio de ser·*vee*·syo
opening hours
hormiga f or·*mee*·ga ant
horno m *or*·no oven
— de microondas de
mee·kro·*on*·das microwave oven
horóscopo m o·*ros*·ko·po horoscope
hospital m os·pee·*tal* hospital
— privado pree·*va*·do private hospital
hotel m o·*tel* hotel
hotelería f o·te·le·*ree*·a hospitality
hoy oy today
hueso m *we*·so bone
humanidades f pl
oo·ma·nee·*da*·des humanities

I

identificación f
ee·den·tee·fee·ka·*syon* identification
idiomas m pl ee·*dyo*·mas
languages
idiota m&f ee·*dyo*·ta idiot
iglesia f ee·*gle*·sya church
igual ee·*gwal* same
igualdad f ee·gwal·*dad* equality
— de oportunidades de
o·por·too·nee·*da*·des equal
opportunity
imbécil m&f eem·*be*·seel fool
impermeable m eem·per·me·a·ble
raincoat
impermeable eem·per·me·a·ble
waterproof
importante eem·por·*tan*·te
important
impuesto m eem·*pwes*·to tax
— sobre la renta so·bre la *ren*·ta
income tax

incendio ⓜ een·*sen*·dyo fire

incluído/a ⓜ/ⓕ een·kloo·ee·do/a included

incómodo/a ⓜ/ⓕ een·*ko*·mo·do/a uncomfortable

indicador ⓜ een·dee·ka·*dor* indicator

indigestión ⓕ een·dee·khes·*tyon* indigestion

industria ⓕ een·*doos*·trya industry

infección ⓕ een·fek·*syon* infection

— de garganta de gar·*gan*·ta thrush

inflamación ⓕ een·fla·ma·*syon* inflammation

informática ⓕ een·for·*ma*·tee·ka IT

informativo ⓜ een·for·ma·*tee*·vo current affairs

ingeniería ⓕ een·khe·nye·*ree*·a engineering

ingeniero/a ⓜ/ⓕ een·khe·*nye*·ro/a engineer

Inglaterra ⓕ een·gla·*te*·ra England

inglés ⓜ een·*gles* English (language)

ingrediente ⓜ een·gre·*dyen*·te ingredient

injusto/a ⓜ/ⓕ een·*khoos*·to/a unfair

inmigración ⓕ een·mee·gra·*syon* immigration

inocente ee·no·*sen*·te innocent

inseguro/a ⓜ/ⓕ een·se·*goo*·ro/a unsafe

inspector(a) ⓜ/ⓕ een·spek·*tor*/ een·spek·*to*·ra ticket collector · inspector

instructor(a) ⓜ/ⓕ een·strook·*tor*/ eens·trook·*to*·ra instructor

intentar een·ten·*tar* try (attempt)

interesante een·te·re·*san*·te interesting

internacional een·ter·na·syo·*nal* international

intérprete ⓜ&ⓕ een·*ter*·pre·te interpreter

inundación ⓕ ee·noon·da·*syon* flooding

invierno ⓜ een·*vyer*·no winter

invitar een·vee·*tar* invite

inyección ⓕ een·yek·*syon* injection

inyectar een·yek·*tar* inject

ir eer go

— de compras de *kom*·pras go shopping

— de excursión de ek·skoor·*syon* hike

irritación ⓕ ee·ree·ta·*syon* rash

isla ⓕ *ees*·la island

itinerario ⓜ ee·tee·ne·*ra*·ryo itinerary

IVA ⓜ *ee*·va sales tax

izquierda ⓕ ees·*kyer*·da left

J

jabón ⓜ kha·*bon* soap

jalar kha·*lar* pull

Japón ⓜ kha·*pon* Japan

jarabe (para la tos) ⓜ kha·*ra*·be (*pa*·ra la tos) cough medicine

jardín ⓜ khar·*deen* garden

— botánico bo·*ta*·nee·ko botanic garden

— de niños de *nee*·nyos kindergarten

jarra ⓕ *kha*·ra jar

jefe/a ⓜ/ⓕ *khe*·fe/a employer · manager

jerga ⓕ *kher*·ga wash cloth

jeringa ⓕ khe·*reen*·ga syringe

joven *kho*·ven young

joyería ⓕ kho·ye·*ree*·a jewellery

jubilado/a ⓜ/ⓕ khoo·bee·*la*·do/a retired · retiree

judío/a ⓜ/ⓕ khoo·*dee*·o/a Jewish

juego ⓜ **de computadora** *khwe*·go de kom·poo·ta·*do*·ra computer game

juez ⓜ&ⓕ khwes judge

jugar khoo·*gar* play (sport/games)

— a las cartas a las *kar*·tas play (cards)

jugo ⓜ *khoo*·go juice

juguetería ⓕ khoo·ge·te·*ree*·a toyshop

juntos/as ⓜ/ⓕ *khoon*·tos/as together

L

L

labios ⓜ pl *la*·byos lips
lado ⓜ *la*·do side
ladrón ⓜ la·*dron* thief
lagartija ⓕ la·gar·*tee*·kha small lizard
lago ⓜ *la*·go lake
lamentar la·men·*tar* regret
lana ⓕ *la*·na wool
lancha ⓕ **de motor** *lan*·cha de mo·*tor* motorboat
lápiz ⓜ *la*·pees pencil
— labial la·*byal* lipstick
larga distancia *lar*·ga dees·*tan*·sya long-distance
largo/a ⓜ/ⓕ *lar*·go/a long
lastimar las·tee·*mar* hurt
lata ⓕ *la*·ta can • tin
lavadora ⓕ la·va·*do*·ra washing machine
lavandería ⓕ la·van·de·*ree*·a laundry • laundrette
lavar la·*var* wash (something)
lavarse la·*var*·se wash (oneself)
leche ⓕ *le*·che milk
leer le·*er* read
legal le·*gal* legal
legislación ⓕ le·khees·la·*syon* legislation
legumbre ⓕ le·*goom*·bre vegetable
lejos *le*·khos far
leña ⓕ *le*·nya firewood
lentes ⓜ&ⓕ pl *len*·tes glasses
— de contacto de kon·*tak*·to contact lenses
— de sol de sol sunglasses
lento/a ⓜ/ⓕ *len*·to/a slow
ley ⓕ lay law
libra ⓕ *lee*·bra pound (money)
libre *lee*·bre free (not bound)
librería ⓕ lee·bre·*ree*·a bookshop
libro ⓜ *lee*·bro book
— de frases de *fra*·ses phrasebook
— de oraciones de o·ra·*syo*·nes prayer book

licencia ⓕ **de manejo** lee·*sen*·sya de ma·*ne*·kho drivers licence
licenciatura ⓕ lee·sen·sya·*too*·ra undergraduate degree
líder ⓜ&ⓕ *lee*·der leader
ligar lee·*gar* chat up • pick up
ligero/a ⓜ/ⓕ lee·*khe*·ro/a light (of weight)
límite ⓜ **de equipaje** *lee*·mee·te de e·kee·*pa*·khe baggage allowance
limosnero/a ⓜ/ⓕ lee·mos·*ne*·ro/a beggar
limpio/a ⓜ/ⓕ *leem*·pyo/a clean
línea ⓕ *lee*·ne·a line • dial tone
linterna ⓕ leen·*ter*·na torch • flashlight
listo/a ⓜ/ⓕ *lees*·to/a ready
llamada ⓕ **por cobrar** ya·*ma*·da por ko·*brar* collect call
llamar ya·*mar* call
— por teléfono por te·*le*·fo·no telephone • ring
llanta ⓕ *yan*·ta tyre
llave ⓕ *ya*·ve key
— del agua del *a*·gwa faucet • tap
llegadas ⓕ pl ye·*ga*·das arrivals
llegar ye·*gar* arrive
llenar ye·*nar* fill
lleno/a ⓜ/ⓕ ye·*no*/a booked out • crowded • full
llevar ye·*var* carry • take (away) • wear
lluvia ⓕ *yoo*·vya rain
local lo·*kal* local
loción ⓕ **para después del afeitado** lo·*syon* pa·ra des·*pwes* del a·*fay*·ta·do aftershave
loco/a ⓜ/ⓕ *lo*·ko/a crazy
lodo ⓜ *lo*·do mud
lombrices ⓕ pl lom·*bree*·ses worms
lubricante ⓜ loo·bree·*kan*·te lubricant
luces ⓕ pl *loo*·ses lights
luchar loo·*char* fight

lugar ⑩ loo·*gar* place
— de nacimiento de na·see·*myen*·to place of birth
lujo ⑩ *loo*·kho luxury
luna ① *loo*·na moon
— de miel de myel honeymoon
— llena *ye*·na full moon
luz ① loos light

M

maceta ① ma·*se*·ta pot (for plant)
madera ① ma·*de*·ra wood
madre ① *ma*·dre mother
maestro/a ⑩/① ma·es·tro/a teacher
mago/a ⑩/① *ma*·go/a magician
maleta ① ma·*le*·ta suitcase
malo/a ⑩/① *ma*·lo/a bad
mamá ① ma·*ma* mum
mamograma ⑩ ma·mo·*gra*·ma mammogram
mañana ① ma·*nya*·na morning
mañana ma·*nya*·na tomorrow
— en la mañana en la ma·*nya*·na tomorrow morning
— en la noche en la *no*·che tomorrow evening
— en la tarde en la *tar*·de tomorrow afternoon
mandíbula ① man·*dee*·boo·la jaw
manifestación ① ma·nee·fes·ta·*syon* demonstration (protest)
mano ① *ma*·no hand
manteca ① man·*te*·ka lard
mantel ⑩ man·*tel* tablecloth
manubrio ⑩ ma·*noo*·bryo handlebar
mapa ⑩ *ma*·pa map
maquillaje ⑩ ma·kee·*ya*·khe make-up
máquina ① *ma*·kee·na machine
— de tabaco de ta·*ba*·ko cigarette machine
mar ⑩ mar sea
maravilloso/a ⑩/① ma·ra·vee·*yo*·so/a wonderful

marcación ① **directa** mar·ka·*syon* dee·*rek*·ta direct-dial
marcador ⑩ mar·ka·*dor* scoreboard
marcapasos ⑩ mar·ka·*pa*·sos pacemaker
marea ① ma·*re*·a tide
mareado/a ⑩/① ma·re·a·do/a dizzy • seasick
mareo ⑩ ma·*re*·o travel sickness
mariposa ① ma·ree·*po*·sa butterfly
martillo ⑩ mar·*tee*·yo hammer
más mas more
— cercano/a ⑩/① mas ser·*ka*·no/a nearest
masaje ⑩ ma·*sa*·khe massage
masajista ⑩&① ma·sa·*khees*·ta masseur/masseuse
matar ma·*tar* kill
matrícula ① ma·*tree*·koo·la car registration
matrimonio ⑩ ma·tree·*mo*·nyo marriage
mecánico/a ⑩/① me·*ka*·nee·ko/a mechanic
medianoche ① me·dya·*no*·che midnight
medicina ① me·dee·*see*·na medicine
medio ambiente ⑩ *me*·dyo am·*byen*·te environment
medio litro *me*·dyo *lee*·tro half a litre
medio/a ⑩/① *me*·dyo/a half
mediodía ⑩ me·dyo·*dee*·a noon
medios ⑩ pl **de comunicación** *me*·dyos de ko·moo·nee·ka·*syon* media
mejor me·*khor* better • best
melodía ① me·lo·*dee*·a tune
menos *me*·nos less
mensaje ⑩ men·*sa*·khe message
menstruación ① men·strwa·*syon* menstruation
mentiroso/a ⑩/① men·tee·*ro*·so/a liar
menú ⑩ me·*noo* set menu
mercado ⑩ mer·*ka*·do market

N

mes ⓜ mes month
mesa ⓕ *me*·sa table
mesero/a ⓜ/ⓕ me·*se*·ro/a waiter
meseta ⓕ me·*se*·ta plateau
meter ⓜ me·*ter* put
— un gol oon gol kick a goal
metro ⓜ *me*·tro metre • subway
mezclar mes·*klar* mix
mezquita ⓕ mes·*kee*·ta mosque
mi mee my
miembro ⓜ *myem*·bro member
migraña ⓕ mee·*gra*·nya migraine
milímetro ⓜ mee·*lee*·me·tro millimetre
militar ⓜ mee·lee·*tar* military
millón ⓜ mee·*yon* million
minuto ⓜ mee·*noo*·to minute
mirador ⓜ mee·ra·*dor* lookout
mirar mee·*rar* look • watch
— los aparadores los a·pa·ra·do·res window-shopping
misa ⓕ *mee*·sa mass
mochila ⓕ mo·*chee*·la backpack • knapsack
mojado/a ⓜ/ⓕ mo·*kha*·do/a wet
monasterio ⓜ mo·nas·*te*·ryo monastery
monedas ⓕ pl mo·*ne*·das coins
monja ⓕ *mon*·kha nun
montaña ⓕ mon·*ta*·nya mountain
montar mon·*tar* ride
monumento ⓜ mo·noo·*men*·to monument
morado/a ⓜ/ⓕ mo·*ra*·do/a purple
mordedura ⓕ mor·de·*doo*·ra bite (dog)
moretón ⓜ mo·re·*ton* bruise
morir mo·*reer* die
mosquitero ⓜ mos·kee·*te*·ro mosquito net
mosquito ⓜ mos·*kee*·to mosquito
mostrador ⓜ mos·tra·*dor* counter
mostrar mos·*trar* show
mota ⓕ *mo*·ta pot (marijuana)
motocicleta ⓕ mo·to·see·*kle*·ta motorcycle
motor ⓜ mo·*tor* engine

muchos/as ⓜ/ⓕ pl *moo*·chos/as many
mudo/a ⓜ/ⓕ *moo*·do/a mute
muebles ⓜ pl *mwe*·bles furniture
muela ⓕ *mwe*·la tooth (back)
muerto/a ⓜ/ⓕ *mwer*·to/a dead
mujer ⓕ moo·*kher* woman
multa ⓕ *mool*·ta fine
mundo ⓜ *moon*·do world
muñeca ⓕ moo·*nye*·ka doll • wrist
murallas ⓕ pl moo·*ra*·yas city walls
músculo ⓜ *moos*·koo·lo muscle
museo ⓜ moo·*se*·o museum
música ⓕ *moo*·see·ka music
músico ⓜ&ⓕ *moo*·see·ko musician
musulmán/musulmana ⓜ/ⓕ moo·sool·*man*/moo·sool·*ma*·na Muslim
muy mooy very

N

nacionalidad ⓕ na·syo·na·lee·*dad* nationality
nada *na*·da none • nothing
nadar na·*dar* swim
naranja na·*ran*·kha orange (colour)
nariz ⓕ na·*rees* nose
naturaleza ⓕ na·too·ra·*le*·sa nature
naturopatía ⓕ na·too·ro·pa·*tee*·a naturopathy
náuseas ⓕ pl **del embarazo** *now*·se·as del em·ba·*ra*·so morning sickness
navaja ⓕ na·*va*·kha penknife
navajas ⓕ pl **de razurar** na·va·khas de ra·soo·*rar* razor blades
neblinoso ne·blee·*no*·so foggy
necesario/a ⓜ/ⓕ ne·se·*sa*·ryo/a necessary
necesitar ne·se·see·*tar* need
negar ne·*gar* deny
negar(se) ne·*gar*·(se) refuse
negativos ⓜ pl ne·ga·*tee*·vos negatives (film)
negocios ⓜ pl ne·*go*·syos business
negro/a ⓜ/ⓕ *ne*·gro/a black

nieto/a ⓜ/ⓕ *nye*·to/a grandchild
nieve ⓕ *nye*·ve snow
niñera ⓕ nee·*nye*·ra babysitter
niño/a ⓜ/ⓕ *nee*·nyo/a child
niños ⓜ&ⓕ pl *nee*·nyos children
no fumar no foo·*mar* non-smoking
noche ⓕ *no*·che evening
nombre ⓜ *nom*·bre name
— de pila de *pee*·la first name
norte ⓜ *nor*·te north
nosotros/as ⓜ/ⓕ pl no·*so*·tros/as we
noticias ⓕ pl no·*tee*·syas news
novia ⓕ *no*·vya girlfriend
novio ⓜ *no*·vyo boyfriend
nube ⓕ *noo*·be cloud
nublado noo·*bla*·do cloudy
nuestro/a ⓜ/ⓕ *nwes*·tro/a our
Nueva ⓕ **Zelandia** *nwe*·va se·*lan*·dya New Zealand
nuevo/a ⓜ/ⓕ *nwe*·vo/a new
número ⓜ *noo*·me·ro number
— de habitación de a·bee·ta·*syon* room number
— de pasaporte de pa·sa·*por*·te passport number
— de placa de *pla*·ka license plate number
nunca *noon*·ka never

O

o o or
objetivo ⓜ ob·khe·*tee*·vo lens
obra ⓕ *o*·bra play
obrero/a ⓜ/ⓕ o·*bre*·ro/a labourer • manual worker
océano ⓜ o·*se*·a·no ocean
ocupado/a ⓜ/ⓕ o·koo·*pa*·do/a busy
oeste ⓜ o·*es*·te west
oficina ⓕ o·fee·*see*·na office
— de correos de ko·*re*·os post office
— de turismo de too·*rees*·mo tourist office
— de objetos perdidos de ob·*khe*·tos per·*dee*·dos lost property office

oír o·*eer* hear
ojo ⓜ o·*kho* eye
ola ⓕ *o*·la wave
oler o·*ler* smell
olor ⓜ o·*lor* smell
olvidar ol·vee·*dar* forget
operación ⓕ o·pe·ra·*syon* operation
operador(a) ⓜ/ⓕ o·pe·ra·*dor*/o·pe·ra·*do*·ra operator
opinión ⓕ o·pee·*nyon* opinion
oportunidad ⓕ o·por·too·nee·*dad* chance • possibility
oración ⓕ o·ra·*syon* prayer
orden ⓜ *or*·den order (placement)
orden ⓕ *or*·den order (command)
ordenar or·de·*nar* order
oreja ⓕ o·*re*·kha ear
orgasmo ⓜ or·*gas*·mo orgasm
original o·ree·khee·*nal* original
orquesta ⓕ or·*kes*·ta orchestra
oscuro/a ⓜ/ⓕ os·*koo*·ro/a dark
otoño ⓜ o·*to*·nyo autumn
otra vez *o*·tra ves again
otro/a ⓜ/ⓕ *o*·tro/a other
oveja ⓕ o·*ve*·kha sheep
oxígeno ⓜ ok·*see*·khe·no oxygen

P

pacheco/a ⓜ/ⓕ pa·*che*·ko/a stoned • high
padre ⓜ *pa*·dre father
padres ⓜ pl *pa*·dres parents
padrísimo/a ⓜ/ⓕ pa·*dree*·see·mo/a great
pagar pa·*gar* pay
página ⓕ *pa*·khee·na page
pago ⓜ *pa*·go payment
país ⓜ pa·*ees* country
pájaro ⓜ *pa*·kha·ro bird
palabra ⓕ pa·*la*·bra word
palacio ⓜ pa·*la*·syo palace
palillo ⓜ pa·*lee*·yo toothpick
pan ⓜ pan bread
panadería ⓕ pa·na·de·*ree*·a bakery
pantaletas ⓕ pl pan·ta·*le*·tas underpants (women)

P

pantalla ⓕ pan·*ta*·ya screen
pantalones ⓜ pl pan·ta·*lo*·nes
pants • trousers
— de mezclilla de mes·*klee*·ya jeans
pantimedias ⓕ pl pan·tee·*me*·dyas
pantyhose • stockings
pantiprotectores ⓜ pl
pan·tee·pro·tek·*to*·res panty liners
pañal ⓜ pa·*nyal* nappy • diaper
papá ⓜ pa·*pa* dad
papanicolaou ⓜ pa·pa·nee·ko·*low*
pap smear
papel ⓜ pa·*pel* paper
— higiénico ee·*khye*·nee·ko toilet
paper
— para cigarros *pa*·ra see·*ga*·ros
cigarette papers
paquete ⓜ pa·*ke*·te package •
packet
para *pa*·ra for
— siempre *syem*·pre forever
parabrisas ⓜ pa·ra·*bree*·sas
windscreen
parada ⓕ pa·*ra*·da stop
— de omnibuses de om·nee·*boo*·ses
bus stop
paraguas ⓜ pa·*ra*·gwas umbrella
parapléjico/a ⓜ/ⓕ
pa·ra·*ple*·khee·ko/a paraplegic
parar pa·*rar* stop
pared ⓕ pa·*red* wall (inside)
pareja ⓕ pa·*re*·kha partner
parlamento ⓜ par·la·*men*·to
parliament
paro ⓜ *pa*·ro dole
parque ⓜ *par*·ke park
— nacional na·syo·*nal* national park
parte ⓕ *par*·te part
partido ⓜ par·*tee*·do match (sport) •
party (political)
pasado ⓜ pa·*sa*·do past
pasado mañana pa·*sa*·do ma·*nya*·na
day after tomorrow
pasajero ⓜ pa·sa·*khe*·ro passenger
pasaporte ⓜ pa·sa·*por*·te passport

pase ⓜ *pa*·se pass
— de abordar de a·bor·*dar* boarding
pass
paseo ⓜ pa·*se*·o ride
paso ⓜ *pa*·so step
pasta ⓕ **de dientes** *pas*·ta de
dyen·tes toothpaste
pastel ⓜ pas·*tel* cake
— de bodas de *bo*·das wedding cake
— de cumpleaños de
koom·ple·*a*·nyos birthday cake
pastelería ⓕ pas·te·le·*ree*·a cake shop
pastillas ⓕ pl pas·*tee*·yas pills
— antipalúdicas
an·tee·pa·*loo*·dee·kas antimalarial
tablets
— de menta de *men*·ta mints
— para dormir *pa*·ra dor·*meer*
sleeping pills
pasto ⓜ *pas*·to grass
patear pa·te·*ar* kick
patinar pa·tee·*nar* rollerblading
patineta ⓕ pa·tee·*ne*·ta skateboard
pato ⓜ *pa*·to duck
pavo ⓜ *pa*·vo turkey
pay ⓜ pay pie
paz ⓕ pas peace
peatón ⓜ pe·a·*ton* pedestrian
pecho ⓜ *pe*·cho chest
pedazo ⓜ pe·*da*·so piece
pedir pe·*deer* ask (for something)
— aventón a·ven·*ton* hitchhike
— prestado pres·*ta*·do borrow
pedo ⓜ *pe*·do fart
peinar pay·*nar* comb
peine ⓜ *pay*·ne comb
pelea ⓕ pe·*le*·a fight • quarrel
película ⓕ pe·*lee*·koo·la film • movie
— en color en ko·*lor* colour film
peligroso/a ⓜ/ⓕ pe·lee·*gro*·so/a
dangerous
pelo ⓜ *pe*·lo hair
pelota ⓕ pe·*lo*·ta ball
peluquero/a ⓜ/ⓕ pe·loo·*ke*·ro/a
hairdresser • barber
pene ⓜ *pe*·ne penis

pensar pen·*sar* think

pensión ⓕ pen·*syon* boarding house

pequeño/a ⓜ/ⓕ pe·ke·nyo/a small • tiny

perder per·*der* lose

perdido/a ⓜ/ⓕ per·dee·do/a lost

perdonar per·do·*nar* forgive

perfume ⓜ per·*foo*·me perfume

periódico ⓜ pe·*ryo*·dee·ko newspaper

periodista ⓜ&ⓕ pe·ryo·*dees*·ta journalist

permiso ⓜ per·*mee*·so permission • permit

— de trabajo de tra·*ba*·kho work permit

permitir per·mee·*teer* allow • permit

pero *pe*·ro but

perro/a ⓜ/ⓕ *pe*·ro/a dog

perro ⓜ **guía** *pe*·ro *gee*·a guide dog

persona ⓕ per·*so*·na person

pesado/a ⓜ/ⓕ pe·*sa*·do/a heavy

pesar pe·*sar* peso (currency) • weight

pesas ⓜ pl *pe*·sas weights

pesca ⓕ *pes*·ka fishing

pescadería ⓕ pes·ka·de·*ree*·a fish shop

peso ⓜ *pe*·so weight

petate ⓜ pe·*ta*·te mat

petición ⓕ pe·tee·*syon* petition

pez ⓜ pes fish

picadura ⓕ pee·ka·*doo*·ra bite (insect)

pico ⓜ *pee*·ko pickaxe

pie ⓜ pye foot

piedra ⓕ *pye*·dra stone

piel ⓕ pyel skin

pierna ⓕ *pyer*·na leg

pila ⓕ *pee*·la battery (small)

píldora ⓕ *peel*·do·ra the Pill

pintar peen·*tar* paint

pintor(a) ⓜ/ⓕ peen·*tor*/peen·*to*·ra painter

pintura ⓕ peen·*too*·ra painting

pinzas ⓕ pl *peen*·sas tweezers

piojos ⓜ pl *pyo*·khos lice

piolet ⓜ pyo·*le* ice axe

piso ⓜ *pee*·so floor

pista ⓕ *pees*·ta racetrack (runners)

plancha ⓕ *plan*·cha iron (for clothing)

planeta ⓜ pla·*ne*·ta planet

plano/a ⓜ/ⓕ *pla*·no/a flat

planta ⓕ *plan*·ta plant

plástico ⓜ *plas*·tee·ko plastic

plata ⓕ *pla*·ta silver • money (slang)

plataforma ⓕ pla·ta·*for*·ma platform

plateado/a ⓜ/ⓕ pla·te·*a*·do/a silver

plato ⓜ *pla*·to plate

playa ⓕ *pla*·ya beach

playera ⓕ pla·*ye*·ra T-shirt

plaza ⓕ *pla*·sa market

— de toros de *to*·ros bullring

pluma ⓕ *ploo*·ma pen

pobre *po*·bre poor

pobreza ⓕ po·*bre*·sa poverty

pocos/as ⓜ/ⓕ pl *po*·kos/as few

poder ⓜ po·*der* power

poder po·*der* (to be) able • can

poesía ⓕ po·e·*see*·a poetry

polen ⓜ *po*·len pollen

policía ⓕ po·lee·*see*·a police

política ⓕ po·lee·*tee*·ka politics • policy

político/a ⓜ/ⓕ po·lee·*tee*·ko/a politician

póliza ⓕ *po*·lee·sa policy (insurance)

ponchar pon·*char* puncture

poner po·*ner* put

popular po·poo·*lar* popular

póquer ⓜ *po*·ker poker

por (día) por (*dee*·a) per (day)

por ciento por *syen*·to percent

por qué por ke why

por vía ⓕ **aérea** por *vee*·a a·*e*·re·a by airmail

porque *por*·ke because

portafolios ⓜ por·ta·*fo*·lyos briefcase

portero/a ⓜ/ⓕ por·*te*·ro/a goalkeeper • concierge

posible po·*see*·ble possible

postal ⓕ pos·*tal* postcard

Q

pozo m *po*·so well
precio m *pre*·syo price
— de entrada de en·*tra*·da admission price
preferir pre·fe·*reer* prefer
pregunta f pre·*goon*·ta question
preguntar pre·goon·*tar* ask (a question)
preocupado/a m/f pre·o·koo·*pa*·do/a worried
preocuparse por pre·o·koo·*par*·se por worry about something • worry
preparar pre·pa·*rar* prepare
presidente/a m/f pre·see·*den*·te/a president
presión f pre·*syon* pressure
— arterial ar·te·*ryal* blood pressure
prevenir pre·ve·*neer* prevent
primavera f pree·ma·*ve*·ra spring (season)
primer ministro m pree·*mer* mee·*nees*·tro prime minister
primera ministra f pree·*me*·ra mee·*nees*·tra prime minister
primera clase pree·*me*·ra *kla*·se first class
primero/a m/f pree·*me*·ro/a first
principal preen·see·*pal* main
prisa *pree*·sa in a hurry
prisionero/a m/f pree·syo·*ne*·ro/a prisoner
privado/a m/f pree·*va*·do/a private
probadores m pl pro·ba·*do*·res changing room
probar pro·*bar* try
producir pro·doo·*seer* produce
productos m pl **congelados** pro·*dook*·tos kon·khe·*la*·dos frozen foods
profundo/a m/f pro·*foon*·do/a deep
programa m pro·*gra*·ma programme
promesa f pro·*me*·sa promise
prometida f pro·me·*tee*·da fiancee
prometido m pro·me·*tee*·do fiance
pronto *pron*·to soon

propietaria f pro·pye·*ta*·rya landlady
propietario m pro·pye·*ta*·ryo landlord
propina f pro·*pee*·na tip (gratuity)
prórroga f *pro*·ro·ga extension (visa)
proteger pro·te·*kher* protect
protegido/a m/f pro·te·*khee*·do/a protected
protesta f pro·*tes*·ta protest
protestar pro·tes·*tar* protest
provisiones f pl pro·vee·*syo*·nes provisions
proyector m pro·yek·*tor* projector
prueba f *prwe*·ba test
— de embarazo de em·ba·*ra*·so pregnancy test kit
pruebas f pl **nucleares** *prwe*·bas noo·kle·*a*·res nuclear testing
pueblo m *pwe*·blo village
puente m *pwen*·te bridge
puerta f *pwer*·ta door
puerto m *pwer*·to harbour • port
puesta f **de sol** *pwes*·ta de sol sunset
puesto m **de periódicos** *pwes*·to de pe·*ryo*·dee·kos news stand
pulga f *pool*·ga flea
pulmones m pl pool·*mo*·nes lungs
punto m *poon*·to point
puro m *poo*·ro cigar
puro/a m/f *poo*·ro/a pure

Q

qué ke what
quedarse ke·*dar*·se stay (remain)
— sin seen run out of
quejarse ke·*khar*·se complain
quemadura f ke·ma·*doo*·ra burn
— de sol de sol sunburn
quemar ke·*mar* burn
querer ke·*rer* want
quién kyen who

quincena ⓕ keen·*se*·na fortnight
quiste ⓜ **ovárico** *kees*·te o·*va*·ree·ko ovarian cyst
quizás kee·*sas* perhaps

R

radiador ⓜ ra·dya·*dor* radiator
rápido/a ⓜ/ⓕ *ra*·pee·do/a fast • quick
raqueta ⓕ ra·*ke*·ta racquet
raro/a ⓜ/ⓕ *ra*·ro/a rare • strange • unusual
rastrillo ⓜ ras·*tree*·yo razor
rastro ⓜ *ras*·tro track (footprints)
rasurarse ra·soo·*rar*·se shave
rata ⓕ *ra*·ta rat
ratón ⓜ ra·*ton* mouse
raza ⓕ *ra*·sa race (people)
razón ⓕ ra·*son* reason • right
realista re·a·*lees*·ta realistic
recámara ⓕ re·*ka*·ma·ra bedroom
recibir re·see·*beer* receive
recibo ⓜ re·*see*·bo receipt
reciclable re·see·*kla*·ble recyclable
reciclar re·see·*klar* recycle
recientemente re·syen·te·*men*·te recently
recolección ⓕ **de fruta** re·ko·lek·*syon* de *froo*·ta fruit picking
recomendar re·ko·men·*dar* recommend
reconocer re·ko·no·*ser* recognise
recordar re·kor·*dar* remember
recorrido ⓜ **guiado** re·ko·*ree*·do gee·a·do guided tour
recostarse re·kos·*tar*·se lie (not stand)
red ⓕ red net
redondo/a ⓜ/ⓕ re·*don*·do/a round
reembolsar re·em·bol·*sar* refund
reembolso ⓜ re·em·*bol*·so refund
referencia ⓕ re·fe·*ren*·sya reference
refresco ⓜ re·*fres*·ko soft drink
refrigerador ⓜ re·free·khe·ra·*dor* refrigerator
refugiado/a ⓜ/ⓕ re·foo·*khya*·do/a refugee

regadera ⓕ re·ga·*de*·ra shower
regalar re·ga·*lar* give a gift
regalo ⓜ re·*ga*·lo gift
— de bodas de *bo*·das wedding present
reglas ⓕ pl *re*·glas rules
reina ⓕ *ray*·na queen
reír re·*eer* laugh
relación ⓕ re·la·*syon* relationship
relajarse re·la·*khar*·se relax
religión ⓕ re·lee·*khyon* religion
religioso/a ⓜ/ⓕ re·lee·*khyo*·so/a religious
reliquia ⓕ re·*lee*·kya relic
reloj ⓜ re·*lokh* clock
— de pulsera de pool·*se*·ra watch
remo ⓜ *re*·mo rowing
remoto/a ⓜ/ⓕ re·*mo*·to/a remote
renta ⓕ *ren*·ta rent
— de coches de *ko*·ches car hire
rentar ren·*tar* hire • rent
reparar re·pa·*rar* repair
repartir re·par·*teer* deal (cards)
repelente ⓜ **contra mosquitos** re·pe·*len*·te *kon*·tra mos·*kee*·tos mosquito repellent
repetir re·pe·*teer* repeat
repisa ⓕ re·*pee*·sa shelf
república ⓕ re·*poo*·blee·ka republic
reservación ⓕ re·ser·va·*syon* reservation
reservar re·ser·*var* book • reserve
resfriado ⓜ res·*free*·a·do cold (illness)
residuos ⓜ pl **tóxicos** re·*see*·dwos *tok*·see·kos toxic waste
resorte ⓜ re·*sor*·te spring (wire)
respaldo ⓜ res·*pal*·do back (of chair)
respirar res·pee·*rar* breathe
respuesta ⓕ res·*pwes*·ta answer
restaurante ⓜ res·tow·*ran*·te restaurant
revisar re·vee·*sar* check
revista ⓕ re·*vees*·ta magazine
rey ⓜ *ray* king

S

rezar re·*sar* worship
rico/a ⓜ/ⓕ *ree*·ko/a rich • wealthy
riesgo ⓜ *ryes*·go risk
río ⓜ *ree*·o river
ritmo ⓜ *reet*·mo rhythm
robar ro·*bar* rob • steal
roca ⓕ *ro*·ka rock
rodilla ⓕ ro·*dee*·ya knee
rojo/a ⓜ/ⓕ *ro*·kho/a red
romántico/a ⓜ/ⓕ ro·*man*·tee·ko/a romantic
romper rom·*per* break
ron ron rum
ropa ⓕ *ro*·pa clothing
— de cama de *ka*·ma bedding
— interior een·te·*ryor* underwear
rosa *ro*·sa pink
rosadura ⓕ ro·sa·*doo*·ra nappy rash
roto/a ⓜ/ⓕ *ro*·to/a broken
rueda ⓕ *rwe*·da wheel
ruidoso/a ⓜ/ⓕ rwee·*do*·so/a loud • noisy
ruinas ⓕ pl *rwee*·nas ruins
ruta ⓕ *roo*·ta route

S

sábana ⓕ *sa*·ba·na sheet (bed)
saber sa·*ber* know (something)
sabroso/a ⓜ/ⓕ sa·*bro*·so/a tasty
sacerdote ⓜ sa·ser·*do*·te priest
sala ⓕ **de espera** *sa*·la de es·*pe*·ra waiting room
sala ⓕ **de tránsito** *sa*·la de *tran*·see·to transit lounge
salario ⓜ sa·*la*·ryo pay rate • salary
saldo ⓜ *sal*·do balance (account)
salida ⓕ sa·*lee*·da exit • departure
saliente ⓕ sa·*lyen*·te ledge
salir sa·*leer* exit
salir con sa·*leer* kon date (a person) • go out with
salir de sa·*leer* de depart
salón ⓜ **de belleza** sa·*lon* de be·*ye*·sa beauty salon
saltar sal·*tar* jump
salud ⓕ sa·*lood* health

salvar sal·*var* save
sandalias ⓕ pl san·*da*·lyas sandals
sangrar san·*grar* bleed
sangre ⓕ *san*·gre blood
santo/a ⓜ/ⓕ *san*·to/a saint
sarampión ⓜ sa·ram·*pyon* measles
sartén ⓕ sar·*ten* frying pan • pan
sastre ⓜ *sas*·tre tailor
secar se·*kar* dry
secretario/a ⓜ/ⓕ se·kre·*ta*·ryo/a secretary
sed ⓕ *sed* thirst
seda ⓕ *se*·da silk
seguido se·*gee*·do often
seguir se·*geer* follow
segundo ⓜ se·*goon*·do second (time)
segundo/a ⓜ/ⓕ se·*goon*·do/a second (place)
seguridad ⓕ **social** se·goo·ree·*dad* so·*syal* social welfare
seguro ⓜ se·*goo*·ro insurance
seguro/a ⓜ/ⓕ se·*goo*·ro/a safe
sello ⓜ *se*·yo stamp
semáforos ⓜ pl se·*ma*·fo·ros traffic lights
sembrar sem·*brar* plant
semidirecto/a ⓜ/ⓕ se·mee·dee·*rek*·to/a non-direct
señal ⓕ se·*nyal* sign
sencillo/a ⓜ/ⓕ sen·*see*·yo/a simple
sendero ⓜ sen·*de*·ro path
senos ⓜ pl *se*·nos breasts
sensibilidad ⓕ sen·see·bee·lee·*dad* film speed
sensible sen·*see*·ble sensible
sensual sen·*swal* sensual
sentarse sen·*tar*·se sit
sentimientos ⓜ pl sen·tee·*myen*·tos feelings
sentir sen·*teer* feel
separado/a ⓜ/ⓕ se·pa·*ra*·do/a separate
separar se·pa·*rar* separate
ser ser be
serie ⓕ *se*·rye series • TV series
serio/a ⓜ/ⓕ *se*·ryo/a serious

seropositivo/a ⓜ/ⓕ se·ro·po·see·*tee*·vo/a HIV positive

serpiente ⓕ ser·*pyen*·te snake

servicio ⓜ **militar** ser·*vee*·syo mee·lee·*tar* military service

servilleta ⓕ ser·vee·*ye*·ta napkin

sexismo ⓜ *sek*·sees·mo sexism

sexo ⓜ *sek*·so sex

— seguro se·*goo*·ro safe sex

si see if

sí see yes

SIDA ⓜ *see*·da AIDS

siempre *syem*·pre always

silla ⓕ *see*·ya chair

— de montar de mon·*tar* saddle

— de ruedas de *rwe*·das wheelchair

similar see·mee·*lar* similar

simpático/a ⓜ/ⓕ seem·*pa*·tee·ko/a nice

sin seen without

— hogar o·*gar* homeless

— plomo *plo*·mo unleaded

sinagoga ⓕ see·na·*go*·ga synagogue

síndrome ⓜ **premenstrual** *seen*·dro·me pre·men·*strwal* premenstrual tension

sintético/a ⓜ/ⓕ seen·*te*·tee·ko/a synthetic

sitio ⓜ **de taxis** *see*·tyo de *tak*·sees taxi stand

sobornar so·bor·*nar* bribe

soborno ⓜ so·*bor*·no bribe

sobre ⓜ *so*·bre envelope

sobre *so*·bre about

sobredosis ⓕ so·bre·*do*·sees overdose

sobrevivir so·bre·vee·*veer* survive

socialista ⓜ&ⓕ so·sya·*lees*·ta socialist

sol ⓜ sol sun

soldado ⓜ&ⓕ sol·*da*·do soldier

soleado so·le·*a*·do sunny

sólo *so*·lo only

solo/a ⓜ/ⓕ *so*·lo/a alone

soltero/a ⓜ/ⓕ sol·*te*·ro/a single (person)

sombra ⓕ *som*·bra shadow

sombrero ⓜ som·*bre*·ro hat

soñar so·*nyar* dream

sonreír son·re·*eer* smile

sordo/a ⓜ/ⓕ *sor*·do/a deaf

sorpresa ⓕ sor·*pre*·sa surprise

su soo his • her • their • your pol

submarinismo ⓜ soob·ma·ree·*nees*·mo diving

subtítulos ⓜ pl soob·*tee*·too·los subtitles

sucio/a ⓜ/ⓕ *soo*·syo/a dirty

sucursal ⓕ soo·koor·*sal* branch office

sudar soo·*dar* perspire

suegra ⓕ *swe*·gra mother-in-law

suegro ⓜ *swe*·gro father-in-law

sueldo ⓜ *swel*·do wage

suelto/a ⓜ/ⓕ *swel*·to/a loose

suerte ⓕ *swer*·te luck

suertudo/a ⓜ/ⓕ swer·*too*·do/a lucky

suéter ⓜ *swe*·ter jumper • sweater

suficiente soo·fee·*syen*·te enough

sufrir soo·*freer* suffer

supermercado ⓜ soo·per·mer·*ka*·do supermarket

superstición ⓕ soo·per·stee·*syon* superstition

sur ⓜ soor south

surfear soor·fe·*ar* surf

suvenir ⓜ soo·ve·*neer* souvenir

T

tabaco ⓜ ta·*ba*·ko tobacco

tabaquería ⓕ ta·ba·ke·*ree*·a tobacconist

tabla ⓕ **de surf** *ta*·bla de soorf surfboard

tablero ⓜ **de ajedrez** ta·*ble*·ro de a·khe·*dres* chess board

tacaño/a ⓜ/ⓕ ta·*ka*·nyo/a stingy

tal vez tal ves maybe

talco ⓜ **para bébe** *tal*·ko *pa*·ra be·*be* baby powder

talla ⓕ *ta*·ya size (clothes)

taller ⓜ ta·*yer* workshop
tamaño ⓜ ta·*ma*·nyo size
también tam·*byen* also
tampoco tam·po·ko neither
tampones ⓜ pl tam·*po*·nes tampons
tapón ⓜ ta·*pon* bath plug
tanga ⓕ *tan*·ga g-string
tapones ⓜ pl **para los oídos** ta·po·nes *pa*·ra los o·ee·dos earplugs
taquilla ⓕ ta·*kee*·ya ticket office
tarde ⓕ *tar*·de afternoon
tarde *tar*·de late
tarjeta ⓕ **de crédito** tar·*khe*·ta de *kre*·dee·to credit card
tarjeta ⓕ **de teléfono** tar·*khe*·ta de te·*le*·fo·no phone card
tasa ⓕ **de aeropuerto** *ta*·sa de a·e·ro·*pwer*·to airport tax
taza ⓕ *ta*·sa cup
té ⓜ te tea
teatro ⓜ te·a·tro theatre
teclado ⓜ te·*kla*·do keyboard
técnica ⓕ *tek*·nee·ka technique
tela ⓕ *te*·la fabric
tele ⓕ *te*·le TV
teleférico ⓜ te·le·*fe*·ree·ko cable car
teléfono ⓜ te·*le*·fo·no telephone
— celular se·loo·*lar* mobile telephone
— público *poo*·blee·ko phone box • public telephone
telegrama ⓜ te·le·*gra*·ma telegram
telenovela ⓕ te·le·no·*ve*·la soap opera
teleobjetivo ⓜ te·le·ob·khe·*tee*·vo telephoto lens
telescopio ⓜ te·les·*ko*·pyo telescope
televisión ⓕ te·le·vee·*syon* television
temperatura ⓕ tem·pe·ra·*too*·ra temperature (weather)
templado/a ⓜ/ⓕ tem·*pla*·do/a warm
templo ⓜ *tem*·plo temple
temporada ⓕ tem·po·*ra*·da season (in sport)

temprano tem·*pra*·no early
tendedero ⓜ ten·de·*de*·ro clothes line
tenedor ⓜ te·ne·*dor* fork
tener te·*ner* have
— gripa *gree*·pa have a cold
— hambre am·bre (be) hungry
— sed sed (be) thirsty
— sueño *swe*·nyo (be) sleepy
tercio ⓜ *ter*·syo third
terco/a ⓜ/ⓕ *ter*·ko/a stubborn
terminar ter·mee·*nar* finish • end
terremoto ⓜ te·re·*mo*·to earthquake
terrible te·*ree*·ble terrible
tía ⓕ *tee*·a aunt
tiempo ⓜ *tyem*·po time • weather
— completo kom·*ple*·to full-time
tienda ⓕ *tyen*·da shop • convenience store
— de abarrotes de a·ba·ro·tes convenience store • grocery store
— de campaña de kam·*pa*·nya tent
— de campismo de cam·*pees*·mo camping store
— de deportes de de·*por*·tes sports store
— de fotografía de fo·to·gra·*fee*·a camera shop
— de ropa de *ro*·pa clothing store
— de suvenirs de soo·ve·*neers* souvenir shop
— departamental de·par·ta·men·*tal* department store
Tierra ⓕ *tye*·ra Earth
tierra ⓕ *tye*·ra land
tijeras ⓕ pl tee·*khe*·ras scissors
tímido/a ⓜ/ⓕ *tee*·mee·do/a shy
tina ⓕ *tee*·na bathtub
típico/a ⓜ/ⓕ *tee*·pee·ko/a typical
tipo ⓜ *tee*·po type
— de cambio de *kam*·byo exchange rate
título ⓜ *tee*·too·lo degree • deed
tlapalería ⓕ tla·pa·le·*ree*·a hardware store

toalla ⓕ to·a·ya towel
toallas ⓕ pl **femeninas** to·a·yas
fe·me·nee·nas sanitary napkins
toallita ⓕ **facial** to·a·yee·ta fa·syal
face cloth
tobillo ⓜ to·bee·yo ankle
tocar to·kar touch • play (instrument)
todavía (no) to·da·vee·a (no) (not)
yet
todo/a ⓜ/ⓕ to·do/a all • everything
todos/as ⓜ/ⓕ to·dos/as all (of them)
tomar to·mar drink • take (the train)
— fotos fo·tos take photographs
torcedura ⓕ tor·se·doo·ra sprain
tormenta ⓕ tor·men·ta storm
toro ⓜ to·ro bull
torre ⓕ to·re tower
tos ⓕ tos cough
tostador ⓜ tos·ta·dor toaster
trabajar tra·ba·khar work
trabajo ⓜ tra·ba·kho job • work
— de casa de ka·sa housework
— de limpieza de leem·pye·sa
cleaning
— eventual e·ven·twal casual work
traducir tra·doo·seer translate
traer tra·er bring
traficante ⓜ&ⓕ **de drogas**
tra·fee·kan·te de dro·gas drug dealer
tráfico ⓜ tra·fee·ko traffic
traje ⓜ **de baño** tra·khe de ba·nyo
bathing suit • swimsuit
trámites ⓜ tra·mee·tes paperwork
tramposo/a ⓜ/ⓕ tram·po·so/a
cheat
tranquilidad ⓕ tran·kee·lee·dad
quiet
tranquilo/a ⓜ/ⓕ tran·kee·lo/a quiet
transparencia ⓕ trans·pa·ren·sya
slide
transporte ⓜ trans·por·te
transport
tranvía ⓜ tran·vee·a tram
tren ⓜ tren train
triste trees·te sad

truzas ⓕ pl troo·sas underpants
(men)
tu sg inf too your
tú sg inf too you
tumba ⓕ toom·ba grave
turista ⓜ&ⓕ too·rees·ta tourist

U

ultrasonido ⓜ ool·tra·so·nee·do
ultrasound
una vez oo·na ves once
uniforme ⓜ oo·nee·for·me uniform
universidad ⓕ oo·nee·ver·see·dad
university • college
universo ⓜ oo·nee·ver·so universe
urgente oor·khen·te urgent
Usted sg pol oos·ted you
Ustedes pl pol oos·te·des you
útil oo·teel useful

V

vaca ⓕ va·ka cow
vacaciones ⓕ pl va·ka·syo·nes
holidays • vacation
vacante va·kan·te vacant
vacío/a ⓜ/ⓕ va·see·o/a empty
vacuna ⓕ va·koo·na vaccination
vagina ⓕ va·khee·na vagina
vagón ⓜ **restaurante** va·gon
res·tow·ran·te dining car
vagoneta ⓕ va·go·ne·ta van
validar va·lee·dar validate
valiente va·lyen·te brave
valioso/a ⓜ/ⓕ va·lyo·so/a
valuable
valle ⓜ va·ye valley
valor ⓜ va·lor value
varios/as ⓜ/ⓕ va·ryos/as several
vaso ⓜ va·so glass
vegetariano/a ⓜ/ⓕ
ve·khe·ta·rya·no/a vegetarian
vela ⓕ ve·la candle
velocidad ⓕ ve·lo·see·dad speed
velocímetro ⓜ ve·lo·see·me·tro
speedometer

Y

velódromo ⓜ ve·*lo*·dro·mo racetrack (bicycles)

vena ⓕ *ve*·na vein

vendaje ⓜ ven·*da*·khe bandage

vendedor(a) ⓜ/ⓕ **de flores** ven·de·*dor*/ven·de·*do*·ra de *flo*·res flower seller

vender ven·*der* sell

venenoso/a ⓜ/ⓕ ve·ne·*no*·so/a poisonous

venir ve·*neer* come

venta ⓕ **automática de boletos** *ven*·ta ow·to·*ma*·tee·ka de bo·*le*·tos ticket machine

ventana ⓕ ven·*ta*·na window

ventilador ⓜ ven·tee·la·*dor* fan (machine)

ver ver see

verano ⓜ ve·*ra*·no summer

verde *ver*·de green

verdulería ⓕ ver·doo·le·*ree*·a greengrocery

verduras ⓕ ver·*doo*·ras vegetables

vestíbulo ⓜ ves·*tee*·boo·lo foyer

vestido ⓜ ves·*tee*·do dress

viajar vya·*khar* travel

viaje ⓜ *vya*·khe trip

vid ⓕ veed vine

vida ⓕ *vee*·da life

viejo/a ⓜ/ⓕ *vye*·kho/a old

viento ⓜ *vyen*·to wind

vinatería ⓕ vee·na·te·*ree*·a liquor store

viñedo ⓜ vee·*nye*·do vineyard

vino ⓜ *vee*·no wine

violar vyo·*lar* rape

virus ⓜ *vee*·roos virus

visa ⓕ *vee*·sa visa

visitar vee·see·*tar* visit

vista ⓕ *vees*·ta view

vitaminas ⓕ pl vee·ta·*mee*·nas vitamins

víveres ⓜ pl *vee*·ve·res food supplies

vivir vee·*veer* live

volar vo·*lar* fly

volumen ⓜ vo·*loo*·men volume

volver vol·*ver* return

votar vo·*tar* vote

voz ⓕ vos voice

vuelo ⓜ **doméstico** *vwe*·lo do·*mes*·tee·ko domestic flight

Y

y ee and

ya ya already

yerbero/a ⓜ/ⓕ yer·*be*·ro/a herbalist

yo yo I

Z

zapatería ⓕ sa·pa·te·*ree*·a shoe shop

zapatos ⓜ pl sa·*pa*·tos shoes

zócalo ⓜ *so*·ka·lo main square

zodíaco ⓜ so·*dee*·a·ko zodiac

zoológico ⓜ so·o·*lo*·khee·ko zoo

Index

For topics that are covered in several sections of this book, we've indicated the most relevant page number in bold.

10 Ways to Start a Sentence

When's (the next flight)?	¿Cuándo sale (el próximo vuelo)?	*kwan*·do sa·le (el *prok*·see·mo vwe·lo)
Where's the (station)?	¿Dónde está (la estación)?	*don*·de es·*ta* (la es·ta·*syon*)
Where can I (buy a ticket)?	¿Dónde puedo (comprar un boleto)?	*don*·de *pwe*·do (kom·*prar* oon bo·*le*·to)
How much is (a room)?	¿Cuánto cuesta (una habitación)?	*kwan*·to *kwes*·ta (*oo*·na a·bee·ta·*syon*)
Do you have (a map)?	¿Tiene (un mapa)?	*tye*·ne (oon *ma*·pa)
Is there (a toilet)?	¿Hay (baño)?	ai (*ba*·nyo)
I'd like (to hire a car).	Quisiera (alquilar un coche).	kee·*sye*·ra (al·kee·*lar* oon *ko*·che)
Can I (enter)?	¿Se puede (entrar)?	se *pwe*·de (en·*trar*)
Could you please (help me)?	¿Puede (ayudarme), por favor?	*pwe*·de (a·yoo·*dar*·me) por fa·*vor*
Do I have to (get a visa)?	¿Necesito (obtener una visa)?	ne·se·*see*·to (ob·te·*ner* *oo*·na vee·sa)